Sorting Out Your Finances

FOR

DUMMIES®

2ND EDITION

Sorting Out Your Finances

FOR DUMMIES®

2ND EDITION

by Melanie Bien

John Wiley & Sons, Ltd

Sorting Out Your Finances For Dummies®, 2nd Edition

Published by
John Wiley & Sons, Ltd
The Atrium
Southern Gate
Chichester
West Sussex
PO19 8SQ
England

E-mail (for orders and customer service enquires): cs-books@wiley.co.uk

Visit our Home Page on www.wiley.com

For general information on our other products and services, please contact our Customer Care Department within the U.S. at 800-762-2974, outside the U.S. at 317-572-3993, or fax 317-572-4002.

For technical support, please visit www.wiley.com/techsupport.

Wiley also publishes its books in a variety of electronic formats. Some content that appears in print may not be available in electronic books.

British Library Cataloguing in Publication Data: A catalogue record for this book is available from the British Library

ISBN-13: 978-0-470-69515-9 (P/B)

Printed and bound in Great Britain by Bell & Bain Ltd, Glasgow

10 9 8 7 6 5 4 3 2

WILEY

About the Author

Melanie Bien is director (head of media relations) at Savills Private Finance, the independent mortgage broker. She was personal finance editor of the *Independent on Sunday* for five years and writes freelance property features for national newspapers, magazines, and websites. She has written several books and pamphlets to accompany television programmes on property makeovers and design, and on buying, renovating, and selling property.

Her other books include *Buying a Home On a Budget For Dummies*, *Buying and Selling Property For Dummies*, and *Renting Out Your Property For Dummies*. She lives in North London with her husband.

Dedication

To my husband, brother and parents, for all your support, enthusiasm, and endless encouragement.

Author's Acknowledgements

I would like to thank Jason Dunne at John Wiley & Sons for having the faith in me to write yet another book for the company! I also acknowledge a depth of gratitude to Rachael Chilvers, my editor, and Kathleen Dobie, my development editor, for their help, direction, feedback, and constructive criticism during the process. Also, many thanks to Sam Spickernell for dealing with my queries patiently and quickly, and to everyone who works behind the scenes at Wiley for their efforts in making this book possible.

Thanks also to my family for their untiring support and encouragement.

Publisher's Acknowledgements

We're proud of this book; please send us your comments through our Dummies online registration form located at www.dummies.com/register/.

Some of the people who helped bring this book to market include the following:

Acquisitions, Editorial, and Media Development

Project Editor: Steve Edwards

(Previous Edition: Rachael Chilvers and Kathleen Dobie)

Content Editor: Nicole Burnett

Commissioning Editor: Wejdan Ismail

Proofreader: Helen Heyes

Publisher: Jason Dunne

Executive Editor: Samantha Spickernell

Executive Project Editor: Daniel Mersey

Cover Photos: ©Thinkstock/Corbis

Cartoons: Ed McLachlan

Composition Services

Project Coordinator: Erin Smith

Layout and Graphics: Reuben W. Davis, Alissa D. Ellet, Melissa K. Jester, Ronald Terry, Christine Williams

Proofreader: Caitie Kelly

Indexer: Estalita Slivoskey

Contents at a Glance

Introduction..*1*

Part 1: Organising Your Finances........................*7*

Chapter 1: Exploring the Basics 9
Chapter 2: Taking Stock of Your Financial Goals
and Seeking Advice..17
Chapter 3: Choosing the Best Current Account for You....................29
Chapter 4: Guarding Against the Unknown: Insurance........................41

Part 11: Dealing with Debt *53*

Chapter 5: Seeing Red: Tackling Your Overdraft 55
Chapter 6: Flexing the Plastic: Choosing a Credit Card......................65
Chapter 7: Navigating Personal Loans...77
Chapter 8: Avoiding Credit Nasties and Getting Out of Debt............89

*Part 111: Building Up Savings
and Investments*...*101*

Chapter 9: Saving for a Rainy Day 103
Chapter 10: Making the Most of Tax-Free Savings
and Investments...113
Chapter 11: Building Up an Investment Portfolio 123
Chapter 12: Finding Safety in Numbers with Collective Funds 137
Chapter 13: DIY Investing: Opting for Shares 153
Chapter 14: Safe as Houses: Choosing a Mortgage 167

Part 1V: Taking Care of the Future...................*185*

Chapter 15: Planning for Retirement and Beyond............................187
Chapter 16: Getting to Grips with Company Pensions 203
Chapter 17: Examining Personal Pensions
and Stakeholder Schemes..219
Chapter 18: Coping in Retirement 235

Part V: The Part of Tens.................................*253*

Chapter 19: Ten Tips to Get Out of Debt and Save Cash 255
Chapter 20: Coping with Ten Events Life May Throw at You............261
Chapter 21: Ten Golden Rules for Sorting Out Your Finances..........267

Appendix: Resources.....................................*273*

Index..*277*

Table of Contents

Introduction *1*

    About This Book 1
    Conventions Used in This Book.................................1
    What You're Not to Read...1
    Foolish Assumptions 2
    How This Book Is Organised......................................2
        Part I: Organising Your Finances...................3
        Part II: Dealing with Debt 3
        Part III: Building Up Savings and Investments 3
        Part IV: Taking Care of the Future...................3
        Part V: The Part of Tens..................................4
    Icons Used in This Book..4
    Where to Go from Here 4

Part 1: Organising Your Finances..........................*7*

  Chapter 1: Exploring the Basics.....................9

    Looking at the Benefits of Being on Top of Your Finances 9
    Pondering Money Matters 10
        Working out how much money you have 11
        Calculating your debts......................................11
    Clearing Your Debt – and Starting to Save.............12
    Establishing Your Financial Goals...........................13
        Assessing how much risk you're happy with...............14
        Planning for retirement 14
    Taking Advantage of the Tax Breaks on Saving
        and Investing 14
    Using a Financial Adviser...15

  **Chapter 2: Taking Stock of Your Financial Goals
  and Seeking Advice...........................17**

    Drawing Up a Budget...17
    Establishing Your Goals 19
        Prioritising your debts.....................................19
        Prioritising your goals......................................20
    Seeking Advice to Help Realise Your Financial Goals...........20
        Considering the benefits...................................20
        Finding out key facts 21
    Considering Advisers 21
        Being truly independent 21
        Taking a more limited approach.......................23

Getting to Grips with Qualifications 24
Becoming advanced 25
Looking beyond bits of paper 25
Paying for Advice 25
Forking out a fee 25
Going with commission 26
Combining fees and commission 26
Going It Alone 26

Chapter 3: Choosing the Best Current Account for You 29

Explaining How Current Accounts Work....................29
Noting interest and taxes..30
Considering safety first...31
Paying the charges 31
Maintaining the ideal balance 32
Finding the Best Current Account 33
Gaining access..34
Weighing balances 36
Accruing interest 36
Viewing overdrafts..36
Switching Your Current Account 37
Completing the application form....................................37
Obtaining a list of direct debits 38
Handling the changeover period 39

Chapter 4: Guarding Against the Unknown: Insurance...................... 41

Arranging Cover 41
Deciding what insurance you need 42
Disclosing information to the insurer 42
Shopping around for insurance 42
Reading the policy carefully..43
Deciding on the excess 43
Making a comeback if things go wrong......................43
Cutting costs – without skimping on cover.................44
Handling Health and Protection....................................44
Insuring your life...45
Protecting your income 47
Covering critical illness 48
Preparing for accident, sickness, and unemployment...49
Purchasing private medical insurance 49
Covering Your Home and Belongings............................50
Safeguarding your home...51
Taking care of contents insurance..............................51
Making sure of your car 51
Travelling under cover..52

Part II: Dealing with Debt 53

Chapter 5: Seeing Red: Tackling Your Overdraft......55

Understanding How Overdrafts Work 56
    Requesting permission 56
    Calculating interest 56
    Looking at fees 58
Deciding Whether an Overdraft Really Is the Answer...........59
Choosing a Current Account for Its Overdraft 60
    Fee-free buffers 60
    Introductory offers 61
Switching Current Accounts When You
    Have an Overdraft...62
Reducing Your Overdraft 62

Chapter 6: Flexing the Plastic:
Choosing a Credit Card 65

Understanding How Credit Cards Work 66
    Calculating interest 66
    Figuring out credit limits 67
    Making the minimum payment 68
Finding Low Rates..68
    Sourcing good introductory rates 69
    Pursuing low lifetime balances 70
Enjoying the Perks of Clearing Your Balance Every Month....70
    Getting cashback 70
    Earning loyalty points and Air Miles 71
    Going for the added extras...71
    Buying for charity and affinity groups 71
Avoiding Certain Credit Card Activities 72
    Paying annual charges 72
    Withdrawing cash 72
    Buying credit card protection......................................72
Protecting Your Purchases 73
Considering Your Credit Rating..73
    Working with credit scoring 74
    Correcting mistakes on your file...................................74
    Failing credit scoring 76

Chapter 7: Navigating Personal Loans 77

Figuring Out When a Loan Makes Perfect Sense....................77
Deciding When a Loan Is Not a Good Idea...............................78
Understanding How Loans Work 79
    Taking out unsecured versus secured loans..............79
    Deciding on the term...81
    Working out the interest 81
    Calculating the total cost...82

Watching out for early redemption penalties 82
Aiming for flexibility.......................................83
Finding the Best Personal Loan 83
Applying for a loan 84
Coping with a poor (or no) credit history.................85
Avoiding Payment Protection Insurance 86
Working out the cost......................................86
Checking the small print..................................86
Deciding whether you need cover...........................87
Taking Action If You Are Struggling with Repayments.........87

**Chapter 8: Avoiding Credit Nasties
and Getting Out of Debt. 89**

Handling Store Cards Smartly 89
Signing up for store cards................................90
Paying extortionate rates of interest 90
Making store cards work for you...........................90
Clearing store card debt 92
Avoiding Debt Consolidation Firms...........................92
Consolidating debts into one loan.........................93
Looking at high rates and arrangement fees................93
Steering Clear of Loan Sharks 94
Escaping the Debt Trap......................................94
Prioritising your debts...................................95
Working out your budget...................................95
Making savings work harder 95
Juggling your mortgage 96
Replacing the plastic.....................................96
Contacting your creditors 97
Going bankrupt 97
Seeking free advice.......................................98

Part III: Building Up Savings and Investments.....101

Chapter 9: Saving for a Rainy Day 103

Dealing with an Emergency 103
Looking at Savings Strengths 104
Making sure your money is easily accessible 105
Minimising risk...105
Deciding How Much You Need to Save 106
Finding the Best Savings Account............................106
Saving with a monthly account............................106
Opting for a cash individual savings account..........107
Watching out for notice periods 108
Considering the impact of bonuses 109
Realising the advantage of tiered rates 109
Fixing the rate and the term..............................109
Offsetting your savings 110

Shopping Around for the Best Deal 110
    Logging on 111
    Telephoning and posting 111
    Accessing savings via a branch 111
Safeguarding Your Savings...112

Chapter 10: Making the Most of Tax-Free Savings and Investments 113

Opting for an Individual Savings Account 113
    Contributing to ISAs...114
    Understanding ISAs 114
    Deciding on your ISA investments 115
    Selecting your own ISA...118
    Transferring your ISA..119
Choosing National Savings Certificates 120
Exploring Venture Capital Trusts...120

Chapter 11: Building Up an Investment Portfolio 123

Planning Your Strategy..124
Understanding Charges..125
Evaluating Your Risk Level 125
    Taking a cautious approach 126
    Taking the middle road 126
    Getting adventurous..127
Balancing Your Investment Portfolio 128
    Covering the basics 128
    Understanding the underlying investments..............129
    Reviewing your holdings 129
    Ditching poorly performing funds 129
Getting to Grips with Bonds 130
    Understanding how bonds work 130
    Working out government bonds 131
    Opting for corporate bonds 134
Building Up a Share Portfolio 135
    Minimising risk...135
    Maximising returns..136

Chapter 12: Finding Safety in Numbers with Collective Funds 137

Pooling Your Investments..137
    Looking at the advantages of pooled investments...138
    Losing out by pooling..139
    Working out the cost 139
Jumping into Different Pools 139
    Understanding unit trusts 140
    Getting to grips with Oeics...144
    Knowing how investment trusts work.......................145

Making Sense of With-Profits Investment Bonds 146
Buying Corporate Bond Funds 147
Choosing Exchange Traded Funds 148
Joining a Pool 149
    Putting past performance in its place 149
    Cutting costs 150
    Being certain of your investment aims 150
    Checking authorisation 150
    Drip-feeding your contributions 151
    Monitoring your investments 151
    Taxing your returns 151

Chapter 13: DIY Investing: Opting for Shares........ 153

Investing Basics 154
    Understanding the process 154
    Being aware of the risks involved 154
Selecting Your Shares 155
    Deciding on growth or income 155
    Spreading your risk 156
    Picking more exotic investments 156
Choosing a Broker 157
    Knowing you're protected 157
    Deciding what service you need 158
Buying and Selling Shares 160
Holding Your Shares 160
Looking Forward to Returns 162
    Generating dividends 162
    Understanding charges 163
    Paying duty 164
Keeping Track of Your Shares 164

Chapter 14: Safe as Houses: Choosing a Mortgage... 167

Working Out How Much You Can Afford to Borrow 168
    Multiplying your income 168
    Coping without a deposit 169
Calculating How Much Cash You Need
    Beyond the Price 169
    Looking out for the lender's fee 170
    Paying a mortgage broker 170
    Commissioning a lender's valuation and survey 170
    Settling legal fees 171
    Sending in your stamp duty 172
Eenie, Meenie, Miney, Mo: Choosing
    the Right Mortgage 172
    Understanding repayment loans 173
    Going interest-only 173
    Combining repayment with interest-only 174
Understanding Rates 174
    Avoiding the standard variable rate 174
    Opting for a fix 175

Tracking the base rate 175
Plumping for a discount...176
Checking out capped rates...176
Offsetting your mortgage...177
Cashing in on a cashback mortgage.........................178
Finding the Best Mortgage..179
Seeking advice...179
Going online 180
Avoiding Unnecessary Costs....................................181
Watching out for HLC...181
Escaping early redemption penalties.......................182
Sidestepping compulsory insurance.......................183

Part IV: Taking Care of the Future.................... 185

Chapter 15: Planning for Retirement and Beyond.... 187

Making Some Vital Decisions about Retirement 188
Planning your retirement age...................................188
Calculating how much income you need
to live (and play)...189
Working out your current position...........................190
Starting saving 191
Reviewing your plan...191
Looking at the Big Pension Picture.................................192
Coping on the state pension – forget about it!.........192
Building up the state second pension.......................194
Getting credit for your pension
and other benefits...195
Supplementing the State Scheme with
a Personal Pension...196
Taking advantage of the tax breaks.........................196
Locking away your cash 196
Guaranteeing an income...197
Mixing and Matching – Alternatives to Pensions.............197
Investing in bricks and mortar.................................197
Utilising individual savings accounts.......................199
Where There's a Will, the Family Know
Where They Stand...199
Delaying writing a will is unwise..............................200
Getting down to business 200
Protecting Your Estate from an Unnecessary Tax Bill........201

Chapter 16: Getting to Grips with
Company Pensions. 203

Being Smart by Joining the Company Scheme.....................203
Benefiting from employer contributions 204
Protecting your family with life cover.......................205
Providing pensions for surviving partners 206

Exploring the Types of Workplace Pensions 207
Figuring out final salary schemes...............................208
Making the most of a money purchase scheme 210
Going with a group personal pension
or stakeholder scheme...211
Looking at Limits on Your Pension.............................213
Bumping into the contribution ceiling......................213
Getting tax relief...214
Increasing your contributions ......,.......................215
Contracting In or Out of the State Second Pension............216
Changing Jobs – And Your Pension 217

Chapter 17: Examining Personal Pensions and Stakeholder Schemes 219

Understanding How Personal Pensions Work....................220
Figuring Out How Stakeholder Schemes
Enter the Equation...221
Choosing the Best Scheme for You.............................222
Searching for sources...223
Seeking advice..224
Deciding where to invest 225
Making Contributions..227
Sticking to the limits...227
Topping up your pension 228
Stopping contributions 229
Transferring to another fund 229
Receiving Your Pension..230
Working out annuities 230
Drawing an income...231
Phasing your retirement 231
Understanding what happens when you die............231
Taking the Bull by the Horns: Self-Invested
Personal Pensions...232

Chapter 18: Coping in Retirement 235

Deciding When to Retire 235
Taking early retirement..237
Retiring at the usual age 237
Working past retirement age 237
Taking the Tax-Free Lump Sum 238
Deciding how much you should take........................238
Working out what to do with it 239
Explaining Annuities..239
Working out annuities 240
Understanding different types of annuities..............241
Deciding between staying level or rising..................242
Deciding when to buy an annuity 244
Shopping around 245

Retiring Gradually..245
Withdrawing Income 246
Dealing with a Trivial Pension.............................247
Getting Money from Your Home..........................248
    Downsizing 248
    Releasing equity...249

Part V: The Part of Tens.................................*253*

Chapter 19: Ten Tips to Get Out of Debt and Save Cash. 255

Taking Scissors to Your Plastic 255
Going Interest-Free...256
Having a Night In..256
Steering Clear of Buying a Round 257
Wearing Last Season's Threads.............................257
Taking on Part-Time Work......................................258
Steering Clear of Lattes and Muffins...................258
Buying Supermarket Own Brands.........................259
Walking to Work 259
Making Your Own Cards and Pressies..................259

Chapter 20: Coping with Ten Events Life May Throw at You. 261

Leaving Home..261
Paying University Costs 261
Joining the Rat Race 262
Getting Hitched 262
Starting a Family 263
Giving Up Your Day Job to Raise the Kids 264
Getting Divorced 264
Going Self-Employed...265
Being Made Redundant 265
Taking Early Retirement...266

Chapter 21: Ten Golden Rules for Sorting Out Your Finances 267

Live within Your Means..267
Start Saving from a Young Age 268
Become a Rate Tart...268
Avoid Store Cards at All Costs...............................269
Get on the Property Ladder....................................269
Put Your Pay Rise towards Your Pension 270
Take Advice before Taking the Plunge 270
File Your Tax Return on Time 271
Provide for Your Dependants 271
Insure Yourself from Risk.......................................272

Appendix: Resources *273*

  Professional and Trade Organisations 273
  Government Agencies 274
  Other Useful Websites 275
  Credit Reference Agencies 275

Index *277*

Introduction

*W*elcome to the second edition of *Sorting Out Your Finances For Dummies*. If you're struggling to clear your debts and build up your savings and investments for the future, you need some sensible tips to help you realise your goals. This book provides all the help you need to enable you to get your debt under control – and start saving for the future.

About This Book

Although these pages are overflowing with useful advice and information, I present it in a light, easy-to-access format. This book helps you decide where your priorities lie when it comes to your finances. I cover debt and how to clear it, and give tips on finding the best savings account so that when you've got some cash you can ensure it works as hard as possible for you. I offer some hints on picking the best investments for building up a nest egg or for a specific outlay, such as buying a car or paying for a holiday. Just as important, this book helps you maintain your sense of humour – as well as your sanity – as you deal with financial challenges.

Conventions Used in This Book

To help you navigate through this book, I've set up a few conventions:

- *Italic* is used for emphasis and to highlight new words or terms that are defined.
- **Boldfaced** text is used to indicate the action part of numbered steps.
- Monofont is used for Web addresses.

What You're Not to Read

I've written this book so that you can:

- Find information easily and
- Easily understand what you find.

And although I'm sure you want to pore over every last word between the two yellow covers, I actually make it easy for you to identify 'skippable' material. This is the stuff that, although interesting and related to the topic at hand, isn't essential for you to know.

- ✔ **Text in sidebars**. The sidebars are the shaded boxes that appear here and there. They share personal stories and observations, but aren't necessary reading.

- ✔ **Anything with a Technical Stuff Icon attached**. This information is interesting but not critical to your understanding of sorting out your finances.

- ✔ **The stuff on the copyright page**. No kidding. There's nothing here of interest unless you are inexplicably enamoured by legal language and reprint information.

Foolish Assumptions

In this book, I make some general assumptions about who you are:

- ✔ You want to tackle your finances but you don't know the first place to start. You're wondering whether – just maybe – it might be possible to get out of debt once and for all. Perhaps your friends are no longer talking about overdrafts and credit cards but are saving for a deposit for their first home, a new car, or to start a family. You may be worried about being left behind or are simply embarrassed by your spending habits and are ready for things to change.

- ✔ You hope to get information on how to start saving for the future – you want to know the pros and cons of pensions, or buying property, or toying with the stock market – or all three.

- ✔ You want easy-to-understand information that explains what you need to know about your finances, but you've got better things to do (like sleeping, participating in your favourite leisure activity, or even relaxing on holiday) than become an expert on annuities and derivatives. In other words, you want to get it right while you retain control over your life.

How This Book Is Organised

Sorting Out Your Finances For Dummies is organised into five parts. The chapters within each part cover specific topic areas in more detail. So you can easily and quickly scan a topic that interests you, or troubleshoot the source of your latest major headache!

Part I: Organising Your Finances

The chapters in this part help you take stock of your financial goals. This part helps you figure out whether you need to use an independent financial adviser to help you organise your finances and, if this is the case, how to select one who's qualified and suitable for the task. I cover making sure you've got the best current account for your needs. This part also includes everything you need to know on insurance, so that you, your family, and your belongings are covered in case the unexpected happens.

Part II: Dealing with Debt

There's not much point starting to save and build up your investments until you've cleared expensive debts, such as unauthorised overdrafts, credit cards with high rates of interest, and uncompetitive personal loans. In this part, I give you the lowdown on debt and how to get out of it. I guide you through all you need to know about choosing the cheapest overdraft, the special deals providers offer on credit cards, and how to shop around for the most competitive personal loan. I also highlight the dangers of store cards and loan sharks so that you don't get into further difficulty.

Part III: Building Up Savings and Investments

This part takes you from putting aside a little cash to tide you over in an emergency to building up serious investments for the future. I look at tax-free savings and investments, and why you'd be mad not to take advantage of these. I cover understanding risk and how to ensure you don't take on more than you're entirely comfortable with. And if you fancy the thrill of investing in shares, I include plenty of tips to get you started. I also address choosing a mortgage and making sure you can raise enough cash to get on the property ladder.

Part IV: Taking Care of the Future

With a decreasing amount of state help available in retirement, you need to start investing as soon as you can afford to do so to ensure you have a comfortable retirement. In this part, I look at the various options available – from occupational and personal pensions, to property or other investment products, such as individual savings accounts. I also include guidelines on coping financially in retirement and ensuring your money stretches as far as possible.

Part V: The Part of Tens

Here, in a concise and lively set of condensed chapters, are tips to make the difference between a prosperous future and one where you struggle. In these chapters, I give you tips on getting out of debt, coping with events life may throw at you, and the golden rules of sorting out your finances.

Icons Used in This Book

Scattered throughout the book are icons to guide you along your way and highlight some of the suggestions, solutions, and cautions of sorting out your finances.

Keep your sights on the target for important advice and critical insights into the best practices in saving, investing, and clearing debt.

Remember these important nuggets of information and you'll stand a better chance of achieving your aims.

This icon highlights the landmines that you need to steer clear of.

Prepare for brain strain when you read these bits – and impress your friends with what you know.

This icon highlights the real-life anecdotes from years of experience and mistakes, made by myself and friends, when tackling our finances. While we should learn from our own mistakes, it's even better to learn from others' – and I share some of them with you here.

Where to Go from Here

This book is organised so that you can go wherever you want to find complete information. Want to know what information is on your credit file? Head to Chapter 6. If you're interested in writing your will, go to Chapter 15. You can use the table of contents to find broad categories of information, or use the index to look up more specific things.

If you're not sure where you want to go, you may want to start with Part I. It gives you all the basic information you need to get started in establishing your financial goals and points to places in the book and beyond where you can find more detailed information.

Part I
Organising Your Finances

'It's nothing to do with the full moon — he
always goes through a change when he tries
to reorganise our finances.'

In this part . . .

Before you sort out your debts and investments, you need to get the basics in order. In this part, I guide you through the process of establishing your financial goals and how an independent financial adviser can help you reach them. I include hints on choosing an adviser and the qualifications to look for.

I also give you tips on choosing the best current account for your circumstances, and making sure you've got enough insurance in place to guard against the unknown.

If you're thinking about getting your finances in order, but are not quite sure where to begin, this is the part for you.

Chapter 1

Exploring the Basics

In This Chapter
▶ Benefiting from getting a grasp on your finances
▶ Looking at your financial picture
▶ Working out how you can get out of debt
▶ Figuring out what you want from your finances
▶ Investing the tax-free way
▶ Understanding the importance of financial advice

Congratulations! You've decided to get to grips with your finances and start building up your savings and investments for the future. Making sure you're in control of your finances enables you to do what you want – upgrade your car, get on the first step of the property ladder, or start building funds for retirement.

In this chapter I start by giving you the lowdown on working out what your financial goals are and how you can achieve them. I offer advice on clearing your debts before you begin building up your savings and investments, and the importance of seeking independent financial advice. Only when you have the basics under your belt can you ensure your finances work for you – rather than limiting you from doing all the things you want to do.

Looking at the Benefits of Being on Top of Your Finances

Sorting out your money by clearing your debt and building up your savings and investments makes you the master of your financial future, and brings several benefits:

 ✔ **You stop paying expensive fees and charges for being in debt.** Debt is pricey, with high rates of interest and often extra fees and charges. If you're in a lot of debt and pay a significant amount of interest on it, you may find that you simply can't clear what you owe as all your money goes towards servicing the debt and paying the interest. Clearing your debt removes the debt itself and the cost of financing it.

- ✔ **You get rid of your guilt.** Being in debt can be a worry, particularly if your debt has got out of hand and you can't see any way of escaping the situation. Some people also regard being in debt as a stigma – something to be ashamed of and hidden from friends, family, and colleagues. Any way you look at it, debt is a burden and getting rid of it can be a huge weight off your shoulders.

- ✔ **You feel more confident about the future.** With the state providing little financial support in retirement (see Chapter 15 for more on this), you may be concerned about how you're going to make ends meet. But if you have savings and investments spread across a range of funds, pensions, and property, you can rest easy with regard to the future. You may even be able to look forward to giving up work, rather than dread it.

- ✔ **You open up a range of financial options.** If your finances are in order, you can afford to take time off to travel or try a new career. But if you have lots of debt or little in the way of savings, you may not have the option to do what you like. This can make you feel rather resentful.

Pondering Money Matters

To stay on top of your finances, you need to review major investments – such as savings accounts, unit and investment trusts, shares, and your pension – at least once a year, to ensure that you're still earning the best returns. Getting into the habit of spending a couple of hours a week keeping things ticking over is also a worthwhile idea: Paying bills before they're late or moving surplus cash from your current account to a high-interest-paying savings account. You should also use this time to plan what you're going to do next.

When you find the best financial products available, keep a careful eye on them. As soon as they start to look uncompetitive, consider switching to a better deal with a more attractive rate of interest. Don't become complacent, or you could lose out.

If you aren't prepared to track your own financial investments, consider using an independent financial adviser (IFA) to do this for you. An IFA can make suggestions as to what you should be investing in and whether you should move out of existing investments. See 'Using a financial adviser' later in this chapter for more details.

In the following sections, I look at how you can start getting on top of your finances.

Working out how much money you have

You should know off the top of your head roughly how much your assets are worth, but if you aren't on top of your finances you may not have a clue. Or if you're in a lot of debt you may know the depressing answer straight away – nothing.

Many people have lots of savings accounts and investments dotted around with a few pounds in each. The money in such accounts often has been languishing there for years and earning a poor rate of interest. If the interest rate is halfway decent, it's more likely to be down to luck than careful financial planning.

 As a first step to getting a clear view of your finances, make an inventory of what you have: List all your savings and investments so that you can see all your assets at a glance. Don't forget those windfall (free) shares you got when your building society demutualised (listed on the stock market), those premium bonds granny bought you when you were born, or that odd £20 sitting in a National Savings account. It all adds up.

 Don't forget payments into your pension (if you have one) and equity in your home (you can work this out by subtracting your outstanding mortgage from the market value of your property). These are all assets.

From there, you can assess whether your money is in the best place to earn you the highest returns.

Calculating your debts

If you're like most people, you have a bit of debt. Or you may have quite a lot of debt, depending on your financial situation and attitude towards credit.

 Debt isn't always bad: The low interest rates of the past few years made it possible to pick up cheap personal loans or credit cards charging 0 per cent for an introductory period on new purchases or balance transfers. Making use of cheap money is a smart financial move, so long as you keep up with the payments and avoid expensive fees. And make sure you switch to another 0 per cent deal when the introductory period on your credit card runs out so that you don't find yourself paying a much higher rate of interest.

On the other hand, you never get out of debt if you ignore bills and credit card statements for fear of what you might find within the envelope. It may not make for pretty reading, but facing up to your debts is the first step to getting rid of them. A bit of short-term pain now leads to stronger finances in the longer term. Bite the bullet and open the envelope.

Before you can attack your debts – getting rid of the most expensive ones and chipping away at the rest – you need to make a list of exactly what you owe.

Compile and arrange a list so that your most expensive – rather than your greatest – debt is at the top. For example, you may owe £150,000 on your mortgage and £2,000 on a store card, but paying off the store card is more of a priority because you pay a lot higher interest on it. While you may be paying around 5 to 6 per cent interest on your mortgage, you might be paying six or seven times this much on the store card. Clearing the store card debt in the short term, and the mortgage debt in the longer term, therefore makes sense. (Go to Chapter 8 for more on store cards and Chapter 14 for the lowdown on mortgages.)

Clearing Your Debt – and Starting to Save

When you know how much debt you've got and what savings you have, use the latter to clear the former. This is particularly worthwhile if your savings are languishing in uncompetitive accounts while your debt is expensive.

If you don't have enough surplus savings to make much of an impact on your debt, at least shift store and credit card balances onto cheaper plastic. This reduces the interest you pay: Instead of paying back just the interest each month, you can chip away at the outstanding debt as well.

Having some savings set aside is always reassuring, but if you've got expensive debt it doesn't make much sense to have money just sitting in an account. Use the savings to clear some of the expensive, short-term debt, as you generally pay more interest on the debt than you earn on your savings. Only after you clear your expensive short-term debts should you start building up savings for an emergency or rainy day. (The chapters in Part II give tips for clearing your debt.)

After you clear your debt, your next step is to start your emergency fund – for if the boiler packs up, for example – which is vital to your financial health. Having an emergency fund prevents you from slipping into expensive debt in the first place.

Make sure your emergency savings are easily accessible. There's no point choosing an account where you have to give 90 days' notice before you can get your money – it defeats the whole object. The amount you save should be the equivalent of three to six months' worth of outgoings: The exact amount you need depends on what you're personally comfortable with and how much you spend each month. If you're the main breadwinner, you may need more cash than someone with a wealthy partner with a good income. Chapter 9 has more on saving for a rainy day.

Establishing Your Financial Goals

Deciding how you should proceed is impossible until you know what you're saving or investing for. Thus, you need to decide what you want before you begin.

When you've got your emergency savings covered, you can be more adventurous with your money. However, before you get carried away, remember that how you invest depends on what you want the money for and when you want it:

- ✔ If you're investing for the **short term** – less than five years – to pay for a holiday or new car, for example, some form of high-interest savings account is your best bet, rather than stocks and shares, which can go down in value as well as up. If you need to raise a set amount of cash in the short term you can't afford to take risks. Instead, opt for low-risk investments so that you end up with enough cash to enable you to achieve your goals.

- ✔ If you want to raise a sum of money for use in 10 or 15 years' time or more, you need to invest for the **long term**. You may want to raise cash to pay for your children's school fees or cash to put towards your pension. You can afford to take on more risk if you don't need the money for a few years. The idea is that you have longer to ride out the ups and downs of the stock market.

Riskier investments should generate greater returns in the long run, but make sure that you don't need to get your hands on the cash in the short term and that you aren't investing cash you can't afford to lose.

Assessing how much risk you're happy with

A crucial factor to finding the right investments to suit you is how much risk you're willing to take on.

You can afford to take on more risk the longer you can allow your money to stay invested. As you near retirement, or need to get hold of your cash, you should switch to less risky investments so you have less chance of losing your money.

Planning for retirement

One of the main reasons people invest is to ensure they have enough income in retirement. You can't rely on the state to provide a generous enough pension – you have to make your own provision.

 A pension is one way of generating retirement income, but not the only one. Diversifying and spreading your risk across a broad range of investments is always a sensible idea.

Pensions come with excellent tax breaks (see Chapter 15 for details) but they are inflexible. If you tie up all your spare cash in a pension, and need some money in an emergency before you reach retirement age, you may not be able to get hold of it.

 A sensible approach is to combine pensions with property, individual savings accounts (ISAs), and other investments to build a broad portfolio of products to provide you with an income in retirement. That way you won't put all your eggs in one basket but will expose yourself to a diverse range of products.

Taking Advantage of the Tax Breaks on Saving and Investing

Never look a gift horse in the mouth, particularly when it comes to savings and investments. You have to pay enough tax to the Government without paying more than you need to. You can save tax on your investment returns – completely legitimately – by opting for tax-free products.

 If you don't pay income tax as a general rule, you don't have to pay tax on your savings. Ensure your savings account provider knows this by filling out form IR85 – available from your bank or building society, or HM Revenue & Customs (www.hmrc.gov.uk).

If you do pay tax, opt for tax-free investments where possible, such as individual savings accounts (ISAs). These enable you to invest in cash or equities up to a maximum of £7,200 each tax year (6 April to 5 April the following year).

Other tax-free investments, such as those offered by National Savings and Investments, are available. But the rates on these aren't always the most competitive (Chapter 10 has more on these) so don't be blinded by the tax-free benefits.

Choosing an investment simply because returns are tax free isn't wise, and may not suit your attitude to risk or your investment aims, or fit in with the other products in your portfolio. Consider each investment as part of the wider picture and you minimise your chances of opting for the wrong product.

Using a Financial Adviser

One of the easiest ways to choose the right investments for you is to use an independent financial adviser (IFA). I advise opting for one who is totally independent and can recommend you any product on the market, rather than a salesperson who is restricted to a limited range of investment products.

You don't always need a financial adviser. If you opt for simple products, such as a savings account, credit card, or personal loan, you should be able to choose one yourself. Do your research beforehand and opt for a product only if you understand exactly how much that product is going to cost you in the long term.

If you're an experienced investor, you may not need advice either. But most people could always use a bit of advice, so paying a bit of cash to ensure you get the best investment may be worthwhile, and could save you money in the long run. (Go to Chapter 2 for more on choosing an IFA.)

Chapter 2

Taking Stock of Your Financial Goals and Seeking Advice

In This Chapter

▶ Working out a budget

▶ Figuring out what you want from your finances

▶ Considering the importance of financial advice

▶ Choosing an adviser or advising yourself

*W*hen you've decided to get to grips with your finances, you might get excited about what shares you're going to buy in which company. But while you may be eager to start dabbling in exotic investments, you must first sort out more mundane matters.

In this chapter I discuss how to establish your financial goals and how to achieve them. I also offer tips on choosing an adviser, deciding whether to opt for fees or commission, and how to make a complaint if you feel you've been given the wrong advice.

Drawing Up a Budget

The only way to manage your finances is to draw up a budget that you can stick to.

People who get into debt generally do so because they live beyond their means – spending more than they earn. Drawing up a budget and sticking to it helps to ensure that this doesn't happen to you. If you're in debt already, following a budget can help you to get out of that situation and develop habits that help you stay out.

In drawing up a budget, record your income and expenditure for a set period – usually a month. You can then calculate how much money you have left over each month after subtracting all your outgoings from your income. This surplus is money you can use to clear away your debts or to start saving or investing.

Table 2-1 lists common outgoings. Go through this and answer honestly how much you spend on each item every month.

Table 2-1	Figuring Your Monthly Budget
MONTHLY INCOME	
Salary (after tax):	£..........
Overtime and bonuses:	£..........
Any other income:	£..........
TOTAL NET INCOME:	£..........
MONTHLY OUTGOINGS	
Rent/Mortgage repayment:	£..........
Pension contribution:	£..........
Gas/electricity/water:	£..........
Council tax:	£..........
Telephone/Mobile:	£..........
Satellite TV:	£..........
Food:	£..........
Insurance – car/home/other:	£..........
Travel:	£..........
Clothing:	£..........
Entertainment:	£..........
Other outgoings:	£..........
TOTAL OUTGOINGS:	£..........
Balance (income minus outgoings):	£..........

If the figures don't add up, and you find that you spend more than you've got coming in, all is not lost. Look for ways to economise in certain areas, though be sure you're realistic about what you can achieve: Don't fool yourself into thinking that you'll be happy to stay in every single night if you're usually a party animal. It simply won't be possible. While you might not be able to stay in every night, saying that you're going to stay in one night a week when you would normally go out may be a realistic goal. This won't have the same dramatic results as staying in all the time but it will save you money in the long term and you are more likely to stick to this.

Establishing Your Goals

Before you can start saving or investing for the future, you need to work out what your aims are. Only if you know what you are saving and investing for can you choose the best products to help you realise your goals. Otherwise, you're likely to end up with completely unsuitable products.

Some of the financial goals you have may include clearing your debts, buying a house, starting a pension, or helping out your children.

Before you can start investing you need to clear your existing debts. In the next sections, I look at how to start clearing your debt and how to put your goals in proper order.

Prioritising your debts

If you have serious debts, your first financial goal has to be to pay them off. Before you can start investing, you need to clear your existing debts.

Debt can be extremely expensive. Having a few hundred pounds in savings if you owe thousands of pounds on a store card that charges you a high rate of interest makes no sense. The interest you're charged on your debts is more expensive than the interest you earn when you're in credit. Struggling to pay high rates of interest on your borrowings makes it even harder to clear the debt itself.

Before you can start whittling away at your debt, compile a list of exactly what you owe. Jot down all your debts, from outstanding store and credit card balances to your overdraft, personal loans, and mortgage, then prioritise them.

Organise your list so that the most expensive debt is at the top. You may be tempted to list your biggest debt – probably your mortgage – first. But bear in mind that more expensive debt – such as store card debt – needs to go before relatively cheaper debt – such as your mortgage. Your aim is to clear the expensive and unneccessary debt, such as pricey plastic and unauthorised overdrafts, first because it's far more of a strain on your pocket.

Prioritising your goals

Most people have short and long-term financial goals. In the short term you might want to buy a new car or pay for a summer holiday, while in the longer term you may be keen to build up savings for retirement. And, you may have more than just your own future to consider: If you have children (or plan to have them at some stage), they may want go to university or need help getting on the housing ladder, and you need to plan to fulfil those goals as well.

Different goals require different investment vehicles so it's important that you work out what you want and then prioritise them. If you're investing for the long term – for retirement, for example – you should invest in equities because, historically, they produce the greatest returns over time. However, they aren't suitable for short-term investment goals because they are extremely volatile – the value of your shares may plummet just when you need the cash to buy your new car. But if you don't need the cash for many years you have plenty of notice as to when you need to sell your shares so can do so when you stand to make a profit. There may well be times during the years you own them when you suffer losses – at least on paper. But it doesn't matter, as potential losses aren't realised unless you actually sell up.

 If you're saving for a holiday or new car – investing for the short term – stick to a savings account paying the highest rate of interest you can find. At least you're guaranteed to get your capital back, plus some return: You aren't risking your cash. You won't make the big returns you might have made on stocks and shares but at least you know there won't be any losses either.

Seeking Advice to Help Realise Your Financial Goals

You're likely to need advice before buying financial products, particularly if you're inexperienced at saving and investing.

Considering the benefits

Life-changing experiences, such as buying your first home, getting married, having children, going self-employed, or retiring, often require professional advice. Potentially, you need a lot of money to see you through each of these stages and generating that money can be hard, particularly if you're inexperienced in such matters.

An independent adviser will metaphorically hold your hand and guide you through the stages. A professional puts distance between himself and your situation so he can assess the situation objectively and recommend the best financial course.

If you've got friends or family who are financially literate, you could ask them for help. But unless they are experienced advisers themselves, and know all the ins and outs of your particular circumstances, they are not in a position to recommend the best products to you. For that you need a qualified adviser.

Finding out key facts

During your first consultation, a potential adviser should give you clear information about what services you're being offered and an indication of what you'll have to pay for them. This enables you to compare the cost of financial advice and shop around for the adviser who is best value for money.

Your adviser can explain the above by giving you two *keyfacts documents* concerning:

- **Services:** This document explains the type of advice you are being offered and the range of products offered.

- **Costs:** This list explains the different ways you can pay for the advice you receive and gives an indication of the fees or commission you may have to pay. If you pay by commission, it shows you how this compares to the average market commission. (See 'Paying for advice' later in this chapter for more information.)

Considering Advisers

Three different types of financial adviser exist: independent, tied, and multi-tied. In the following sections, I explain these in more detail.

Being truly independent

If you want unbiased financial advice and access to all the products on the market, then opt for an independent financial adviser (IFA). An IFA researches the whole market and takes his pick from what's available to ensure that you get the best product for your needs.

Benefiting from independent advice

The big advantage of using an IFA is that you're using a qualified practitioner to find the best products for your circumstances. Your IFA asks you a number of questions about your situation, your financial goals, and attitude to risk to ensure that he finds the most suitable products.

IFAs are answerable to the Financial Services Authority (FSA), the City regulator. IFAs have to follow FSA rules, so you have the comfort of knowing that your adviser is governed by certain procedures. If he falls foul of these rules, he will be brought to task by the FSA, and may be fined and could even lose his licence to trade. Hence, abiding by these rules is extremely important to IFAs.

 When your IFA recommends products to you, he must provide reasons, in writing, as to why he suggests certain funds and investments and not others. This is to avoid the chance of mis-selling, when you are advised to take out products that aren't suitable for you.

Avoiding the pitfalls

Not all advisers can offer independent advice on every investment product. One advisory company may offer advice on mortgages from the whole market but not be authorised to offer investment advice (see 'Taking a more limited approach' in the next section).

 Check that your adviser is authorised with the FSA: Don't assume this is the case – the unscrupulous have been known to lie about this. Check that he is authorised even if he has been recommended to you by a friend or relative. You can do this by checking the FSA Central Register at www.fsa.gov.uk/register or telephone 0845 606 1234 for further information.

 If you sign on with an unauthorised adviser and he loses your money through negligence, you can't claim compensation as you could in the same circumstances with an authorised IFA.

If a firm is authorised by the FSA, and you feel that the advice you have been given is wrong, take up your complaint with the firm in question. If it isn't answered to your satisfaction and you wish to pursue your complaint, contact the Financial Ombudsman Service on 0845 080 1800 or at www.financial-ombudsman.org.uk.

Finding an IFA

 If you've decided to opt for independent advice – even if it means paying a fee to ensure the service is completely unbiased – it defeats the object if you opt for the first IFA you come across. Do your research beforehand and choose an adviser who is most suitable for your needs.

To find an IFA, contact IFA Promotion on 0800 085 3250 or go to www.unbiased.co.uk to search for a local IFA or one that matches your specific requirements. Or you could try the Personal Finance Society at www.findanadviser.org.

When you first meet your IFA, the initial consultation is often free to allow you both to get to know each other. Try to assess whether you could see yourself working with this person as you'll be expected to reveal lots of personal information about your finances: If you don't get on with or trust your IFA, you won't get the best results and it will be a largely unfruitful relationship. Shop around – if you don't get the right vibes, say 'thanks but no thanks' and keep on looking.

Taking a more limited approach

Some advisers can give advice only on a limited number of products: In other words, they are not independent because they don't have access to the whole market. Such an adviser may be able to advise you on the investment products – pensions, life insurance, and unit trusts – of just one company or a specified panel of companies.

I explain how this works in more detail in the following sections.

Tying yourself down

An adviser who can only recommend products from one provider is known as a *tied agent*. Most people buy their financial products through tied agents, usually salespeople at their bank or building society.

Just because it's easy doesn't make tied advice the best way to buy your financial products. In doing so, you're limiting your choice so much that you're highly unlikely to end up with the most competitive product – if you do, it will be a stroke of luck rather than the result of sound judgement.

The salesperson in the bank or building society is acting on behalf of the product provider. He is not acting in your interests, as an IFA should, and can give no really independent advice. All he can do is provide information about the product you're already interested in buying, or other products provided by his company He can't tell you whether it is the best product for your circumstances, or indeed right for you at all. He can only talk you through the application process and how the product works.

If you're an inexperienced investor, using a tied agent can be a recipe for disaster. You desperately need advice yet you aren't going to get it so how can you possibly make the right investment decision? You may not lose your cash because you are investing with a reputable company, but you're unlikely to generate the highest returns from it either.

Multiplying your options

Halfway between a tied adviser and an IFA is a *multi-tied agent.* A multi-tied agent can sell you products from a panel of companies, rather than just one. The adviser has an agreement with the companies whose products he sells before he starts advising clients: He can't suddenly pluck one out of the air when consulting a client and decide to sell you its products. Multi-tied agents are intended to offer consumers more choice without having to fork out for an IFA, if they can't afford it or aren't prepared to pay for financial advice.

Banks and building societies, which sold only their own products in the past, can now broaden their range to include products from several other providers. The idea is that this will be quicker than using an IFA because the multi-tied agent doesn't have to do a comprehensive search yet can still benefit customers by offering exposure to a wider range of products.

Don't assume that the panel the multi-tied agent is using offers the best buys on the market. There could well be better deals out there. The panel are simply providers the adviser has a relationship with – usually of the financial variety. To guarantee access to the best products on the market you must use an independent financial adviser.

Find out about the breadth of products on offer before using a multi-tied agent and decide whether the choice is wide enough. If not, try another multi-tied agent or IFA.

Getting to Grips with Qualifications

All advisers – independent, tied, or multi-tied – must pass the Certificate in Financial Planning (Cert.FP) exam, or equivalent, before they can provide financial advice. The FSA requires that they pass this. An adviser can't sit back on their laurels and assume they've nothing more to learn once they've achieved this benchmark, either: They are obliged to keep up to date with relevant developments.

Becoming advanced

Advisers can stick with the basic Cert.FP or choose to take a more advanced exam. The most popular are the Advanced Financial Planning Certificate (AFPC) and Certified Financial Planner (CFP) licence.

If you're buying a pension, look for an adviser with G60 and AF3; for investments, look for G70 and AF4 along with the Investment Management Certificate (IMC). If you require specialist mortgage advice, look for a Certificate in Mortgage Advice and the Certificate in Mortgage Advice and Practice (CeMap).

Looking beyond bits of paper

Although advisers with lots of qualifications look encouraging, they aren't the be-all and end-all. You need to get on with your adviser because you could well have to spend a lot of time with him and trusting him is important.

You also need to ensure that your adviser specialises in the areas that you're keen to invest in. Experience can also be important so find out how long they've been in the business. An adviser who is wet behind the ears may not have enough knowledge to instil confidence in you.

Paying for Advice

Advice doesn't come free, which is why lots of people are put off from seeking it: They think it will be expensive. But it doesn't have to be.

Advisers must give you a menu of charges when you first seek advice. This enables you to compare the cost of advice and to shop around for a better service.

Three main ways of paying for advice exist, explained in the following sections.

Forking out a fee

Fees are either charged by the hour or as a set price for the whole job. This is known as *fees-only* advice and is the most expensive option, with fees costing anything from £50 to £200 an hour (depending on how experienced your adviser is). You may get the first half-hour free; the initial meeting is often an introductory session where you simply get to know one another better and figure out whether you're happy to work with the adviser.

You have to pay a fee even if you don't end up taking out a financial product. This isn't the case if you pay by commission (see 'Going with commission' in the following section).

If you do pay an hourly fee, make sure you get a rough idea of how many hours' work is required and how much the total cost is likely to be. Ask your adviser for an estimate of how much he might charge you. You can also request that he doesn't exceed a given amount without checking with you first.

If you use an IFA, you can choose to pay a fee rather than commission. Only an IFA has to offer the choice of payment options. Tied and multi-tied agents don't have to offer a choice, although they may decide to anyhow.

Going with commission

If you aren't prepared to pay a fee, or can't afford to, some advisers charge commission instead – and all IFAs must offer this option. The commission is deducted by the product provider when you invest money in a product. As well as an initial commission for setting up a plan, you may also be charged an annual commission on top, which is known as *trail commission*. Check with your adviser whether this applies before signing up.

Combining fees and commission

You don't have to choose fees or commission – you can have a combination of both. Some product providers pay your adviser commission when you buy a product, which he may pass onto you in one of a number of ways. These include passing on the full value of that commission to you by reducing his fee; reducing the product charges; increasing your investment amount; or refunding the commission to you.

Going It Alone

In some circumstances, you may decide that you don't need advice. If you're opting for a simple product, such as a credit card or savings account, you don't need to pay an adviser for help in choosing the best product: You should simply do the research yourself. Likewise, if you're an experienced investor and have plenty of time to devote to your investments, you may not need advice.

The advantages of not using an adviser are:

- **Low cost:** The only money you spend is on phone calls.

- **Convenience:** You can buy where you like and when you like. You don't have to wait until you've made an appointment or for your adviser to do the necessary research.

- **Broad access:** You can deal with a wider range of firms. You aren't restricted to dealing just with those in your local area.

- **Speed:** You can buy over the phone or Internet, without having to queue to see an adviser in your local bank branch.

You should only go it alone if you know what you're doing. Not taking advice can save you money in the short term but it's also a risky business if you're inexperienced and could cost you in the long run.

Chapter 3

Choosing the Best Current Account for You

In This Chapter

▶ Understanding how current accounts operate

▶ Choosing a current account that suits you

▶ Changing accounts

A current account is the most common type of financial product: Most people have one. If you're like the majority of
account owners, you didn't give much thought to what you want
from a current account before signing up for one, which means
your current account may be unsuitable for your needs. For example, if you frequently go overdrawn you don't want an account with
expensive overdraft charges, or if your account is usually in credit
you don't want one with a poor rate of interest on balances.

The good news is that if you're not happy with your account – for
whatever reason – it's easier than ever to switch. The Internet has
opened up competition in the current account market with scores
of new providers offering attractive products. And the rules mean
that banks have to co-operate within days rather than weeks if you
express a desire to move an account. In this chapter I show you
how to make sure you find the best current account for your particular needs.

Explaining How Current Accounts Work

Unless you're happy to deal in cash all the time, you need a *current
account*, which is where your wages are usually paid by your
employer so that you can pay bills, your rent or mortgage, and
withdraw cash for everyday spending. Banks, building societies,
and even supermarkets offer these.

Most people have their salary, state benefits, and tax credits (where applicable) paid into their current account.

You can arrange to pay your bills, mortgage, rent, and so on directly from your account through one of two methods:

✔ A *standing order* is an instruction you give your bank to pay a fixed amount, usually each month, to a particular person or supplier. The amount can be changed only if you give instructions to your bank.

✔ A *direct debit* is an instruction to pay a particular person or supplier an amount that can fluctuate. The person or supplier informs your bank how much it is taking out of your account that particular month (after informing you).

Most current accounts come with a cash card so you can withdraw money from automated teller machines (ATMs). This card usually doubles up as a debit card so you can pay for goods in shops with the money debited from your account – usually the next day. Most current accounts also offer a cheque book, although a number of shops now refuse to accept cheques, so they are going out of fashion. If you're over 18 you can also apply for an overdraft (see Chapter 5 for more details on these).

I give you more of the specifics of current accounts in the following sections.

Noting interest and taxes

The interest you receive on the balance in your current account is subject to income tax and usually paid monthly. Interest on some accounts is calculated annually.

You receive interest after it has been taxed at 20 per cent (your current account provider deducts interest and pays it to HM Revenue & Customs on your behalf). If you're a basic rate taxpayer this is the full extent of your tax liability, but if you're a higher-rate taxpayer you have to pay 40 per cent tax – the rest is collected via your self-assessment tax return.

If you don't have a job or are on a low income, you don't have to pay tax on the interest you earn. However, you need to inform your bank or building society of your circumstances by filling out form R85, which is available from your current account provider or local tax office.

Considering safety first

A current account is a safe home for your money: The biggest threat to your money is your spending habit! With a current account, you don't assume any stock market risk or stand much chance of the bank or building society going bust and you 'losing' your cash. Even if your bank or building society goes bust, because it is registered with the Financial Services Authority (FSA) and subject to the Financial Services Compensation Scheme (FSCS) you would receive back 100 per cent of the first £2,000 you had on deposit and 90 per cent of the next £33,000 (up to a limit of £31,700).

Only firms registered with the FSA are covered by the FSCS. To check that a current account provider is covered *before* you open an account, go to the FSA's Web site (www.fsa.gov.uk) or call the consumer helpline on 0845 606 1234. The majority of banks and building societies in the UK have signed up to the voluntary Banking Code. This sets out the standards for dealing fairly with customers. A copy of the Banking Code is available on the British Bankers Association Web site (www.bba.org.uk or telephone 020 7216 8800).

If you aren't happy with the service you've received from your bank or building society, complain first to the institution concerned. If the problem isn't rectified, contact the Financial Ombudsman Service, which was set up to settle disputes between customers and financial firms, on 0845 080 1800.

The main risk to your money is the rate of inflation, which indicates how much the cost of living is going up. So when the rate of inflation is higher than the interest you're earning on your account, you are losing money in real terms. For example, if inflation is at 2 per cent and you are earning 0.1 per cent interest on your current account, you are losing money. This is why shopping around for the best rate of interest (see 'Switching your current account' later in this chapter) and ensuring you don't keep huge sums of money sitting in your current account is worthwhile. Move that money to a savings account paying a better rate of interest instead.

Paying the charges

You pay no charges on most current accounts if you're in credit, although packaged accounts impose a monthly fee for a range of additional services (see the nearby 'Paying for packaged accounts' sidebar).

Paying for packaged accounts

A number of banks provide packaged accounts that offer a range of benefits and services above and beyond your standard current account. Most charge a fee – of around £7 a month – but not all do: You may end up paying a higher rate on your overdraft instead (if you have one), so check the rates before signing up if you regularly go overdrawn.

A packaged account is worth the fee only if you make use of the perks available. These can include free annual travel insurance, free commission on foreign currency, and free breakdown recovery. But before taking up offers such as discounts on holidays and flights, or preferential deals on savings, credit cards, or loans, shop around to see whether you can find a better deal elsewhere.

If you don't use the perks and can get a cheaper deal elsewhere on other products, think carefully before opting for a packaged account.

You may have to pay a fee of £1.50 to £2 for using 'convenience' cash machines to withdraw money in small shops and service stations, however, and will be charged for special services such as sending money abroad.

Most banks charge for going overdrawn. As well as the overdraft rate, you may also have to pay a monthly or quarterly fee. Some banks also charge a fee for every day you have an *unauthorised overdraft* – where you go into the red without permission. One bank charges £20 a day up to a maximum of £80 in any one month, for example. Many banks offer a fee-free overdraft buffer of a few hundred pounds, while others charge as much as 30 per cent for unauthorised borrowing.

You may – or may not – have to pay fees for other services such as requesting a duplicate statement, using an ATM abroad, or stopping a cheque. So, for example, if you travel frequently, finding an account that doesn't make you pay to use an ATM when you're outside the country makes sense.

Maintaining the ideal balance

There are no restrictions on how long you keep your cash in your account or on withdrawing money from it, apart from the availability of funds and the limit on how much cash you can withdraw from an ATM in any one day (usually £250 or £300).

You may be required to keep a minimum balance in your account, however. Some accounts have tiered rates of interest, so if your balance falls below a certain level you earn a lower rate of interest.

Even if your current account does pay a good rate of interest, keeping a big balance in your account is a bad idea. You could almost certainly get a better deal elsewhere in an instant-access mini cash individual savings account (ISA), because returns are tax-free. See Chapter 10 for more on these.

The ideal balance in a current account differs from person to person, but as a general rule you shouldn't have more than you need to cover the month's outgoings. Keeping tens of thousands of pounds in your current account makes no sense because your money can earn more interest in a savings account or mini cash ISA.

Work out how much you need to cover your bills and expenses each month, allow a couple of hundred pounds as a buffer in case of unexpected outgoings (the exact amount will depend on what you feel comfortable with), and put the rest where it earns a better rate of interest.

Finding the Best Current Account

When opening your first current account, opting for the same account your parents have is the easy move. Or if you're heading off to university and opening your first current account you may choose the one that offers the best perks: Such as a free five-year Young Person's Railcard, which gives you one-third off rail travel. Few people give any more thought to opening a current account than that. But seeing that a current account fulfils such a crucial role in your finances because most of your cash flows through it at some stage, think about what you want from a current account before signing up.

Some banks pay extremely poor rates of interest on current accounts and charge extortionate rates of interest on overdrafts, yet those offering the worst deals also have the largest number of customers. Some of the biggest banks pay as little as 0.1 per cent interest on balances. Other banks pay 30 times this amount of interest. Some banks charge around 18 per cent interest on authorised overdrafts, even though you can get an overdraft rate of around 7 per cent if you shop around. Yet despite this, some 70 per cent of all current accounts remain with one of the big four banks – Barclays, HSBC, Lloyds TSB, and NatWest.

No bank or building society offers the best deal on every single product. One bank may have a fantastic mortgage range but offer a low interest rate on its current accounts. Product providers specialise in certain areas, offering one or two really attractive deals to pull in the punters. Other customers end up paying for this great deal – usually those stuck with an uncompetitive current account.

Check for an introductory offer. Some banks pay a lump sum or charge 0 per cent on overdrafts for a limited period when you open an account. Find out whether you qualify for preferential rates on other products offered by the bank, such as insurance or personal loans.

When scouting financial institutions, discover what other services are on offer, such as the ability to buy or sell shares (see Chapter 13 for more on this) or free financial advice. If you're keen on being green, determine whether you can get an ethical banking account, which are provided by socially responsible banks that don't invest in companies involved in tobacco, gaming, gambling, or pornography (see Chapter 12).

To compare the best current accounts, use the best buy calculator at www.switchwithwhich.co.uk.

When choosing a current account, you need to consider how you'll use it. I give you information on several issues to bear in mind in the following sections.

Gaining access

Having money sitting in your current account is all well and good, but you need to be able to get to your money. Fortunately, modern banking methods offer you a multitude of ways to access your dough, from stepping into a solid building and getting money from a live person to choosing the virtual route of a standalone Internet bank (keep in mind that the money is all too real).

In the following sections, I take you through the various access methods and highlight points to consider when choosing a current account to meet your individual needs.

Going automated with ATMs

A growing number of ATMs charge you for withdrawing your cash. This is usually a flat fee of about £1.50 or £1.75 – regardless of how much you withdraw. A message flashes up on the screen just before you complete your transaction warning you of this fee. If you don't wish to pay the fee, you simply cancel the transaction and don't get your cash.

If your bank charges you for using other banks' ATMs, make sure you choose one that has cash points close to your home or place of work so you won't have to pay for using them.

You should check the maximum amount of cash you can withdraw from an ATM in a single day. This is usually around £300, subject to available funds or an arranged overdraft, but the amount can vary. If you're likely to deposit cash or cheques into your account, find out whether you can do this via your bank's ATMs to avoid queuing for hours in your local branch.

Scouting locations

A branch close to your home or workplace is useful, even if you prefer to do your banking over the telephone or Internet. Times occur when you need to visit your local branch to collect travellers' cheques or foreign currency, for example, or to pick up some literature about a new account or talk to an adviser. Not having far to go makes things much more convenient.

Writing cheques and using cheque cards

Most current accounts offer a cheque book and cheque guarantee card (which often doubles up as a debit card). However, many people no longer pay by cheque, so there are a number of current account providers – usually online – who don't offer a cheque book (in exchange, you might get a slightly higher rate of interest on balances).

If you do want the option of paying by cheque, make sure the account you sign up for offers this. Check what limit is on the cheque guarantee card – it may be as low as £50, although some accounts go as high as £250.

Clicking through the Internet

The growth of Internet banking has been phenomenal. A number of high-street banks are behind the various Internet banks, although the latter are run as standalone operations. So, for example, Halifax owns Intelligent Finance, Abbey owns Cahoot, and insurer Prudential owns Egg.

Standalone Internet banks offer better rates of interest on balances and overdrafts than high-street banks. They can do this because they have lower overheads (no branches). Instead, you get 24-hour access, 365 days a year. But the accounts on offer are more limited than on the high street and there are times when you might want to speak to someone face to face. With many standalone Internet banks you have to rely on the phone or email, which doesn't suit everyone.

You won't get a monthly statement in the post either: Instead, you'll be able to access an electronic statement online. If you really want a paper statement for your records, print this off and file it.

Before opening an Internet bank account, check the security it has in place. Hackers often try to access online accounts but are very rarely successful, as extremely sophisticated security systems are employed by the banks. The FSA warns customers to be wary of banks based outside the European Economic Area because you may not be as well protected as with a UK bank. And make sure you don't give your passwords to anyone or write them down.

Banking by phone

Find out whether the bank has a free or local-rate number for telephone banking and what services you can access by phone. This could make a difference if you contact your bank on a regular basis.

Weighing balances

Many banks require only £1 to open a current account, but some providers insist that you deposit a minimum amount of cash and that your balance doesn't dip below a set amount. If you don't have much cash to spare, steer clear of such accounts because if your balance dips below, say, £250 you may forfeit your interest. Find out whether the bank imposes any penalties for not maintaining a minimum balance before signing up.

Accruing interest

If your current account is usually in the black, opt for one paying a good rate of interest – 3 per cent or above – to maximise your returns.

Some accounts pay tiered rates of interest, so the more cash you have in your account, the greater the rate. But this also usually means that such accounts pay a low rate of interest on small balances so they're not worth bothering with. You shouldn't be keeping the large sums of money in your current account that qualify you for the higher rate of interest on a tiered account in the first place.

Viewing overdrafts

If a chance exists that you might go overdrawn, check what the charges are for doing so. Overdraft rates vary significantly between account providers, so shop around for the lowest one if you need an overdraft and inform your bank before going over-drawn. Unauthorised overdrafts are far more expensive than authorised ones.

Find out how much you can go overdrawn by if you may need more than a few hundred pounds. Ask whether you can go overdrawn by a certain amount without having to notify your bank beforehand and not have to pay over the odds for this. You may need to pay an arrangement fee for setting up the overdraft. See Chapter 5 for more on overdrafts.

If you never go overdrawn, you don't need to worry about the overdraft rate – the interest you earn on your balance is far more important.

Switching Your Current Account

Switching accounts is easier and quicker than ever, thanks to Banking Code standards. The good news is that you don't actually have to do very much as your new bank does all the legwork. An automated system swaps customer information between banks and building societies. And the revised Banking Code means your old bank has to provide your new bank with details of all your direct debits and standing orders within three working days of being asked for them. All you do is choose the current account you wish to switch to, fill out an application form, and your new bank does the rest.

Completing the application form

When you decide to switch current account and find one that suits your needs, you must fill out an application form, which you get from your new bank by popping into your local branch, ordering one over the telephone, or downloading it from the Internet. If you download a form, when you've completed it you must print it off, sign it, and return it to the bank. You're asked for your name and address and details of your existing current account, such as the name and address of the bank it's with, your sort code, and account number.

Along with the completed form, you must supply proof of your identity and address. Proof of identity can be a passport or driving licence, while a council tax or utility bill will provide proof of where you live. You can't use the same document to prove your identity and address.

Connected accounts

To really make your current account work for you, you can opt for a connected account. This enables you to connect your current account to several products, such as your mortgage, credit card, savings account, and even personal loans you have with the same provider. The advantage of linking your accounts is that your savings and current account balance is offset against your debts, reducing the interest you pay. For example, if you've got £5,000 in your current and savings accounts, and owe £3,000 on your credit card, you won't pay any interest on the debt because your savings cancel it out.

Similarly, if your salary of £2,500 a month is paid into your current account, and this is connected with your £70,000 mortgage, it can be offset against your outstanding debt so you will be charged interest on £67,500. Interest is calculated daily, so even though you won't maintain this balance in your current account for long, and even if you have nothing left in your account at the end of the month, while there is cash in there you pay less interest on your mortgage. This makes a difference in the long run, knocking years off your mortgage.

The big advantage of linking savings with debits is that because you don't receive interest on your savings, you aren't taxed on them either.

Send important documents by recorded delivery to ensure they're not lost in the post.

Obtaining a list of direct debits

When your application to open a current account has been accepted, you're asked to sign a mandate allowing your new bank to ask your old provider for details of your direct debits and standing orders. When your new bank has this information, it usually sends you the list so you can check it. Ensure that nothing is missing (and that you aren't still making a payment you no longer need to). If anything is missing, contact your new bank or building society to ensure it gets paid.

Your new provider will contact all the companies you have direct debits and standing orders with and give them your new account details.

Your new bank may contact your employer and arrange for your salary to be paid into your new account. Other banks expect you to arrange this. Check whether you are expected to do so. If your bank takes care of this, check that it has done so or you could face a serious shortfall at the end of the month.

Handling the changeover period

The length of time for the changeover to be completed depends on the banks involved. The Banking Code says your existing bank should provide your account details to your new provider within three working days, but allow six weeks for the switch to be fully completed.

Keep some cash in your old account for three months after you open the new one and don't close that account until everything has been finalised. That way, if any payments do slip through the net, you've got the funds to cover them.

Chapter 4

Guarding Against the Unknown: Insurance

In This Chapter

▶ Deciding what cover you need

▶ Protecting your life, health, and income

▶ Covering your home and belongings

*A*lthough we assume it will never happen to us, accidents will happen and illness can strike. Ensuring that you're adequately insured for the unknown makes it easier to deal with the events life may throw at you.

Many people consider insurance to be a waste of money, as you could end up paying hundreds of pounds of premiums and yet never make a claim. But although you could get nothing but peace of mind – which alone is worth the price to some – if you do have to make a claim, you'll be glad you bothered getting cover.

This chapter examines the main types of insurance available, what suits your needs, and how to ensure you don't pay over the odds.

Arranging Cover

Insurance works by offering you cover against injury or loss in return for a monthly, annual, or one-off payment called a *premium*. The insurer calculates your premium by assessing the risk of something happening to you – such as your home being flooded – and what it would cost to right the damage. The higher the likelihood of an event occurring, and therefore of you making a claim, the greater your premium.

Deciding what insurance you need

Some types of cover are compulsory, such as buildings insurance for those with a mortgage or third-party cover for motorists (see upcoming sections titled 'Safeguarding your home' and 'Making sure of your car' respectively). But the majority of insurance isn't compulsory; it simply brings peace of mind and makes life easier if disaster strikes.

When deciding whether you need non-compulsory cover, consider the impact of something happening to you and whether you could cope if it did. For example, if you were burgled could you afford to replace all your belongings? If not, you need contents insurance.

 What you can afford also dictates the cover you opt for. Draw up a short list of the insurance you would buy if money were no object and rank it in order of importance, with the cover you have to buy at the top. After compulsory cover, most people opt for life assurance, but this isn't relevant if you don't have dependants (see 'Insuring your life' later in this chapter). Consider your needs as well as cost. When checking whether you've got enough cover, remember that most insurers state a maximum limit they pay out in the event of a claim: Check whether this would cover your loss.

Disclosing information to the insurer

You have to fill out an application form to obtain cover. This involves answering a series of questions, depending on the type of insurance you are buying.

 Answer truthfully, even if you know this will bump up your premiums. For example, if you're applying for home contents insurance and the insurer asks if you are a smoker, don't lie and say you aren't if you are. Even though being a smoker increases your risk and your premiums, tell the truth because if you lie, the insurer may refuse to pay out on a claim. Pay higher premiums to ensure that you're covered.

If you have pre-existing medical conditions, mention them to the insurer or broker: Don't wait to be asked. It's better to be safe than sorry.

Shopping around for insurance

You can buy insurance direct from the provider, your bank or building society, a supermarket, or broker. You can also buy insurance from the provider of another product (such as travel insurance from your travel agent). For straightforward insurance, direct providers such as supermarkets often offer the best deal. For the best price for less straightforward cover, use a broker with access to hundreds of policies who can find the best deal for your circumstances. Log onto www.insuresupermarket. com, www.moneyextra.com, or www.moneyfacts.co.uk to search hundreds of policies for the best deal.

If you're struggling to get cover because, say, your home is at risk of flooding, a broker will probably know which providers are most likely to insure you. Using a broker saves you wasting time ringing several insurers yourself only to be told they can't cover you.

Reading the policy carefully

It sounds obvious, but you must read the insurance policy carefully. The policy sets out the legal obligations on both you and the insurer. Check that it provides the cover you need and ensure you understand the excess – the amount you have to pay your insurer every time you make a claim (see the next section). Make sure you're happy with what is excluded from the cover: If not, try getting this changed. You may have to pay extra to do so but it may be worth it. If you need clarification, ask your insurer.

Deciding on the excess

When you claim on your insurance policy, you usually make a small payment, known as an *excess*, before you get money from the insurer. Some policies have several different excesses, depending on what you are claiming for. For example, if your home has suffered from subsidence in the past, you may have to pay a higher excess on a subsidence-related claim than you would if your laptop was stolen. The standard excess can be anything between £50 and £250, but you can get this raised or removed completely. The higher the excess, the lower your premiums, but don't opt for a greater excess than you are comfortable paying.

Making a comeback if things go wrong

Your policy documents spell out how you make a claim. If you're unsatisfied with the way your insurer handles your claim, inform your insurer in writing. If you aren't happy with the way the insurer deals with your complaint, contact the Financial Ombudsman

Service (FOS), which can intervene on your behalf and make a binding ruling. Telephone 0845 080 1800 or log onto `www.financial-ombudsman.org.uk/consumer/complaints.htm`.

Cutting costs – without skimping on cover

Insurance can be pricey but ways exist of cutting your premiums – without slashing your cover:

- Pay premiums annually rather than monthly. Insurers offer a discount for this.

- Don't double up on cover. You can only claim on one policy. So if you take out baggage cover as part of your travel insurance, check you aren't already covered by your contents insurance. Read the small print on your existing cover first before buying any more.

- Shop around for cover using a broker or comparison websites. But don't be guided solely by price; price is important but enough cover is more vital.

Handling Health and Protection

If you lose your job or become ill and can't work, the state provides very little help in making your mortgage repayments. If you took out your mortgage before October 1995, the Government provides no financial help until you've been out of work for eight weeks; for the following 18 weeks you get up to 50 per cent of the eligible interest. If you took out your mortgage since October 1995, you get even less cover: You have to wait 39 weeks before you get full assistance with the mortgage interest. Even then what is available is capped and means tested: You must be on income support or jobseeker's allowance.

With such a limited safety net provided by the Government, it is vital that you take out your own cover in case you lose your job or become ill and unable to work (see 'Preparing for accident, sickness, and unemployment' later in this chapter).

If you need more advice about insurance, and which policies are right for you, contact an independent financial adviser.

Insuring your life

The most basic type of cover is *life assurance*, also known as *life insurance*. It pays out a lump sum on your death, which your dependants (usually a partner and/or children under the age of 18) can use as they please – pay off the mortgage, clear debts, or provide an income. The lump sum is usually tax-free. Taking out life assurance is vital if you're the main breadwinner. Be sure, too, that you take out enough cover; otherwise, your dependants will suffer financially after you die.

If you're single, you don't have a real need for life cover unless you have special circumstances (for example you plan to leave your home to a friend or sibling and want the mortgage paid off before they receive it). Life assurance can do this.

When applying for life cover you must complete an application form, giving details of your age, job, and health. Answer these truthfully, no matter how this affects your premiums. If you don't, your policy may not pay out, which could be disastrous for your dependants.

Most life providers can also tack *critical illness cover*, which pays out on diagnosis of certain illnesses, onto your policy for an extra premium, which is quite expensive. This cover can also be bought separately (see 'Covering critical illness' later in this chapter).

I explain the different types of life assurance in more detail in the following sections.

Beginning term assurance

Term assurance is the cheapest form of life protection, and is getting cheaper all the time as people live longer, giving insurers less risk of having to pay out.

Term assurance is available from traditional providers such as insurance companies and banks and building societies to retailers. Because competition is fierce, the cost of cover is reasonable: a 30-year-old non-smoking female buying £100,000 worth of level cover for a term of 20 years could purchase cover for £6.80 a month.

Term assurance works like this: You choose the *term* – how long the policy runs for, which can be anything between 1 and 30 years. Many people choose a term that coincides with the length of their mortgage so that their payments are covered if they die before they clear this debt. So if you have 20 years before your outstanding mortgage is cleared, you take term assurance for the same period.

How much the insurer pays out if you die during the term depends upon the type of term assurance:

- ✔ **Level term:** Covers you for the same amount throughout the term of the policy (your premiums also remain the same). As it doesn't take into account the effect of inflation, level term assurance can put your beneficiaries at a disadvantage.

- ✔ **Renewable term:** A renewable term is shorter than a level term – usually five years. You can then renew it if you wish, although you can't increase the sum assured and your premiums rise with age.

- ✔ **Convertible term:** Can be converted to whole of life or endowment insurance without giving further medical evidence of the state of your health. The new policy should cost the same as a normal whole of life or endowment policy based on your age when you exercise this option. This may be worth doing if you don't have much cash initially (so can only afford level term) but have a greater income and more responsibilities, such as kids, later on.

- ✔ **Decreasing term:** The payout sum falls by a fixed amount every year, so by the end of the term you get nothing. However, your premiums remain the same throughout the term, although they are set lower than level term to account for the decline in the sum insured. Popular for covering a repayment mortgage.

- ✔ **Increasing term:** The payout sum, and possibly your premium, increases every year by a fixed percentage of the original sum insured or the retail price index. This ensures there's enough to cover the rising cost of living.

- ✔ **Family income benefit:** Instead of paying a lump sum on your death, your family receives an income until the end of the term. This is paid monthly, every three months, or once a year. You can also have this increase by 3 or 5 per cent each year, but your premiums will be higher to accommodate this.

The downside with term assurance is that your family is protected only if you die during the term. If you take out a policy with a 20-year term and live longer than this, your family won't see a penny of your outlay returned. There is no surrender value either, so if you stop paying the premiums the cover ceases and you don't get back the premiums you have paid.

Just as making sure that you take out enough cover – ensuring the lump sum is big enough to clear all your debts and provide an income as necessary – is important, you must review your policy on a regular basis to ensure you still have enough cover. Do this at least every two years, and when something significant happens, such as you get married, move house, or have children. An independent financial adviser can help decide how much cover you need. While checking that you have enough cover, ensure your premiums remain competitive as well. No penalties exist for switching policy, so do so if you find the same cover for less money – just make sure the new policy is properly in force before terminating the old one.

Getting whole of life insurance

If you want to ensure your family is covered whenever you die – not just during a set term – opt for *whole of life insurance*. Premiums are higher than for term assurance because the insurer will definitely pay out. Some insurers require you to pay premiums until death; others require premiums only until you reach a certain age, such as 65 or older, but your beneficiaries still get the sum insured when you die. The size of the payment your family gets depends on how long you pay premiums for and the performance of any investments within that policy.

Protecting your income

Also known as *permanent health insurance, income protection* pays out a monthly tax-free sum if you suffer loss of earnings because you are injured or too ill to work. You pay a monthly premium in return. The payout is less than your normal earnings because it is free of tax and the insurer doesn't want to give you too much incentive to stay off work.

Decide whether you need income protection by working out what will happen if you can't work. Your employer may pay Statutory Sick Pay or something more generous. Find out what you're entitled to, as this affects whether you need income protection. If you're self-employed, your income may almost certainly cease so you need some income protection.

The state offers some benefits, such as Long Term Incapacity Benefit, but they don't pay out in the short term, and may be means tested. Find out what you qualify for from your local Jobcentre Plus or log onto www.jobcentreplus.gov.uk.

After you work out how much money you receive if you become sick or injured, think about how much you need to cover your outgoings, such as your mortgage, council tax, and other bills. If you have savings and/or investments, or your employer provides generous sick pay, covering these may not be a problem. But if you can't cope with a loss of income, you need income protection.

You have several decisions to make when buying income protection:

- ✓ **Whether you want *own occupation* or *any occupation* cover.** The former pays out if you can't do your normal job, the latter you can't claim on unless you are too ill to carry out any job. The former is more expensive but usually worth having.

- ✓ **How long you want the *deferred period* to be.** This is the length of time after your incapacity before you get a payout. The longer the deferred period is, the lower your premiums. If your employer will give you sick pay for six months, you could defer your policy to pay out after this, for example. Avoid opting for a longer deferred period than you can comfortably cope with just to reduce your premiums, as it could be a struggle.

- ✓ **How long you want the policy to pay out for.** Tying this in with your normal retirement date is a wise move. The longer the period, the more expensive your premiums.

- ✓ **Whether your premiums are fixed or variable.** If you opt for a *guaranteed* rate, your insurer can't increase your premiums, except in line with inflation, so you get certainty. If your rate is *reviewable*, the insurer can raise premiums to reflect its overall costs, which may mean you have to pay out significantly more than you'd budgeted for. A *renewable* rate means premiums are set for a fixed period, which again buys peace of mind.

Covering critical illness

Critical illness cover (CIC) pays out a tax-free lump sum if you are diagnosed with a specific illness or condition, such as cancer, a heart attack, or a stroke. Full details of the conditions covered are listed in the insurer's key features leaflet.

CIC is more restrictive than income protection because the latter pays out a monthly income if you are too ill to work regardless of the illness, whereas CIC is quite limited in the conditions it covers. And receiving a monthly income until you can return to work via income protection insurance may be more useful than a lump sum via CIC, because you may spend the lump sum and be left with no income.

You can arrange for CIC to cover you for a set number of years, perhaps until you clear your mortgage. Or you can opt for a plan without a fixed period.

Most policies charge a regular monthly or yearly premium, depending on your age, sex, health, occupation, whether you smoke, the cover you need, and for how long. Your doctor may be asked to confirm your medical history. If you're already seriously ill, you may not be able to get cover or the provider may cover you but not that particular illness. Alternatively, you may be charged a higher premium. You may also have to pay higher premiums if certain illnesses run in your family.

Premiums may increase over the life of the policy or you can opt for a guarantee that they won't.

Preparing for accident, sickness, and unemployment

Also known as *mortgage payment protection insurance, accident, sickness, and unemployment insurance (ASU)* is the most comprehensive and expensive cover available. ASU pays out for a limited period – usually 12 or 24 months – and you must wait 30, 60, or 90 days before receiving payment. If you take out all three elements, this type of policy is expensive. But you may not need every element: Work out what you require and take out only enough to cover what you need. For example, if your employer provides sick pay for six months, you don't need accident or sickness cover and may need only the unemployment part.

Income protection is cheaper than ASU and pays out until you return to work, whereas ASU pays out only for a limited period, so income protection may be a better option. You can buy ASU from your mortgage lender but see whether you can find a better deal first by consulting a mortgage broker or financial adviser.

Purchasing private medical insurance

If you have private medical insurance (PMI), you don't have to wait months to be treated on the NHS. You pay a monthly or yearly premium in exchange for cover for the cost of private medical treatment for curable short-term illnesses or injuries, otherwise known as *acute conditions*.

A long list of illnesses and conditions aren't covered by PMI, including drug abuse, self-inflicted injuries, pregnancy, cosmetic surgery, and organ transplants. For a full list of exclusions, check the insurer's key features leaflet. Treatment by accident and emergency isn't covered under PMI, as private hospitals don't have the facilities to cope with it.

Accounting for the cost

PMI can be extremely expensive and you should be prepared for your premium to rise each year, usually above the rate of general inflation. The cost is the result of the increasing number of people claiming for private medical treatment and the increasingly sophisticated and expensive procedures available. According to the Association of British Insurers (ABI) a hip replacement – a common procedure – costs £6,000, for example.

The number of claims you make doesn't influence your premiums, unless your cover includes a no-claims discount. However, your premiums increase as you get older because you are more likely to make a claim. A 45-year-old should expect to pay 25 per cent higher premiums than a 35-year-old, according to the ABI. A 65-year-old would pay more than twice the premium of a 45-year-old.

Your premiums depend on your level of cover: A limited policy costs less than a comprehensive one. Most schemes cover in-patient and day-patient treatment, but not all offer outpatient treatment. Consider how important this is to you when choosing a policy.

Declaring your medical history

The most common type of policy requires you to fill out a form with details of your medical history. Your doctor may be contacted for further information and you won't be covered for pre-existing conditions.

An alternative to declaring your medical history is the *moratorium* option, which is offered by a number of insurers. You don't have to fill in a medical history form, but if treatment for a pre-existing condition (something you suffered from in the past five years) is required within two years after the policy starts, the costs are not covered. If you haven't had any symptoms or received treatment for this condition for two years after starting your policy, the insurer covers you as normal.

Declaring any medical conditions you have suffered from in the past five years is down to you if you don't opt for the moratorium. Resist the temptation to conceal this information, as the insurer may refuse to pay out if you make a claim.

Covering Your Home and Belongings

As well as covering your life and mortgage payments, covering your belongings in case disaster strikes is a wise move.

Safeguarding your home

In return for a monthly or annual premium, buildings insurance pays out if the structure of your home and/or its fixtures and fittings are damaged by fire, subsidence, flood, or storm. Premiums are calculated according to your postcode, previous claims history, the sum insured, and the nature of what you are insuring.

If you have a mortgage, this cover is compulsory. Lenders insist on proof that you have cover before releasing the mortgage, so purchase insurance before contracts are exchanged. If you own a leasehold property, your freeholder – the landlord – is responsible for arranging buildings insurance. You repay him via your service charge.

Taking care of contents insurance

Contents insurance protects you against damage or loss of your moveable possessions due to theft, fire, or flood. For an extra premium, you can get accidental damage cover, which pays out if you spill a pot of paint on the carpet, for example. Consider whether you need this extra protection. You also pay extra for *all risks*: cover for items you regularly take out of the home, such as a laptop or digital camera.

You can get lower premiums by beefing up your security, fitting alarms and British Standard locks. Ask your insurer for details.

Making sure of your car

If you cause an accident, *third-party cover* protects you against liability to other people and their property. You can also get *fully comprehensive* insurance, which also pays out for repairs to your car if you cause an accident as well as for theft and fire damage. An inbetween policy – *third-party fire and theft* – is available that covers you for liability to other people and their property, and if your car is stolen or damaged by fire.

Driving a car without third-party cover is an offence.

Motor insurance can be expensive, but there are ways of cutting the cost rather than the cover. Premiums are calculated according to your age and driving experience, occupation, and where you live – you can do little about these. But you can choose a car with a low insurance group rating; ensure an alarm is fitted; travel fewer miles; and keep the car in a garage.

You can also get a discount on your premiums if you build up a no-claims record – usually around 30 per cent for one claim-free year to 60 per cent after four or five years. Discounts differ between insurers, so shop around for the best deal. Some insurers offer a *protected discount policy* to drivers with a good claims record. For an extra premium, you can typically make two claims in a three- to five-year period without affecting your discount.

Travelling under cover

Buying travel cover before going on holiday is a good idea. You might be intending to rely on the E111 form, which gives UK residents free or discounted medical treatment in another European country if it has signed a reciprocal agreement for health services. However, the E111 doesn't cover many countries, such as the US, and few EU countries pay the full cost of reciprocal health care.

What's more, the E111 doesn't cover loss of luggage, money, or passport, or expenses caused by flight delays. With travel insurance, you get recompense if your trip is cancelled or curtailed for reasons beyond your control or you have to be repatriated (flown back) to the UK.

You can take out an annual policy or single-trip policy every time you travel. The former is cheaper if you make at least two trips a year. You can buy cover from travel agents or tour operators, but can get a better deal via a broker. Insurers, retailers, banks, and building societies all offer travel cover, so it's a competitive market.

Ensure you have enough cover. If you are participating in winter sports or bungee jumping, make sure your policy covers you before you go. Having more cover than you need is often worthwhile if you might undertake a dangerous sport or activity: Extending your cover when you're abroad could be either difficult or impossible.

Part II
Dealing with Debt

'I don't care how big the bank is, it doesn't frighten me.'

In this part . . .

*C*learing your outstanding debt may be the biggest challenge you face and the chapters in this part show you how. Here you find ways of tackling your overdraft, tips on choosing a credit card, and useful info on personal loans. I also include tips on steering clear of store cards, loan sharks, and other credit nasties.

Chapter 5

Seeing Red: Tackling Your Overdraft

....

In This Chapter

▶ Going overdrawn

▶ Working out whether an overdraft is the answer

▶ Going for a current account with the best overdraft

▶ Changing current accounts

▶ Whittling down your overdraft

....

*E*ven the best-laid plans can go awry, and even the most careful budget-follower can overspend on occasion. One of the easiest ways of spending more cash than you have is to go overdrawn on your current account. But if you do so without asking the bank's permission beforehand, you're likely to get a nasty shock when you receive your next bank statement.

Unauthorised borrowing is expensive and also unnecessary. With a bit of careful planning, you should have no need for an unauthorised overdraft. This chapter shows you what you need to bear in mind before going overdrawn.

Increased competition in the current account market means that if you're already overdrawn, and have been for some time, you may be paying more in charges than absolutely necessary. Shopping around for a cheaper overdraft – and switching current account – is straightforward, will save you on charges, and enable you to clear your borrowings more quickly. In this chapter, I help you choose the best overdraft for your needs and show you how to manage it to best advantage.

Understanding How Overdrafts Work

Going *overdrawn* – also known as slipping into the red, as opposed to the black – happens when you spend more money than you have in your current account. You're using the bank's money instead of your own and are charged interest for doing so. The amount differs between banks and also depends on whether you asked permission beforehand or not.

You can only get an overdraft on your current account. Overdrafts are not available on regular savings accounts.

Requesting permission

You must ask your bank for permission before going overdrawn: This is known as an *authorised* overdraft. You should do this as soon as you realise that you are getting short of funds and may need some extra cash. Contact your bank: You have to fill out an application form or put your request in writing. Your bank decides how big your overdraft can be, according to status and general rules.

Even if you aren't planning on going overdrawn, there's no harm in applying to your bank for an overdraft just in case. You don't have to pay for it if you're not using it and you never know when you might need extra funds in an emergency. If you've already got the overdraft facility set up, slipping into the red doesn't present a problem.

Most current accounts have an overdraft facility so, in theory, you could slip into the red without notifying your bank first. But this isn't a good idea, as *unauthorised* overdrafts usually have punitive interest charges. And you could well be charged other fees on top (see 'Looking at fees' later in this chapter).

Calculating interest

An overdraft is a form of borrowing because you are using the bank's money, so you usually have to pay interest on it. However, you may not be charged interest on an overdraft if your bank is charging 0 per cent for an introductory period, the account has an interest-free buffer, or you have a student or graduate bank account.

Connecting interest and credit rating

You may find that you apply for a current account only to be told that the rate of interest on overdrafts is higher than the advertised rate. This happens when the account provider bases its overdraft rate on your credit rating.

The rate advertised is the *typical* rate, which means you may be charged that amount of interest or a higher rate, depending on how you score in a credit check. For example, one bank offers a typical overdraft rate of 10 per cent (authorised) or 21 per cent (unauthorised), but people deemed to be higher risk are charged between 11 and 15 per cent for an authorised overdraft. (Chapter 6 has more details on how your credit rating is checked and how you can improve this rating, thereby qualifying for a lower rate of interest.)

If your overdraft is authorised, you pay around half as much interest as you would on an unauthorised overdraft – sometimes less. You may still have to pay a fee for being overdrawn, however, depending on the account provider.

Take care not to exceed an authorised overdraft without requesting further permission from your bank beforehand. Otherwise, you could be penalised more heavily than you imagine: Some banks charge the higher, unauthorised rate on the full amount you are overdrawn – not just the portion over and above your authorised limit.

Say, for example, your bank charges 10 per cent interest on authorised overdrafts and 30 per cent on unauthorised ones. If you have a £250 authorised overdraft but go £1 over this limit, you could be charged 30 per cent interest on the full £251 if your bank follows this practice.

Finding out how interest is calculated on your overdraft is vital. If a chance exists that you may run up a small, unauthorised overdraft for a short period of time, find a bank that won't penalise you by charging high rates of interest on your total borrowings.

A couple of banks have the same rate on authorised and unauthorised overdrafts, which can save you the agony of paying twice as much interest for going overdrawn without seeking permission first. But a considerable difference exists between what the two banks charge – one charges 6.9 per cent on authorised and unauthorised borrowing; the other 18.4 per cent on both – so you still need to shop around for the best deal.

Looking at fees

Many people don't realise that interest charges on their overdrafts are just the beginning. Many banks charge an array of other fees and charges, which can be buried in the small print. At the time of writing, some customers are successfully challenging what they consider to be unfair overdraft fees and obtaining refunds. But be wary of fees when signing up for a new current account, as one with a low rate of interest may not look quite such a good deal after fees and charges are added.

You may discover that the overdraft with the higher rate of interest and no fees is actually a better deal than the lower rate with lots of hidden fees and charges. For example, one bank may charge 29.8 per cent on unauthorised overdrafts, while another charges 35 per cent. But if the former bank also charges you £20 a day up to a maximum of £80 a month for an unauthorised overdraft, whereas the latter has no additional fees, the bank with the higher rate of interest may work out cheaper in the long run. Take all fees and charges into account as well as rates of interest when making your choice.

Daily charges

If you go overdrawn without authorisation your account provider may charge you a fee for each day you are overdrawn – up to a maximum amount. This is charged on top of the higher rate of interest, which is why unauthorised borrowing can be so pricey. For example, many account providers charge £30 a day for every day you are overdrawn in one month (up to a maximum of around £90 a month). This charge can be imposed even if you are only a few pounds overdrawn.

Item charges

As well as a daily charge, you may get stung with an item charge every time your bank pays a direct debit, standing order, or cheque on your unauthorised overdraft. This can be as much as £25 per item.

Charges for bouncing payments

Some banks charge a fee every time they bounce a payment – in other words, refuse to pay it. This can cost around £25 or £30 a time, even if the amount isn't paid. So if your bank bounces five cheques or direct debits in one month, you're stung with a £150 bill – and still have to find the cash to make the original payments.

Administration or arrangement fees

Some banks charge a fee for setting up an overdraft, so check whether this is the case – and how much it is – before applying.

This is usually a one-off fee of £25. Many banks don't charge such a fee, however, so there really is no need to pay it. Shop around for an account that won't charge you.

Monthly or quarterly usage fees

Some banks pump up the cost of an overdraft by charging a monthly or quarterly usage fee of around £10 (some refer to this as a management fee) on authorised as well as unauthorised overdrafts (although most banks have dropped the practice of charging this on the former).

Deciding Whether an Overdraft Really Is the Answer

Your current account may have an overdraft facility, but that doesn't automatically mean you have to take advantage of it. An overdraft can be a flexible and convenient way of borrowing, but might not be the best way of doing so. Table 5-1 weighs up some of the pros and cons of taking out an overdraft.

Table 5-1	Pros and Cons of Overdrafts
Advantages	*Disadvantages*
Easy to arrange: A letter or call to your bank is usually enough to arrange an overdraft or extend it as required.	Too much flexibility: Slipping into the red is easy to do, and if you do so without seeking authorisation before-hand, you're penalised through heavy charges.
Great for borrowing small amounts of cash in the short term: Some banks even offer a small interest-free overdraft facility, which may be enough to tide you over.	Cost: You may get stung by high rates of interest, plus monthly and arrangement fees if you don't shop around for a good deal. If you exceed your authorised limit, charges are particularly high.
No fixed repayment schedule: You can pay back the money as and when you can afford to do so.	Danger of having a never-ending overdraft: You may have every intention of using your overdraft only in the short-term, but because there is no repayment schedule, you may find it becoming a permanent fixture.

Overdrafts are excellent for short-term borrowing of relatively small amounts of cash. But if you need to borrow money for a long period of time, an overdraft may not be the answer. Even if your overdraft is authorised, you could still pay considerably more interest in the long run than you would on a cheap personal loan. To decide whether a personal loan may be a better choice, consider how much cash you need and how long you're likely to take to repay it. If you need more than say, £3,000, a personal loan may be a better bet than an overdraft: Some banks may not let you go overdrawn by this amount, for example, whereas it's usually not a problem obtaining a loan this size.

If you're borrowing a sizeable amount of money, a personal loan's structured monthly repayments might make it easier to clear your debt more quickly. See Chapter 7 for more information on choosing a personal loan.

Choosing a Current Account for Its Overdraft

If you regularly go overdrawn, searching for a current account that pays the best rate of interest on balances is pointless. If you're rarely in credit, you simply won't make the most of this facility so there's little point in having it. What you do need is a current account with a cheap overdraft. Historically, overdrafts were an extremely expensive form of borrowing, but as part of their drive to attract new business, many banks are realising that it's not just the rate of interest paid to customers in credit that is important but overdraft rates as well. When looking for an overdraft, avoid the big four banks as they are among the most expensive providers. Instead, shop around for another current account offering a good deal on overdrafts: You should be able to find one charging less than 10 per cent interest.

Check out comparison site www.moneysupermarket.com, which enables you to compare overdrafts offered by 300 banks.

Fee-free buffers

If you only slip into the red by a couple of hundred pounds a month you may be able to avoid paying any interest or charges at all, as some banks offer fee- and interest-free overdraft buffers. This enables you to go overdrawn by a certain amount – whether it is £10, £50, £250, or even £500 – without charge. This amount varies considerably, so check before signing up for a new current account.

An aid to the forgetful

My bank lets me go overdrawn by up to £100 every month interest free. It's a handy feature, because even with the most careful budgeting, unexpected expenses can crop up and catch you unawares.

One month a magazine subscription I'd forgotten about – because I pay annually by direct debit – was debited from my account, pushing me into the red. Luckily, I had the £100 interest- and fee-free buffer to call upon, so didn't rack up any costs for my oversight.

If your account has a sizeable interest-free overdraft buffer, resist the temptation to see it as an extra £250 or £500 to spend every single month. Try and think of it as an extra for emergencies instead. Otherwise, you're immediately down by your overdraft amount when your salary is paid into your account, which means you're likely to dip into your overdraft again the following month, leaving you no reserves to cope with a genuine emergency.

Watch out for the distinction between fee-free and interest-free when comparing overdrafts. If a bank is offering a £250 fee-free buffer, for example, you may find you're still charged interest on this amount. However, if the buffer is interest-free, you won't be charged interest although you may incur a fee. One bank has a £2,500 interest-free overdraft limit but just a £20 fee-free limit, which means you have to pay a flat fee if you go overdrawn by more than £20, although you won't have to pay interest if it's less than £2,500. Check the small print and ask the current account provider if you still aren't sure of the difference.

Introductory offers

Several banks charge 0 per cent on overdrafts for an introductory period of up to 12 months to encourage you to open a current account. They place a limit on the size of overdraft you're allowed – one account has a £1,000 limit, another £2,500. To qualify for such deals, you may have to meet certain criteria, such as agreeing to have your salary paid into your account every month. Check the small print.

Such interest-free limits are not automatic: You must still apply for them, just as you would any other authorised borrowing.

If you're tempted by a 0 per cent overdraft for an introductory period, check what rate of interest you have to pay once this ends, even if it's a long way off. If the standard rate is extremely high, and you haven't cleared your overdraft before you're charged interest at this rate, you may be better off opting for a low standard overdraft rate in the first place.

Switching Current Accounts When You Have an Overdraft

If you have a sizeable overdraft, you may well find that another account provider offers a cheaper deal. Checking whether this is the case is always worthwhile and, if so, think about switching bank accounts so that you can benefit from the lower rate.

While banks tend to welcome new current account customers with open arms, they are not usually so keen to have your existing overdraft as well – unless you have a business account or are a recent graduate. But this doesn't necessarily mean that you have to be stuck with a bank charging hefty overdraft rates for the rest of your life.

One way of switching current accounts if you've already got an overdraft is to use funds from a new account to clear your old one. You can then work at reducing the overdraft on your new account (which will hopefully have a lower rate of interest, making it easier to achieve). First, find a new account with a 0 per cent overdraft for 12 months or a lower rate of interest than the one you're currently being charged, at least. Open your new account and withdraw enough cash to clear your existing overdraft: Pay this into your existing current account, before closing this account. Whittling away your overdraft will then be easier because the rate of interest will be lower (or there might not be any interest to pay at all for a while).

Reducing Your Overdraft

Although it pays to shop around for the cheapest overdraft, in an ideal world you wouldn't go overdrawn in the first place. Borrowing money is an expensive business: Even if you do your research carefully and find the cheapest overdraft available, you still pay out money in interest charges every month. The sensible approach is to work out how you can cut your overdraft and therefore the charges you pay.

If you're slipping into debt, you may find it easy to bury your head in the sand, ignore the problem, and hope it goes away. But it won't – and such an attitude simply makes matters worse.

If you have savings in a separate account, which you may be keeping for an emergency, you should use this cash to clear or at least reduce your overdraft. You're unlikely to be earning as much interest on your savings as you're paying on your overdraft, so it makes no financial sense to clear your debts before starting to build up your savings.

If you don't have savings to call upon, consider taking out a personal loan to clear your overdraft. This may be a good idea if you've run up a big overdraft and are paying a lot of interest on it: Personal loan rates are likely to be quite a bit cheaper. A loan can also replace what could be unwieldy borrowing with a fixed repayment plan, which can be easier to manage and clear.

When you whittle away your overdraft, make a budget and stick to it. This enables you to get in control of your spending and ensure you don't slip back into the red. See Chapter 2 for more on budgeting.

Chapter 6

Flexing the Plastic: Choosing a Credit Card

In This Chapter

▶ Getting to grips with how credit cards work

▶ Finding the best rate of interest

▶ Seeking out perks and benefits

▶ Steering clear of unnecessary charges

▶ Checking your credit file

*C*redit cards have replaced cash as the most convenient way to pay for goods and services. Part of the reason for the growing popularity of credit cards is that they are becoming far cheaper. With an increasing number of issuers, including petrol stations, supermarkets, and football clubs as well as traditional high-street banks, interest rates are being forced down. Annual fees are thankfully becoming a thing of the past and a range of benefits is available if you clear your balance every month. In other words, using a credit card is a smart way of keeping track of your spending, not necessarily a sign that it is out of control.

However, not all credit cards have low interest rates, no annual fees, and excellent perks. Some are still rather disappointing, charging interest at four or more times the Bank of England base rate. This chapter shows you how to avoid such cards – and where to seek out the better ones. I also look at how your credit rating affects the amount of interest you're charged on your card – and how you can improve it.

The world of finance is a fast-moving one. Facts and figures can change rapidly, so treat the examples in this chapter as a guide only.

Understanding How Credit Cards Work

You can use a credit card instead of cash to purchase goods or services. A credit card is more convenient than cash because you don't have to go to an ATM to withdraw money every time you need to buy something or carry round lots of cash. However, unlike a debit card, you are, in effect, borrowing money as you're spending the card issuer's cash: You pay this back at the end of the month when you get a statement listing your purchases. So if you don't clear the balance, you usually have to pay interest on your outstanding debt – unless you have a card with a 0 per cent offer.

If you have a large balance you wish to chip away at, you should switch to a card charging 0 per cent on balance transfers for 9 or 12 months to give you time to reduce the debt. Or if you wish to support your favourite charity while you spend, you need a card that donates a percentage of your purchases to a specific charity. If you clear your balance every month, you need a card with perks such as a proportion of what you spend returned to you in the form of cash or AirMiles.

Calculating interest

Every credit card has an *annual percentage rate (APR)*, the interest the issuer charges you on purchases you don't pay off every month. You can use the APR to compare different cards: All issuers are obliged to tell you what the APR is when you apply.

Generally speaking, the lower the APR the better, although the rate of interest isn't important if you always clear your balance (see 'Enjoying the perks of clearing your balance every month' later in this chapter). APRs vary considerably between providers, so shop around for a competitive deal. Credit cards from the big four banks – Barclays, HSBC, Lloyds TSB, and NatWest – can have rather high APRs, ranging from 0 per cent to 15.9 per cent.

Some cards offer a 0 per cent introductory offer (see 'Sourcing good introductory rates' later in this chapter). Even if this is the case, you must still make the minimum payment (see 'Making the minimum payment' later in this chapter) or you'll be charged a penalty.

Most credit cards have an interest-free credit period of up to 59 days, depending on the issuer (some interest-free credit periods last just 46 days). However, if you don't clear your balance within the interest-free period, your interest is normally calculated from the date the item is charged to your account – not the payment due date – usually the same day as you made the purchase or a couple of days later at most.

If you withdraw cash from an ATM using your credit card or ask for it from a retailer, interest is charged straight away – even if you clear the balance when you receive your statement. You're also charged a fee (see 'Withdrawing cash' later in this chapter for more on this).

Figuring out credit limits

Your *credit limit* is the maximum, cumulative amount you can spend on your card. If you try to exceed your limit, your card is refused at the point of sale.

A credit limit of £6,000 is not a monthly limit but the total amount you can spend. So, if you spend £800 one month and don't clear the balance when your statement arrives, your *available credit* is £5,200 (£6,000 minus £800). After you pay back the £800, your full limit is restored.

Credit limits aren't set in stone. They vary from customer to customer. Your card issuer calculates your limit by checking your credit file and giving you a credit score. The company giving you a card wants to be assured that you have a regular income and aren't over-committed with other loans, credit cards, and a mortgage. If you score well, you may get a credit limit of thousands of pounds. (Check out 'Considering your credit rating' later in this chapter).

Even if your card issuer grants you a credit limit beyond your wildest dreams, it doesn't mean you should spend every last penny of it. Doing so may lead to debt problems. Your credit limit is simply the card issuer's assessment of what it can comfortably let you borrow, and doesn't necessarily mean you should borrow that much.

Your card issuer reviews your credit limit on a regular basis and may raise – or even lower – your limit from time to time. You can also apply for an increase. You may want a higher limit if you have a particularly low limit or a one-off expense that you have no other way of paying. But if the latter is the case, take care. Borrowing on a credit card can be very expensive (unless you have a 0 per cent introductory offer), so consider whether this is the best method of getting your hands on extra cash.

Card issuers often raise your credit limit whether you ask for an increase or not. Credit card companies do this to encourage you to spend more money. Of course, your issuer dresses it up as though it is doing you the favour, writing you a letter in which you are 'congratulated' on your higher limit. Simply ignore the increase and resist the temptation to spend more just because extra credit is available to you.

Making the minimum payment

Although you don't have to clear your card balance every month, card issuers insist that you pay a minimum amount. This minimum is set out on your statement, either a fixed minimum payment or a percentage of the outstanding balance. It is usually no more than a token amount, so if you owe £600, say, you may be required to make a minimum payment of around £13.

Although it seems such a piddling sum that you might not bother paying it, a penalty is applied if you don't pay the minimum amount. If you're on an introductory offer, the rate may be withdrawn and you'll be switched to the issuer's standard rate. For example, Barclays withdraws the introductory offer rate and your card reverts to the standard rate – from 0 per cent to 14.9 per cent – if you don't pay the minimum amount.

The minimum payment is never much so you should have no problem paying it. If you're struggling to do so, it means your debts have got out of control and you're unlikely to be able to clear the full balance on your card any time soon, running up further interest. If this is the case, see it as a wake-up call and look at ways of clearing your balance (see 'Sourcing good introductory rates' in the following section). If you don't pay the minimum amount, this will be reflected in your credit rating, which may make it difficult to get other finance such as a mortgage at a later date (see 'Considering your credit rating' later in this chapter).

If you make only the minimum payment each month, you'll run up an even bigger balance because of the interest you'll be charged. Even if you can't clear the entire balance, try at least to pay more than the minimum each month.

Finding Low Rates

If you regularly use your credit card but rarely or never pay off the full debt each month, the APR is extremely important. You need a card with a 0 per cent introductory rate of interest or a low long-term standard rate.

Sourcing good introductory rates

Many card providers offer 0 per cent introductory deals to new customers for a period of 5 to 12 months. This rate usually applies to new purchases, *balance transfers* (moving an existing balance from one card to another, although a one-off charge is often applied for this), or both. This rate may even apply to cash advances, although usually this isn't the case.

Find out exactly what charges apply to your card: Claiming ignorance when you've been stung with outrageous interest charges won't change the situation.

The advantage of a 0 per cent deal is that it can help you clear or reduce a large outstanding debt. If you have a £2,000 balance on a card with a standard APR of 14.9, you may be able to pay only the interest on your debt each month. But if you transfer to a card offering 0 per cent for nine months, you can clear some of the balance: Instead of paying off the interest, you can now chip away at the debt itself, reducing your outstanding balance. When the offer ends, switch the remaining balance to a card offering a similar deal and continue until the debt is cleared.

If you continue spending on your card, you have to pay back the money eventually – it isn't free. So resist the temptation to run up huge debts simply because you aren't being charged any interest initially. This won't always be the case.

When the introductory period ends, the card reverts to the issuer's standard rate. This could be quite a lot higher than 0 per cent and if you've run up a sizeable balance, you could be stung for quite a hefty interest bill. To get round this, find another card offering 0 per cent on balance transfers and switch your debt to this new card.

Most cards charge a one-off fee for balance transfers of up to 3 per cent of the outstanding balance so you won't want to switch the balance too often.

If the issuer charges 0 per cent on balance transfers but not on new purchases, be wary of spending on the card or you could run up a lot of interest – at a rather higher rate than 0 per cent. Not only that but if you make any payments, the cheaper debt is usually cleared first – in this case, your transferred debt at 0 per cent – not the higher rate on new purchases.

You can own more than one card; so take out another offering 0 per cent on new purchases for spending.

Pursuing low lifetime balances

If you have serious debt, don't feel that a six-month introductory period isn't long enough to whittle it down, and you can't face the hassle of switching again when the offer ends, consider a card with a low lifetime balance. Any balance transferred to the card is charged interest at a low rate – one issuer charges 8.9 per cent, for example – until the balance has been cleared in full. This gives you time to chip away at it at your own pace while still paying a fairly low rate of interest.

While the balance transfer rate may be very competitive, the rate on new purchases might not be quite as attractive: It is usually the standard APR. If this is the case, get a second card for new purchases.

Enjoying the Perks of Clearing Your Balance Every Month

If you clear the balance on your credit card(s) every month, the rate of interest is irrelevant. Instead, look for cards that offer incentives that match your spending habits. Make sure you choose a card that doesn't charge an annual fee and then look for other benefits that provide a worthwhile return. Some schemes are more generous than others, so shop around till you find the best one for you.

Ensure you do pay your balance in full each month – thereby incurring no interest – by setting up a direct debit with your bank for the full amount each month. Then, all you have to make sure is that you've enough cash in your account to cover this.

Getting cashback

A number of card providers offer *cashback* – a percentage of what you spend – which is paid to you via an annual cheque or subtracted from the balance on your card. Shop around for a good deal, as card issuers have been cutting their rates. Only a couple of providers offer 1 per cent cashback and this is only for a limited period (one issuer pays it for the first 6 months, the other for the first £2,000 spent on your card). After this, both revert to 0.5 per cent.

Earning loyalty points and Air Miles

You may prefer incentives such as a number of Air Miles related to how much you spend on your card or loyalty points for using your plastic in certain stores or to buy certain products. If you shop in Marks & Spencer or John Lewis on a regular basis, for example, it may be worth opting for one of their cards.

Going for the added extras

Card issuers sometimes attach a range of added benefits to your plastic, which may be attractive to you if you regularly travel or make purchases on your card. These may include:

- ✓ **Domestic warranty cover:** Protects electrical purchases bought with your card for up to a year after the manufacturer's warranty expires.

- ✓ **Price promise cover:** Ensures you're refunded the difference should you purchase an item and then find it cheaper elsewhere.

- ✓ **Free purchase protection insurance:** Covers your purchases against loss, theft, or accidental damage for a limited period.

- ✓ **Free travel accident insurance:** Provides a limited form of travel insurance. Don't assume that this means you don't need to take out travel insurance; check the small print and buy a standalone policy as necessary.

Buying for charity and affinity groups

Instead of receiving something yourself, you may prefer to help a charity or organisation you feel strongly about. These affinity cards are issued in partnership with the charity or organisation, which receives a one-off donation when you first apply for the card or first use it. The initial donation tends to be between £10 and £20. An ongoing donation is also made based on a percentage of your spending – usually 0.25 per cent. The APR on such cards tends to be about average and you're unlikely to find a 0 per cent introductory offer.

Don't be fooled into thinking that cards that benefit charity have charitable terms and conditions. For example, one card has an APR of 12.9 on purchases, which is average, but on cash withdrawals it charges 25.4 per cent. Keep an eye on the small print and don't assume anything.

Avoiding Certain Credit Card Activities

To use your credit card effectively, you need to watch out for hidden charges and stick to your debit card when making cash withdrawals. The following sections point out some credit card pitfalls to avoid.

Paying annual charges

Many card providers used to charge an annual fee for owning a credit card, though this practice has declined as the market has become more competitive. However, some providers still charge a fee, arguing that you get value-added goods and services in return. But in most cases, these aren't worth what you pay, particularly if you never use these services.

Withdrawing cash

Withdrawing cash using your credit card is never a good idea, because a *cash advance* is very expensive, with providers charging high rates of interest and fees. Even if your issuer is offering 0 per cent on new purchases and balance transfers on your card, this usually doesn't apply to cash advances. Most issuers charge a percentage of the amount withdrawn – 1.5 to 2 per cent, with a minimum charge of £1.50 to £2, every time.

The APR on cash advances tends to be far higher than on new purchases or balance transfers. For example, Halifax charges 0 per cent on purchases for 12 months, followed by an APR of 15.9 per cent and 22.95 per cent on cash withdrawals, plus a 3 per cent fee. You're also charged interest from the date of the transaction – there is no interest-free period.

Buying credit card protection

Another waste of money, credit card protection is offered by issuers for an annual fee of around £15. If your card is lost or stolen, this protection ensures that you aren't liable if your card is used fraudulently before you have a chance to cancel it, as long as you aren't responsible for the loss or theft. But the same is true if you don't have this protection.

Have credit card, don't necessarily travel

If you think using your card to withdraw cash in the UK is expensive, wait till you hit foreign shores. If you withdraw cash abroad, you're charged a *loading fee* – typically 2.75 per cent of the amount withdrawn. (This loading fee is also charged when you make purchases abroad using your card.) On top of this is an added ATM charge – around 2 per cent of the amount withdrawn (minimum £2). The problem is that you probably won't be aware of these charges until you receive your card statement back home and get a nasty shock.

Credit cards do have their advantages abroad: They are fairly safe, as fraudsters can't use them easily, and they are quick and simple to replace if they are lost or stolen. But to save money, stick to a debit card when withdrawing cash, preferably the Nationwide Flex account, which imposes no charges at all for withdrawing cash abroad. Or at least limit the number of withdrawals you make using your credit card.

Card protection can come in handy if you have several cards, and they're all lost or stolen at the same time – one call cancels them all. But you can just as easily make the calls yourself: Keep a list of all the issuers' numbers near the phone so if you need to cancel your cards, you can do so quickly and easily, without paying for unnecessary insurance.

Protecting Your Purchases

If you purchase goods or services costing between £100 and £30,000 using a credit card, you are protected under Section 75 of the Consumer Credit Act 1974. Both the supplier and your card issuer are responsible if there's a problem. So if the supplier goes bust, for example, you should be able to get a refund from your card issuer.

Only credit cards are covered by this protection – not debit cards – so think carefully before making a purchase on one of these, as you may be better off using your credit card.

Considering Your Credit Rating

When you apply for a credit card or any other form of loan, the lender checks your credit rating and assigns you a credit score before granting the card or loan.

If you have no previous credit history (no mortgage, other credit cards, or loans), have county court judgements (CCJs) against you, are in arrears or default, or are self-employed, you may find it difficult to get a credit card. Some card issuers specialise in such cases but charge a higher rate of interest than the typical rate. If you use such a card properly and repay at least the minimum amount each month, you can build or rebuild your credit rating before switching to a card with a more attractive rate.

Working with credit scoring

With credit scoring you are awarded points depending on your answers to questions on the card application form. The questions help the issuer assess how big a risk you are. How many points you earn determines whether the issuer lets you have a card at all and, if so, what your credit limit is.

If you don't have a high enough score, the issuer does one of the following:

- Refuses your application outright.

- Offers you a lower credit limit than you hoped for. You may be able to apply for a higher credit limit after you prove that you can repay what you owe.

- Charges a higher rate of interest. The advertised rate is not necessarily the one you receive. Many lenders treat the advertised rate as a *typical* rate and decide what to charge you according to your credit score. The riskier you are deemed to be, the more interest you have to pay. Check whether your rate can be reduced once you prove that you can meet your repayments.

If you fail the credit score, the issuer doesn't have to explain why. Scoring systems are commercially sensitive, so issuers prefer to keep them under wraps. Anyway, if you knew what answers they were looking for, you may fill out your application form accordingly so it wouldn't be a fair assessment.

While it may not go into details, the issuer should give you a general indication of why you failed the credit score, if you ask. Do so, as this may help you with further applications.

Correcting mistakes on your file

Credit card issuers check your credit file by applying to a credit reference agency. If you have a good credit history – haven't been declared bankrupt and have no CCJs against you – this helps your application.

Credit reference agencies hold all sorts of information on their files, including:

- ✔ **Public record information:** The UK electoral roll is used for checking names and addresses, CCJs, bankruptcies, and repossession orders.

- ✔ **Credit account information:** Includes information such as whether you've kept up to date with other payments and other borrowings you have, such as loans and credit cards.

- ✔ **Search information:** Every time you apply for credit, a *footprint* is recorded on your file. If you make a lot of applications over a short period of time, you appear desperate for credit. The card issuer will wonder why: Are you over-committed or committing fraud?

Obtaining a copy of your credit file is a good idea, so that you can check it for errors and correct them. The Data Protection Act 1988 gives you the right to correct inaccurate information held about you. If you spot a mistake, contact the reference agency to find out how to remove or amend it. A note of correction may be added to your file.

To order a copy of your file, contact the three main agencies: Callcredit, Equifax, and Experian. You can get a copy of your file online (Equifax and Experian) or by phone (Experian), using a credit or debit card. Or you can send a cheque (payable to Callcredit, Equifax, or Experian) for £2 to get each file. This should take seven working days. Don't forget to include:

- ✔ Your full name and current address

- ✔ Date of birth

- ✔ Any addresses you have had in the past six years

- ✔ Whether you've changed your name in the past six years

Details for the three agencies are:

- ✔ Consumer Services Team, **Callcredit** plc, PO Box 491, Leeds, LS3 1WZ. Telephone 0870 060 1414 or visit www.callcredit.co.uk

- ✔ Credit File Advice Centre, **Equifax** plc, PO Box 1140, Bradford, BD1 5US. Telephone 08705 143 700 or visit www.econsumer.equifax.co.uk

✔ Consumer Help Service, **Experian** Ltd, PO Box 8000, Nottingham, NG1 5GX. Telephone 0870 241 6212 or visit www. experian.com

 Plenty of credit repair companies promise to clean up your credit file or help you obtain credit. Avoid them. These companies charge expensive fees but are limited in what they can do because only genuinely incorrect information can be removed, which you can do yourself using the information in this section.

Failing credit scoring

If you fail the credit score, it doesn't necessarily mean that no issuer will let you have a credit card. Issuers use different criteria in assessing whether to lend to you or not, and some may give more points to certain aspects of your score than others.

 You could try other issuers to see whether they'll consider your credit card application. But remember, each application is recorded on your credit file, so if you try several issuers to no avail, you harm your credit rating.

If you do fail, you may be over-committed. Look candidly at your debts to assess whether this is the case. If it is, work out how you can cut back on the debt you already have before taking on even more. This enables you to pass the credit score next time, and to manage your debts more easily.

Chapter 7

Navigating Personal Loans

· ·

In This Chapter

▶ Deciding whether a loan is the answer

▶ Investigating loans and how they work

▶ Searching for a loan that suits

▶ Ensuring you don't get stung on insurance

▶ Managing repayment problems

· ·

*N*o matter how good you are at managing your finances, from time to time you may need to borrow money. You may need to cover the cost of a big outgoing, such as a new car or kitchen for example, where the alternative is years of saving. In such a situation, you may want to consider a personal loan.

 Redemption penalties for repaying some loans ahead of schedule and expensive payment protection insurance lie in wait to trip up the unwary. In this chapter I show you what to look out for when choosing a loan to avoid spending more than you absolutely need to. If you're looking for a mortgage, you won't find the necessary information in this chapter: You need to go to Chapter 14 for that.

Figuring Out When a Loan Makes Perfect Sense

If you need at least a couple of thousand pounds in the medium term to buy anything from plastic surgery to a new kitchen or a cruise, a loan can be a good choice. Loans are useful because:

✔ **You can borrow more than you can on a credit card or overdraft:** You can take out a personal loan for any amount, usually between £500 and £25,000. You may even be able to borrow more than this via a secured loan (see 'Taking out unsecured versus secured loans' later in this chapter for more details).

✔ **The rate of interest is normally fixed:** You know exactly how much you have to pay back over the term of the loan, making budgeting easy to do.

✔ **You know when the debt will be cleared:** Loans have a fixed repayment schedule, unlike an overdraft or credit card where you pay the money back as and when you can. If you lack the discipline to do this, a loan could be the answer.

✔ **A loan is easy to arrange:** Loans can be arranged through the post, over the telephone, or via the Internet. You don't need to make an appointment to see your bank manager. The money is sent to you by cheque or transferred to your bank account within days.

✔ **Your borrowing is limited:** You get a specified amount of cash – you can't keep dipping in and taking more, as you can with an overdraft or credit card.

As long as you can afford the monthly repayments and shop around for the cheapest deal you can find, a loan can be a good choice for borrowing money.

Deciding When a Loan Is Not a Good Idea

A personal loan isn't always the ideal way of borrowing money. You might want to think twice if:

✔ **You need to borrow only a few hundred pounds:** The smaller the sum you borrow, the higher the rate of interest you pay. Borrowing an amount under £1,000 is extremely expensive in terms of interest charges and not all lenders let you do this. Most lenders have a minimum that you can borrow: If you need less, you may find yourself taking out a bigger loan simply in order to get the money in the first place. This isn't a wise move. You may be better off borrowing smaller sums on a credit card or extending your overdraft instead of opting for a loan.

✔ **You can repay the money in a couple of months:** The shorter the loan's term, the bigger your monthly repayments, so work out whether you could afford them if you take a loan out for just a year or so. If a chance exists that you'll be able to clear the loan even sooner, you probably won't be charged a redemption penalty for doing so (see 'Understanding how loans work' later in this chapter).

✔ **You're borrowing £20,000 or so to improve your property:**
If you already have a mortgage, asking your mortgage lender
to extend your home loan rather than take out a personal
loan could be the cheaper option – particularly if you need
money to build an extension or otherwise fix up your home.
Although interest rates on personal loans have fallen, they
still tend to be higher than mortgage rates (the cheapest loan
is around 6.7 per cent compared with mortgage rates starting
from around 5.5 per cent). So you pay less interest if you
increase your mortgage instead. This may also be easier to
arrange than a personal loan because you already have a
relationship with the lender.

Think carefully before extending your mortgage and overbur-
dening yourself. Your home is at risk if you can't keep up the
repayments on it, whereas if you take out an unsecured loan
to pay for your extension, your home is safe (even if you
default on the loan payments). Don't gamble with the roof
over your head.

Understanding How Loans Work

You can borrow between £500 and £25,000 on a personal loan.
Some lenders let you borrow more than £25,000 if you opt for a
secured loan (the next section addresses secured and unsecured
loans). You choose the repayment period, which can be anything
from six months to ten years.

Repayments are monthly, usually by direct debit from your bank
account. If you opt for a flexible loan, you may be allowed to
overpay or make lump-sum payments in order to clear the debt
more quickly. This could save you hundreds of pounds in interest.
However, some loans have a penalty for early repayment. This
applies to fixed-sum loans taken out on or after 31 May 2005, which
are regulated by the Consumer Credit Act 1974. The lender may
charge a penalty of 30 days' or one calendar month's interest if the
loan term is more than one year. If the loan term is less than one
year, you don't pay a redemption penalty. Personal loans taken out
before 31 May 2005 may have higher penalties.

Taking out unsecured versus secured loans

Two main types of loan are available: unsecured and secured.
The former offers the lender no security, the latter offers the security

of your home. So if you fail to keep up the repayments for a loan secured on your home, the lender has a claim on it. I explain this in more detail in the following sections.

You might opt for a secured loan if you have a poor credit rating, but you may be able to find a cheaper, unsecured loan if you're prepared to shop around instead.

Unsecured loans

Most personal loans are *unsecured*, which means that the lender has no security for your debt. If you fail to make your repayments, the lender doesn't have the automatic right to seize an asset, such as your home. The lender can pursue you through the courts for an unpaid loan, however, so you aren't totally off the hook if you don't pay up.

Unsecured loans of up to £25,000 are governed by the Consumer Credit Act 1974, so are also known as *regulated loans*. This is not the case with secured loans, which aren't covered by the Act. The Act strictly regulates how money is lent and ensures that the lender must give you seven days to change your mind about taking out a loan.

Secured loans

On *secured loans*, your assets, such as property or investments, provide the lender with some security. If you default on your repayments, your lender can take you to court and demand repossession of the property you used to secure the loan.

If the loan is secured against your home, and your home is still mortgaged, the loan is known as a *second charge loan*.

Secured loans have a lower APR than unsecured loans because they are less risky from the lender's perspective. They are also easier to come by for this reason.

Secured loans are not regulated by the Consumer Credit Act, so make sure you read the terms and conditions extremely carefully before signing the credit agreement, as the agreement is binding. The lender is not obliged to give you seven days to change your mind, as is the case with unsecured loans.

You can usually borrow more on a secured loan as the lender is taking on less risk because it knows it will get its money back if you default. Most lenders offering secured loans let you borrow up to £50,000 – although some may let you borrow up to £100,000. However, if you need to borrow this much, consider remortgaging instead, as you should be able to get a cheaper rate.

The term of a secured loan can be longer than an unsecured loan – up to 25 years in some cases. You'll be charged a penalty for repaying the loan early, so check with the lender what the penalty is before signing on the dotted line.

Deciding on the term

You can choose how long you want to pay off the loan within the minimum and maximum terms on offer. The longer the term of the loan, the lower your monthly repayments (so if you opt for five years rather than two, you pay less each month) but you end up paying in the long run. You pay more interest and make more payments over a longer term.

Consider the term of the loan carefully. If you need cash to pay for a dream holiday this summer, for example, do you really want to still be paying it back in four years' time? But whatever term you choose, make sure it's realistic: Don't overstretch yourself with massive monthly payments just to clear the loan within a year if there's no way you will be able to cope.

Working out the interest

The lender charges interest on the amount you borrow, known as the *annual percentage rate (APR)*. The APR is usually a fixed percentage, but may be variable. Every loan has an APR, which you can use to compare deals to find the cheapest one. How much you borrow, for how long, and the lender's perception of your chances of repaying it all affect the APR you're charged.

The advertised APR can be misleading. This headline rate is usually the best deal available. To qualify for this rate, you may have to take out the biggest loan that the lender offers, which may be far more than you need. Borrow a smaller amount and you're likely to be charged a higher APR. However, this shouldn't be seen as an excuse for taking out a bigger loan than you need.

Whether your interest rate is fixed or variable can make quite a difference to your repayments, so ensure you understand which type you're signing up for:

 ✔ **Fixed rate:** Interest is the same throughout the term of the loan, no matter what happens to the Bank of England base rate. This enables you to budget, as your monthly repayments are always the same.

✔ **Variable rate:** The APR rises or falls in line with changes to the base rate. Your monthly repayments are therefore not fixed, which makes budgeting harder. However, if the base rate goes down, and the APR on your loan falls accordingly, your repayments are lower than if you'd opted for a fixed-rate loan. However, the reverse can also happen if rates increase, so you're taking a risk. If this would be a struggle for you, opt for a fixed-rate loan.

Some lenders charge a lower APR if you apply for a loan over the Internet rather than the telephone, post, or in a branch. Find out whether this is the case: If it is, apply online if you can.

Calculating the total cost

In order to compare loans from different providers, find out exactly what the lender charges for the amount of cash you want to borrow. Otherwise, the comparison is meaningless. The lender may simply provide you with the monthly cost, rather than the full amount. Check how much you pay in total to compare with other providers and work out whether it's a good deal or not.

Doing the sums yourself is a good idea, so that you know exactly how much you're paying in the long run. Then you can consider whether it *is* such a good deal. For example, if you want to borrow £5,000 over three years, you may find two lenders charging you £150.89 and £168.68 a month respectively. The latter may not seem that much more and you may well be able to afford the extra. But if you consider how much extra you'll pay over the term of the loan, you might think twice: £5,432 on the first loan and £6,072 on the latter. That's a difference of £640 – a significant amount.

Watching out for early redemption penalties

A low APR is important when choosing a loan, but you should also watch out for early redemption penalties, also known as *early settlement charges*, which can push up the overall cost.

Some lenders charge a redemption penalty if you clear your loan ahead of schedule. This comes as a shock to many borrowers.

Lenders can charge a penalty of no more than 30 days' or one month's interest if you took the loan out on or after 31 May 2005 for at least a year. If the loan duration is less than one year and you took it out on or after 31 May 2005, the lender can't charge you a penalty for paying the loan off early. While these limits are encouraging, you're better off selecting a lender who doesn't charge a redemption penalty: Several lenders have scrapped this practice. When shopping around for a loan, make sure you ask lenders whether they charge a redemption penalty.

You may be charged a higher APR for taking on a loan with no early settlement charges, but if a chance exists that you might repay your loan ahead of schedule, it's still worth considering.

Aiming for flexibility

Most loans are fixed, so you borrow a set amount over a certain period and pay the same amount each month to clear the debt. But a smaller number of flexible deals are available that allow you to overpay or pay a lump sum to clear your debt early (without penalty).

You may also be able to take a repayment holiday (which means you don't have to make a repayment for anything up to several months). You can do this at the start of the loan or at an agreed date during the loan. But you must arrange this with your lender: You can't simply stop making your repayments without warning.

Even when you take a payment holiday, your outstanding balance continues to accrue interest. This may result in higher monthly payments to ensure that your debt is still repaid over the term of the loan as agreed at the outset.

With a flexible deal, you don't have to take all the cash in one go. Instead, you may also be able to withdraw funds from the account on a rolling basis, as long as you stay within your credit limit. So you apply for the full extent of the cash you need in the first instance and then take it as and when you require it.

Finding the Best Personal Loan

Long gone are the days when you had to put on your best suit, polish your shoes, and make an appointment to visit your bank manager to grovel for a loan. Nowadays, you can apply online in a matter of minutes and receive the cash within hours.

Shopping around is also easier than ever if you have access to the Internet, as there are a number of sites that enable you to compare the cost of products. Check out www.moneyextra.com, www.moneyfacts.co.uk, and www.moneysupermarket.com for more details. Most of these sites have direct links through to lenders, so you can click on a button and up pops an application form immediately. It couldn't be simpler, so think carefully before taking the plunge and committing yourself to something you can't really afford.

If you don't have Internet access, keep an eye on loan adverts and 'best-buy' tables in the quality weekend newspapers for the cheapest deals. You can get loans for as little as 6.7 per cent, so anything around this mark is good value. If the APR is in double digits, it should be avoided.

If you're buying a new car or kitchen, the retailer will probably try to persuade you to take out its finance deal. This may be tempting, as doing so saves you the bother of searching for finance, but it's unlikely to be the cheapest solution. You're better off searching for a cheap personal loan instead.

The advantage of arranging a loan before making your purchase is that you'll be, in effect, a cash buyer as far as the retailer is concerned. You should be able to drive a bargain and perhaps get a discount, as well as saving interest on the loan.

Applying for a loan

After choosing the loan you want, you have to complete an application form. The application asks for details of your existing financial commitments and income. The lender uses this to assess whether you can afford to take on and repay the loan. If you're married, both you and your spouse must be named on the application form: The lender insists upon this.

The lender also contacts credit reference agencies to obtain a copy of your credit file. Your credit file indicates whether you have any outstanding county court judgments against you, are bankrupt, or have a history of defaulting on debts. (See Chapter 6 for more on your credit file and obtaining a copy to check this information.)

Lenders also use credit scoring, enabling them to work out what category of borrower you are, according to your personal circumstances (see Chapter 6 for more details). This enables them to work out what APR to charge you: The higher risk you appear, the higher the APR will be.

When the lender is happy with the result of its checks, it offers you a loan. Processing an application usually takes only a few hours or days, depending on the lender. If the lender isn't happy with its findings, you may be refused a loan.

As well as being a great place to search for a loan, the Internet also provides the easiest way of applying to borrow cash. And because fewer administration costs are involved, lenders tend to offer a lower APR if you apply for your loan online rather than via the post, in person at your local branch, or over the telephone.

Coping with a poor (or no) credit history

If you've had difficulty repaying credit in the past, you may have a bad credit history. This history is unearthed when you apply for a new loan and the lender runs a credit check on you. As a result, your application may be turned down.

Not only people with bad credit histories are refused credit. If you don't have a credit history because you've never had a credit card, loan, or mortgage before, the lender won't be able to figure out whether you're a good risk or not. How can the lender tell whether you're going to make your repayments every month if you haven't done this before? If you're self-employed or if you've changed jobs recently, you may also find getting credit to be more difficult. And moving around frequently doesn't look good either.

If any of these apply to you, don't give up just yet. A number of lenders specifically target people with bad credit histories or those who have difficulty getting a loan. If you apply to one of these lenders, you increase your chances of success but you also have to pay a higher APR – because you're perceived as being higher risk. This could be more than twice as much as the cheapest loan on the market, so the extra cost can be considerable.

Even if you do pay a higher APR initially, you may not always have to pay over the odds. When you build up a payment history, it has the same effect as rebuilding your credit history (or creating a new one). This goes on your credit file, so when you apply for credit in the future it will count in your favour and you should be able to qualify for a standard loan with a lower APR.

Alternatively, if you're having difficulty getting an unsecured loan and are a homeowner, you can opt for a secured loan. Because the lender has the added benefit of security – in other words an ultimate claim to your property if you default on your repayments – it is more likely to consider lending you money. (See 'Taking out unsecured versus secured loans' earlier in this chapter for more details.)

Avoiding Payment Protection Insurance

When you take out a personal loan, you must sign a binding credit agreement. This commits you to making the repayments each month, even if you lose your job, or become ill or sick so you can no longer work. To protect yourself, you can take out a form of insurance called *payment protection* to ensure that your repayments are still made – even if you personally can't afford to do so. Some policies also clear your debt if you die leaving an outstanding loan, making life easier for your dependants.

Working out the cost

While you may think this cover is vital, it is expensive and largely unnecessary. To make matters worse, many lenders conceal the true cost by automatically adding the cost of cover to the loan, whether you request it or not. The danger is that you assume you have to take the cover out, which is nonsense. And you also don't appreciate exactly how much the insurance is costing you.

Do the sums to find out the true cost of cover. For example, borrowing £5,000 over three years with payment protection could cost you £176.28 a month (for a 6.8 per cent loan from Barclaycard). But if you opt not to take out the cover, your monthly repayments would be £153.57, a saving of £22.71. Over three years, the insurance would cost you £817.56.

Checking the small print

Both the level of cover and cost of protection vary considerably between lenders, so check individual policies so you know exactly what is included – and what isn't. Most policies don't let you claim immediately after you're out of work: They usually have an excess period of 60 days or longer before you can make a claim. Decide whether you could cope without an income for this period of time. If you can't, shop around for another policy that doesn't have such a long excess: A number of providers have an excess of 30 days, for example.

Loan payment protection can be comforting, but it's also usually extremely expensive, particularly if you buy cover from your loan provider. Standalone payment protection policies offer much better value for money. For example, if a person borrowing £5,000 over three years from Barclaycard at 6.8 per cent shopped around for cover instead of buying it from the lender, they could pay £5.91 a month for insurance from a broker via an online search. This is a saving of £16.80 a month, or £604.80 over the term of the loan.

Deciding whether you need cover

You may wonder whether this insurance is just another method devised by the industry to make money out of you, or if it is worth having. Much depends on your personal circumstances and whether you have other savings or investments, which could be used to clear your loan if you lose your job or can't work.

If you're seriously worried about losing your job, think about whether now is the best time to take on extra borrowing. Perhaps waiting until the situation is clearer and knowing where you stand with your employer would be wiser.

Check whether you already have some cover for sickness or accident – perhaps from your employer. If this is the case, you don't need to purchase further cover: You may only need the unemployment element. There is no point doubling up on cover, as it will just cost you more than you need to pay.

If you're self-employed, there's little point taking out this cover because it usually only pays out if you wind up your business – not if you don't have any work on. Don't waste your money.

Taking Action If You Are Struggling with Repayments

If you have problems meeting your loan repayments – and have no payment protection – resist the temptation to ignore the problem and hope it goes away. Ask your lender for advice: The earlier you get in touch and explain the situation, the more understanding the lender is likely to be.

If your home is secured against your loan, seeking help as soon as possible is particularly important. Otherwise, you're at risk of losing the roof over your head.

If you don't feel you can speak to your lender for whatever reason, a number of organisations provide free advice and contact the lender to negotiate on your behalf. Try your local Citizens Advice Bureau (details in your local phone book). Alternatively, try the National Debtline (www.nationaldebtline.co.uk) or the Consumer Credit Counselling Service (www.cccs.co.uk).

Steer clear of debt management companies that organise your debts into one monthly payment for a fee. Try the free advice services instead of going down this route, particularly if it's just your loan you're having trouble repaying. (Chapter 8 has more information on debt management companies.)

Chapter 8

Avoiding Credit Nasties and Getting Out of Debt

● ●

In This Chapter

▶ Handling store card debt

▶ Steering clear of debt management companies

▶ Consolidating your own debts

▶ Avoiding bankruptcy

● ●

*C*heap overdrafts, credit cards, personal loans, and mortgages have made borrowing much cheaper than in the past, but not all debt is inexpensive. Cards issued by stores have remained largely untouched by the downward trend in interest rates and charges – remaining as expensive as ever. And despite the growing number of cheap personal loans, loan sharks still operate, preying on the desperate.

But debt management companies, expensive consolidation loans, and bankruptcy aren't the answer. In this chapter I show you where to get free advice and how to get on top of your debt.

Handling Store Cards Smartly

Plastic is a convenient form of spending, but when it comes to store cards it can be extremely expensive. A *store card* is a credit card branded with the name of the store that issues it and is useful to purchase only goods in that store, or chain of stores. Store cards work much the same as credit cards from major companies, although store cards generally have high annual percentage rates (APRs) and often have short interest-free grace periods.

Signing up for store cards

The big incentive to sign up for a store card is a discount on your purchases the day you apply: Up to 10 or even 15 per cent in some cases, which can be quite a saving if you're spending a lot of cash. But if you don't clear the balance when your statement arrives, that initial discount could easily be eaten up in interest because store cards have high APRs.

Store cards are 'sold' to you by sales assistants, many of whom are on commission so the more customers they can persuade to sign up, the more lucrative it is for them. The sales assistant usually fills out the application form on your behalf while you supply your details, then calls to check your credit rating while you wait. If you're deemed a good enough risk, the card is authorised.

The Office of Fair Trading (OFT) is concerned about hard-sell tactics. Although sales assistants never suggest that you take the application form away with you to read carefully before deciding whether to sign up or not, the OFT advises that you do so to ensure you understand what you're getting into. However, if you take the form away you won't get your 10 per cent discount, which may be the only reason you're signing up in the first place.

Paying extortionate rates of interest

The main problem with store cards is that it often isn't clear when you sign up in store exactly what the APR is – the amount of interest you pay. The APR is rarely clearly advertised, and the rate could mean a nasty shock when your statement arrives because rates tend to be extremely high. And if you don't pay off the balance in full, you could pay a lot extra.

With all but a couple of exceptions, store cards are a very expensive method of borrowing. While APRs on credit cards have fallen dramatically in recent years, rates on the majority of store cards still hover around the 30 per cent mark – more than double those on most credit cards.

Making store cards work for you

If you can comfortably clear the outstanding amount on your store card when the bill arrives and are a regular customer of that particular retailer, using a store card may be worthwhile, as doing so could bring plenty of benefits. Not only do you get a discount on your first purchase, the cards usually come with other perks too, such as bonus reward schemes, free catalogues or magazines, and special shopping days, where you can avoid the crowds and shop in peace. John Lewis gives customers 1 per cent of what they spend in store back in the form of vouchers, for example, so if you're a regular customer this could be worth having.

Some retailers have launched credit cards alongside their store cards so you get the usual rewards of a store card for spending on the retailer-branded credit card. The danger is that while the APR tends to be lower than on a store card, it isn't as cheap as some of the best credit cards. And as you aren't restricted to one store but can use it in whatever outlets you like, you could run up more debt on it than you were able to before. Check the APR before spending – and if it isn't that competitive (and you don't clear your balance every month) don't use it at all.

Set up a direct debit to pay the full amount due on your store card each month. Then, if you forget to pay one month – perhaps because you're on holiday – it'll be paid regardless so you won't run up any interest.

As well as persuading you to take out a store card, many retailers will try to force you to buy *card protection* and, just for good measure, *card payment protection* as well:

- ✔ **Card protection:** Covers you if your card is lost or stolen. A single call from you can cancel all your plastic and usually costs around £12 a year.

- ✔ **Card payment protection:** Covers your store card repayments if you lose your job or become ill and can't work.

Refusing to bow to pressure

Although store cards have high APRs, I know only too well the allure of a 10 per cent discount. I signed up for one in a major department store when I bought a £150 outfit for a wedding because it seemed an easy way of saving £15. However, when I was still standing there 20 minutes later, worrying about my car on the meter and the disgruntled queue building up behind me, it no longer seemed such a good idea.

I passed the credit check though and got my discount. A few weeks later I got a call from the store advising me to take out its card protection plan: For £45 I would get three years' cover. I was told that it was a good idea and everyone was being advised to buy it. I said I wasn't interested and the salesperson grew quite pushy. I was unimpressed and stuck to my guns.

Don't bow to pressure, whether it's over buying insurance – or applying for the store card in the first place.

I would avoid both types of cover, as they are expensive and usually a waste of money. Don't be talked into signing up, no matter how persuasive the salesperson is. If you really want some card or payment protection, shop around for a good deal rather than automatically taking out the policy the store card provider offers: You are not obliged to do so and you can find better deals elsewhere. Make sure you read the small print before signing anything (Chapters 6 and 7 have more details on this type of cover).

Clearing store card debt

If you run up debt on your store card that you can't clear at the end of the month, you will be charged a lot of interest – usually from the day you made the purchase, rather than the statement date. To avoid paying the interest, take out a regular credit card with a 0 per cent introductory offer period on balance transfers and switch your outstanding store card debt to the new card. This is a simple process: You contact your new card provider with your store card account number and how much you want to transfer. Processing the payment usually takes a few working days.

When you've transferred your store card debt, use the money that would've gone towards paying off the interest to chip away at the balance. If you haven't cleared the balance by the end of the introductory period (anything from five to twelve months), switch to another card offering a similar deal, and so on until the debt is cleared.

 When you've transferred the debt from your store card, cut the card up and write to the issuer closing your account. This takes away the temptation to spend further on the card. Stick to cheaper forms of credit in future.

Avoiding Debt Consolidation Firms

The fact that rising levels of debt have been accompanied by a growth in the number of debt management or debt consolidation companies is no coincidence. Their services are advertised everywhere – from the television to radio and national newspapers, promising to help with all your nasty debt problems. Need £25,000, £50,000, or £100,000 as soon as possible, no questions asked? If you're a homeowner, a debt management company will be happy to oblige.

The reason debt management companies are interested in home-owners is that the companies replace your debts, which are *unsecured*, with a *secured* loan. In other words, the lender can repossess your home if you don't keep up your monthly repayments. This is extremely risky and should be avoided at all costs. (See Chapter 7 for more on the difference between secured and unsecured loans and the risks associated with the former.)

Consolidating debts into one loan

Debt management companies reorganise your debts into one *consolidation loan*. In other words, they take out yet another loan to pay off your existing debt, thereby increasing your borrowing. You make a single monthly payment: This may be lower than your current payments (particularly if your existing debts are expensive), but you pay more in the long run as you take longer to pay it off.

Consolidation loans can be tempting if you owe money to several creditors who all want paying at the same time. Instead of making payments here, there, and everywhere, you only have to worry about one payment. The debt management company plays on this. But some consolidation loans extend your term of borrowing by as long as 25 years. Ask yourself whether you'd be happy paying off credit card debt and other bills over such a long period of time.

Work out the total cost of the consolidation loan to see how much it will be in the long run, rather than just the monthly amount. And avoid expensive payment protection insurance, which the lender may try to sell you, as it often isn't worth having and will simply bump up the cost. (Chapter 7 has more on this type of cover.)

Be wary of borrowing more money to pay off existing debt. Despite your efforts to improve matters, you may find you make the situation worse.

Looking at high rates and arrangement fees

Unlike consumer groups and charities that help you get on top of your debts for free, debt management companies charge around 15 per cent, plus VAT (at 17.5 per cent) for arranging a consolidation loan. It's no wonder there are so many debt management companies out there: It's a lucrative business to be in right now.

Working out the cost of consolidation

One Citizens Advice Bureau client saw his debt quadruple when he took out a consolidation loan for £24,200. This came with payment protection insurance of £4,823, which covered him if he lost his job or became ill and couldn't meet his repayments. He ended up with monthly repayments of £350 for 25 years – a grand total of £105,078!

To avoid paying fees to a debt management company, consider whether a consolidation loan is what you need to get out of your debt mess. You may be able to get an unsecured loan with a lower APR than a secured one if you shop around. You can then use this money to pay off your debts, just as you would if a debt management company set up a consolidated loan for you, and make your monthly payment to your new lender each month. Chapter 7 has the lowdown on shopping around for personal loans.

Steering Clear of Loan Sharks

If you're desperate for cash and have a bad credit rating, which makes it difficult to get a credit card, bank loan, or overdraft, you may be tempted to borrow from a loan shark. But don't be fooled into thinking that you can control such a loan and won't go the way of all those other borrowers who fall behind with their repayments and find themselves intimidated and threatened with violence.

Loan sharks are illegal moneylenders who give out quick cash loans, so they are convenient if you need money as soon as possible. But the rates of interest they charge are astronomical – up to 200 per cent in some cases. This would be hard enough to repay even if your finances were in a strong position.

If you're in such a dire position that you're even contemplating using a loan shark, you must seek advice before you do anything else. (Check out 'Seeking free advice' at the end of this chapter.)

Escaping the Debt Trap

Although debt management companies do a good job of persuading you that you really must use their services to get out of debt, this isn't the case. When you've faced up to your debt problem – the sooner you do this the better – you can take steps to get out of it yourself.

Prioritising your debts

The first step is to prioritise your debts, deciding which ones you must pay first. This helps you separate the urgent debts from the not-so-urgent ones, so you clear the ones that carry the severest penalty for defaulting first.

Priority debts include:

- ✔ **Your rent or mortgage:** If you don't pay this, your landlord can evict you or your mortgage lender can apply to a court to have your home repossessed and sell it to cover your debts. Either way, you end up without a roof over your head.
- ✔ **Gas and electricity bills:** If you don't pay these, your supply will be cut off.
- ✔ **Telephone bill:** Again, the supplier will simply cut you off if you don't pay.
- ✔ **Council tax:** You can go to prison if you don't pay up.

When you've identified your priority debts, see whether there are any areas where you can make savings (perhaps by switching to a cheaper utility supplier, for example).

Don't pay any secondary debts, such as credit or store card bills or unsecured loans, until you've reached agreement with your priority creditors.

Working out your budget

The next step is to work out how much cash you have left over once you pay your priority debts. Subtract the cost of these from your monthly income: Any money left over can be divided between your remaining (or secondary) creditors.

If you haven't got a surplus, or enough of one to clear all your bills, contact one of the free advice services (see 'Seeking free advice' at the end of this chapter) for help.

Making savings work harder

If you have any savings or investments, such as a few windfall shares from the demutualisation of a building society, work out whether you could put this money to better use clearing your debts rather than leaving it where it is. If you earn less interest on your savings than you pay on your debts, use this cash to pay some bills. Even if you earn 5 per cent tax free on your savings in a mini cash individual savings account, if you're paying 30 per cent interest on store card debt, it doesn't make sense to keep the savings. Reduce your debt instead – and the interest you pay.

Juggling your mortgage

If you're struggling to repay your mortgage, you could reduce your monthly repayments by extending the term of your loan. Alternatively, you might be able to reduce your payments, and stick to the same term, by remortgaging at a cheaper rate. If you've had the same deal for several years, you could almost certainly save money by remortgaging. Check first whether you'll incur an early redemption penalty for switching: This could be the case if you're on a fixed or discounted deal, or have recently come to the end of such an offer.

 Even if you do have to pay a penalty, you may still save cash in the long run. Ask an independent mortgage broker to do the calculations for you (Chapter 14 has more on finding a broker).

While you're remortgaging you could increase the size of your home loan (if you have enough equity in your home to do so), and use the cash you raise to clear other loans or credit card debts. The advantage of this is that mortgage rates tend to be lower than other forms of borrowing, so you pay less interest.

 Avoid increasing your mortgage by an unnecessarily large amount, otherwise you could struggle to repay it and could lose your home. Calculate how much you absolutely need to clear your debts and don't borrow more than this. Remortgaging shouldn't be seen as a chance of raising money to fritter away, but only for the serious matter of clearing your existing debt.

Replacing the plastic

If you've got store and credit cards with high APRs and don't clear the balance each month, transfer the outstanding debt to a cheap credit card charging 0 per cent for an introductory period. Then cut up the expensive cards so you won't be tempted to use them again.

Alternatively, take out a cheap personal loan. This cash can be used to pay all your debts in return for a manageable monthly payment. This is, in effect, what a consolidation loan organised by a debt management company does, but by doing it yourself, you save on the management charge and don't have to secure the loan against your home. Chapter 7 has tips on shopping around for a loan.

Contacting your creditors

When you're in debt, you could be tempted to stick your head in the sand and pretend you haven't got a problem. The last people you may feel like telling are those you owe money to: Surely they'll pull the rug from under you if you 'fess up? But in actual fact, these are the very people you should be talking to if you have problems.

The sooner you contact your creditors and explain the situation to them, the more sympathetic they're likely to be. Tell them you're having difficulty paying what you owe and offer to pay a smaller amount each week or month. Even if this is only a tiny proportion of your debt, the lender may welcome it as a sign that you are determined to honour what you owe. Most creditors also realise that a court would only order small payments anyway, so they might as well accept your offer.

If you can't repay what you owe because you've lost your job or your marriage has broken down, the lender may be prepared to reduce or freeze your payments until you get back on your feet.

Don't agree to pay back more than you can realistically afford or you'll simply be back where you started.

Going bankrupt

As the stigma surrounding bankruptcy lessens, it is an increasingly attractive alternative to those struggling with debt. It used to be the case that you were automatically discharged from bankruptcy two to three years after the bankruptcy order, but this has been reduced to one year.

By going bankrupt you finally put an end to harassment from your creditors – the people you owe money to – which can come as a blessed relief. When a bankruptcy order has been made, a third party or trustee – the *Official Receiver* or an *insolvency practitioner* – takes over your estate. Any financial interest you have in your home is transferred to the trustee: He recovers the value of this for the benefit of your creditors. Your creditors contact him and he decides who gets what, when your possessions have been sold.

When you're discharged from bankruptcy, your creditors can't come after you for any outstanding debts.

However, it isn't as straightforward as all that. Bankruptcy shouldn't be taken lightly because:

- ✔ If you have a home, you could lose it. The administrator will sell your assets, such as shares and investments, as well as property, to raise the cash to pay your creditors.
- ✔ If you own a business this will almost certainly be sold.
- ✔ Getting a bank account or mortgage is difficult when you're a bankrupt.
- ✔ Bankruptcy is extremely expensive. All court and insolvency service fees are taken out of your assets and the Official Receiver also levies a 15 per cent charge on all sums received.
- ✔ If you want more than £250 credit, you must declare that you're an undischarged bankrupt.
- ✔ You can't hold public office or be an MP, solicitor, or accountant.
- ✔ Your name will be published in the local press, bringing unwanted publicity.

Bankruptcy is a last resort. Take advice before declaring yourself bankrupt by contacting one of the debt counselling groups listed in the following section.

Seeking free advice

When it comes to getting out of debt and the problems it causes, numerous companies are out there offering to help you, although you must steer clear of debt management companies for the reasons I detail in the previous sections. You should also steer clear of credit repair companies, which promise to improve your credit rating. They can practically do very little, and you can do all that yourself – for free. See Chapter 6 for ways of improving your credit file.

A number of organisations offer free advice if you get into debt difficulties. They will negotiate with your creditors on your behalf, so contact one of these before approaching any debt management companies or loan sharks:

- ✔ Citizens Advice Bureau: Check your local phone book for your local branch or go to www.citizensadvice.org.uk.

- ✔ Consumer Credit Counselling Service on 0800 138 1111 or www.cccs.co.uk.

- ✔ National Debtline on 0808 808 4000 or www.nationaldebt line.co.uk.

Part III
Building Up Savings and Investments

'Your stock market investments, at this very moment, are being chosen with meticulous care by our team of approved experts.'

In this part . . .

*T*he chapters in this part guide you through growing
money, from establishing a savings account for emergencies to investing for the future. They also offer heaps
of tips on paying the taxman as little as possible!

Because investing in stocks and shares can be risky, you
want to make sure that you go about it the right way. In these
chapters, I guide you through building up an investment
portfolio.

You'll also find a chapter on choosing a mortgage.

Chapter 9

Saving for a Rainy Day

· ·

In This Chapter

▶ Working out how much cash you need for emergencies

▶ Searching for the best rates

▶ Deciding what type of account you're after

▶ Protecting your savings

· ·

Saving seems to have gone right out of fashion, with the nation more than £1 trillion in debt – and rising. Debt appears to be far more tempting and dangerous, while boring old saving doesn't excite in the same way as getting what you want, right now. Saving is looking increasingly old-fashioned while debt is rather cooler.

However, in an emergency, it's far better to rely on savings than your credit card or overdraft to see you through. If you need money here and now, getting hold of cash sitting in a savings account is much easier than having to arrange credit at short notice.

In this chapter I look at the importance of building up an emergency pot of savings that you can use to pay for any emergency that arises – repairs to your car should it fail its MOT or to replace the boiler when it packs in.

Dealing with an Emergency

 If you don't have cash put by for an emergency, your options may be limited should one arise. Your disposable income is unlikely to generate enough of a surplus to pay for this, given the other demands on your incomings each month.

You may be able to extend your overdraft, slap the cost on a credit card, or take out a personal loan. But these all cost money and may take time to arrange. The overdraft rate depends on your lender but could be very high, particularly if you forget to ask permission for extending it first. Even shopping around for a cheap credit card

may be difficult if you need the money immediately: Your application to be approved and processed will take a couple of weeks, at
least. And taking out a personal loan for just £1,000 will cost you a
lot in interest.

When you're desperate, you're more likely to opt for higher rates
of interest than you would normally when you've got time to shop
around for a competitive deal. And if you've already maxed out on
your credit, you may find you simply can't get your hands on the
extra cash you require.

The big advantage of having emergency savings is that they negate
the need to take out pricey payment protection insurance or
income protection. If you've enough cash to see you through several months with no income, you don't need to have cover for that
period. Or if you do opt for income protection, you can arrange for
an excess period to kick in after your savings run out – whether it's
one, three, or six months. (See Chapter 4 for more on these types
of insurance.)

Looking at Savings Strengths

Having a few grand stashed in an easily accessible place to cover
emergencies is a good idea. Common sense dictates that at some
point you'll encounter an unforeseen expense; research says the
average cost of such expenses is £3,000.

Making sure your rainy day fund is easily accessible doesn't mean
shoving it under the floorboards though: The smart way to save
this cash is in an instant access savings account paying the highest
rate of interest you can find – preferably tax-free. Your savings
vehicle must also be risk free, i.e. an instant access savings
account rather than an investment in the stock market, so that
nothing can happen to your money.

The interest your rainy day savings earn is a bonus, not the main
reason to have such an account. The key is to be able to access
your cash in an emergency – interest is a nice little extra. Beware
of keeping thousands of pounds in this account because finding
the best rate of interest will become more of an issue. Only keep
enough for a rainy day and invest the remainder more wisely
elsewhere.

Avoid using your current account to build up a fund for emergencies. You may be tempted to dip into it for everyday expenses,
which could mean you don't have enough money left when you're
faced with a real emergency. Current accounts don't pay the

highest rates of interest either: You earn better returns in a savings account. Keep your current account for day-to-day bills and expenses.

Clear any debts before you start saving, because you pay more interest on your debt than you can earn on your savings. Having a few hundred pounds earning 4 per cent interest in a savings account when you are paying 30 per cent interest on your store card makes no sense. Clear your debts first.

Making sure your money is easily accessible

Saving up emergency cash if you have to give the bank a month's notice before you can get your hands on it is pointless. The whole point of an emergency fund is that you're able to access it in an emergency, so aim for an instant access account that enables you to get the cash the same day or in a couple of days at most (if it's an Internet account).

Building societies were the traditional choice for savings accounts, but you're likely to find a better deal from one of the newer providers, such as a telephone- or Internet-based account. These often come with cash cards so you can withdraw your cash from an ATM without hassle, or you can transfer money to your current account where you'll be able to access it.

Minimising risk

If you leave thousands of pounds lying around at home, you are at risk of being burgled. Lock that money away in a savings account so you don't lose it or are tempted to spend it.

It is important that you don't take on any risk with your emergency savings. A deposit-based savings vehicle is perfect for this purpose because it guarantees your capital back when you need it, preferably with some added interest on top.

Stock market investments may grow more quickly over time than cash, but steer clear of equities when it comes to your emergency fund. Your aim shouldn't be to generate the biggest return possible but to keep your money safe. Stash your money where you aren't going to lose any of it, and that means a bank or building society account.

Deciding How Much You Need to Save

A reassuring amount of cash for one person may not be nearly enough for another. Your personal situation largely dictates how much cash you need in your emergency fund. The amount depends on your resources and how much you can afford to put by, as well as your responsibilities and how much you need to cover your usual outgoings. For example, if you're single and in your twenties, renting a flat with no dependants, you're likely to need much less cash in an emergency than if you're the main breadwinner for a spouse and four children, with a large mortgage and two cars.

Most financial advisers suggest stashing enough to cover between three and six months' worth of outgoings in an instant access savings account. Tailor the amount to suit you and your family's needs.

If you're self-employed you may need more cash put by because you won't qualify for sick pay, as you would if you were employed. Taking out some income protection to cover you if you can't work may also be worthwhile. (See Chapter 4 for more information.)

Finding the Best Savings Account

Just because your emergency cash is easily accessible in a low-risk deposit account doesn't mean that you can't earn a decent amount of interest on it. The vast majority of savings accounts are variable, which means that the rate of interest loosely reflects movements in the Bank of England base rate. With so many lenders competing for your business, some excellent rates are available, particularly if you're prepared to go save via the Internet.

In the past, you had to tie your savings up for a year or more if you wanted to get the best rates. But that's no longer necessary: You can get an attractive rate of interest and no restrictions on accessing your money – good news for generating returns on your emergency fund.

Saving with a monthly account

The best way of building up emergency savings if you're starting from scratch is to get in the habit of putting a small sum of cash aside every month. A monthly savings account can discipline you into doing this by requiring you to make a deposit each month – no excuses. This is a set amount, somewhere between the minimum and maximum amounts set by the account provider.

You can't invest a lump sum, so if you have surplus cash one month you still can't put away more than your set monthly limit.

What access you get to your savings with a monthly account depends on the provider, so check the small print before opening one. Some are instant access, which is what you need, while others have notice periods or a fixed term, which is not what you need.

Monthly savings accounts often have bonuses, which you earn once you've made enough deposits or paid a certain amount of cash into your account. The bonus often also depends on you not making any withdrawals from your account or less than a certain amount. But as you don't know when you're going to need to make a withdrawal or how many you might have to make, you might not want these restrictions.

If you're building up an emergency savings fund from scratch, rather than signing up to a monthly savings account, why not pretend that's what you've got? Open an instant or easy access account and then decide on a realistic monthly amount that you can afford to save. Then, set up a direct debit from your bank account to your savings account for this amount of cash, ensuring it is transferred over the day after you get paid. That way you won't miss it, you're making regular contributions, and you don't have any of the restrictions of a monthly savings account.

Opting for a cash individual savings account

The advantage of a cash individual savings account (ISA) is that you can build up your interest free of tax. Make sure you opt for one that is easy access and doesn't require that you give notice before accessing your cash, as quite a few of them do – particularly those paying the highest rates of interest. Also, make sure the provider doesn't require you to maintain a minimum balance, as you may need to drop below this on occasion should you withdraw some cash from your account.

The amount you can invest in a cash ISA in any one tax year (6 April to 5 April the following year) is limited to £3,600. So if you need more than £3,600 in your emergency fund, you may need two or three ISAs (taken out over consecutive years) to build this up.

Understanding interest on savings

If you're a taxpayer you must pay income tax on the interest you earn on your savings. This is currently 20 per cent for basic-rate taxpayers and 40 per cent for higher-rate taxpayers. Savings rates are usually quoted gross (without the tax deducted).

Some providers also refer to an *annual equivalent rate* (AER) on their savings and investments. This demonstrates what interest you would get if interest was compounded and paid annually: In other words, each interest payment is added to your balance so the next interest payment is calculated on your original deposit plus interest already earned.

If you aren't a taxpayer or your total income is less than your personal allowance (£5,435 for those aged up to 64 years in 2008–9), you don't have to pay tax on your savings. But you must alert the bank to this fact, otherwise tax will be deducted automatically before the interest is paid to you. Fill out form IR85, which is available from your bank or building society, to ensure this happens.

If you've already had tax deducted from your account when it shouldn't have been, you can claim this back by filling out form IR40. Both IR40 and IR85 can be downloaded from HM Revenue & Customs' Web site (www.hmrc.gov.uk).

Watching out for notice periods

Some of the accounts offering better rates of interest require you to give notice – of anything from a week to 30, 60, or 90 days – if you want to withdraw your cash. If you don't give this notice, you're likely to be penalised by losing the same amount of interest as the notice period. In other words, if you have to give 90 days' notice to get your money and you don't, you lose 90 days' interest.

If you need your money in an emergency you won't be able to give the required notice, resulting in a loss of interest. So steer clear of notice accounts when saving for a rainy day.

Notice accounts also tend to require a minimum balance of several hundred pounds, which may be difficult if you need most of your fund in an emergency. If you fall below the minimum amount, the account may be automatically closed.

Choose an account that lets you have your cash when you need it without notice or having to pay a penalty. The best choice is an *instant access* or *easy access* account, also referred to as a *no notice* account. These tend to have a minimum investment of as little as £1, which can be useful if you need to withdraw most of your cash in an emergency, and handy when you are just starting to build up your emergency fund.

With an instant access account, your money is available on demand; with an easy access account you can get your cash within a few days. You'll earn less interest on these accounts than you would with a notice account, but it may be worth it for not having to pay a penalty when you want your money.

Considering the impact of bonuses

Some account providers cynically propel themselves to the top of the 'best buy' tables by offering a tasty bonus for the first 6 or 12 months after you open an account. This can make the rate highly attractive, but remember that it won't last forever. When the bonus period ends, the account may look far more ordinary and no longer competitive.

Only opt for an account offering a bonus if you're prepared to move your cash once the bonus runs out. If you don't want the hassle, opt for an account that is regularly near the top of the best buy tables and has a good rate of interest all year round – not just because it is offering a bonus.

Realising the advantage of tiered rates

Some savings accounts have tiered rates of interest, so the more you save the better the rate of interest you receive. This can mean a significant amount of interest if you have a few thousand pounds stashed in your emergency account. But remember, if the balance falls (perhaps you have to withdraw some cash to pay for some emergency repairs) the amount of interest you earn will also fall.

Fixing the rate and the term

Fixed-rate accounts usually pay a higher rate of interest than variable easy or instant access accounts. But this higher rate comes at a cost: With a fixed-rate account you have to invest a certain amount of money for a set period of time – usually one to five years.

Most providers don't allow any withdrawals before the maturity date, which rather misses the point of emergency savings. If you are allowed to make withdrawals, you'll have to pay a penalty. And you usually can't add to your balance during the term, so it's not a place for building up your emergency savings. Steer clear of such products in this instance.

Offsetting your savings

If you've got a mortgage, you can use an offset account to build up your emergency savings. Instead of earning interest on your savings, you reduce the amount of interest you pay on your home loan. You pay interest only on the difference between your savings and mortgage debt, reducing the length of your mortgage term.

For example, if you have a £150,000 mortgage and £3,000 in your emergency savings account, offset against your home loan, you only pay interest on £147,000 (and earn no interest on your savings). But as your repayments are calculated on the £150,000 loan, you will be overpaying each month (if you don't ask your lender to reduce the payments accordingly) so you pay off your mortgage more quickly.

Because the interest on your mortgage is likely to be higher than what you can earn on your savings, an offset account makes a lot of sense. And you can still access your savings whenever you need them, without notice, so it's ideal for a rainy day fund.

Shopping Around for the Best Deal

As with any financial product, it's important to shop around for the best deal available. Although your bank will offer a savings account, this is unlikely to offer you the best rate of interest: Indeed, it's far more likely that this will be one of the worst rates on the market, particularly if you bank with one of the 'big four' – Barclays, HSBC, Lloyds TSB, and NatWest.

When you've picked the account with the most competitive rate, don't just rest on your laurels and pat yourself on the back for being astute. Review your account and the rate of interest it earns on a regular basis – at least once a year – to ensure you're still getting a competitive deal. New accounts offering better rates of interest may be available, or other providers may have increased their rate of interest while yours hasn't.

Log onto www.moneysupermarket.com to use its free savings calculator: You tap in how much you've saved up and the rate of interest you're currently earning – you'll then be told how much extra interest you could earn elsewhere.

If you do decide to switch to another account paying a better rate of interest, check that you won't lose interest or pay a penalty for doing so. If you do have to give notice, make sure you give enough before moving your money. Losing interest in order to move to gain interest is pointless: It defeats the whole object.

Logging on

The best rates for savings accounts are to be found online. The Internet is also the easiest place to research the best savings deals. Although strictly speaking such accounts are not instant access, because you can't get your hands on your money immediately, they are easy access, which is almost as good.

When you need to access your cash, you can arrange for it to be transferred to your current account, so you can withdraw the cash from an ATM, write a cheque, or use your debit card. Some online accounts also come with a cash card, making it even easier to get your money because you don't have to transfer it anywhere first.

 Use comparison sites such as www.find.co.uk, www.moneyfacts. co.uk, www.moneyextra.com, or www.moneysupermarket.com to find the best savings account for you.

Telephoning and posting

Any savings account that isn't operated from a branch is more likely to have a tasty rate of interest than one that is, because the overheads are reduced. Having operators in a call centre dealing with applications and enquiries helps keep costs down.

Check that access isn't a problem when signing up: If you get a cheque in the post when you make a withdrawal, this could take a week or so to arrive, which isn't as convenient as being able to get your hands on the money immediately.

Look at 'best buy' tables published in newspapers or finance magazines, and online, for the best postal and telephone savings accounts.

Accessing savings via a branch

The most immediate type of account is the one where you can walk into a branch and come out with your money. But you sacrifice interest for this convenience because of the overheads incurred in running a branch network. Thus, such accounts rarely pay the highest rates of interest.

Avoiding National Savings and Investments

If you want the best rate of interest on your instant or easy access savings, you're unlikely to get this if you take out a National Savings and Investments (NS&I) product. These are possibly the safest type of investment you can buy because you are, in effect, lending money to the Government, which is highly unlikely to default on its debts.

All NS&I products are deposit based, with a wide range of different savings accounts and bonds to choose from, depending on whether you want a fixed or variable return, tax-free, instant access, or a fixed term. Accessing your cash is easy, as you can withdraw it from your local post office or receive a cheque in the post.

But the rates of interest are rarely competitive. You'll never find NS&I products at the top of the best buy tables and can nearly always get a better deal elsewhere with enough security to satisfy most people. So don't feel that you have to opt for NS&I products for a safe home for your rainy day money: Shop around and earn more interest.

Safeguarding Your Savings

As you're saving for an emergency you'll want to be assured that your cash is safe. Thankfully, most UK banks and building societies are stable institutions, but a safety net is in place in case the worst does come to the worst and the provider of your savings account goes bust.

The Financial Services Compensation Scheme protects you if your provider goes into liquidation or out of business. If you have more than £35,000 in savings, you won't get the full amount back, but you will get the first £35,000.

You should, therefore, think twice about having more than this in your emergency savings account!

Chapter 10

Making the Most of Tax-Free Savings and Investments

In This Chapter

▶ Figuring out whether ISAs are the answer

▶ Saving with National Savings

▶ Looking at venture capital trusts

*O*ne of the easiest ways of making your money work harder for you is to ensure that your interest and returns are free of tax. The Chancellor of the Exchequer demands that you pay income tax on your earnings, including your profits from shares, managed funds, and savings accounts. But you can get round this – completely legitimately – by opting for a certain number of tax-free products, of which individual savings accounts (ISAs) are the most popular type.

Saving tax should be seen as an added bonus, not the be-all and end-all of investing. Don't choose products that don't suit your risk profile or goals, simply for the tax breaks.

Tax-free investments are useful if you pay tax, particularly if you're a higher-rate taxpayer as you have the most to gain (because you pay 40 per cent tax compared to the basic-rate taxpayer's 20 per cent). But if you don't pay tax, you gain no advantage from opting for tax-free investments, apart from the fact that you won't be automatically taxed and have to claim the money back.

Opting for an Individual Savings Account

The easiest way to save tax-free is via an *individual savings account (ISA)*. An ISA is a tax-free wrapper that enables you to invest in a wide range of products from cash to stocks and shares (also known as equities). ISAs replaced *tax-exempt special savings accounts (Tessas)* and *personal equity plans (Peps)* in April 1999.

ISAs are available from a range of sources, including banks, building societies, supermarkets, National Savings, investment firms, insurers, stockbrokers, and financial advisers. Shop around until you find the best deal for your needs.

ISAs are a good way of regular saving because the minimum investment amounts tend to be fairly small – as low as £10 in some cases. And you don't even have to declare them on your tax return because you don't pay any tax on your ISA profits, giving you one less thing to worry about.

Contributing to ISAs

You can invest up to £7,200 in an equity ISA or up to £3,600 in a cash ISA.

The investment limits apply regardless of any withdrawals you make. So if you invest £7,200 in one tax year, and then withdraw £500, you can't invest another £500 before the end of the tax year to top your allowance back up to £7,200. Unused allowance can't be carried forward either, so plan ahead and use it before the end of the tax year – or you lose it forever.

If you opt for an equity ISA, you can invest your full allowance totally in equities or put some of it in a separate cash ISA, as long as you don't exceed the £7,200 limit in any one tax year.

Understanding ISAs

Two types of ISA are available: *cash ISAs* and *equity ISAs*. You can have a cash ISA and an equity ISA in the same tax year as long as you don't invest more than a total of £7,200 – your annual ISA allowance.

The main thing to remember is that you aren't allowed to invest more than £7,200 in the same tax year. HM Revenue & Customs is very strict on this: Break this rule and the excess money will be returned to you, plus, you lose the tax breaks on any interest you earned.

Deciding on your ISA investments

ISAs have two investment components:

- **Cash:** Cash is invested in deposit-based accounts, such as bank and building society accounts. You can also include National Savings under this (see 'Cashing in' later in this chapter for more details).

- **Stocks and shares:** As well as shares, unit and investment trusts, and open-ended investment companies (Oeics), you can also invest in Government bonds or gilts, and corporate bonds.

Cashing in

Cash ISAs are the most popular type of ISA because they are low risk and require small amounts of money to get started. They also don't require you to commit your funds for any length of time (as long as you don't opt for one with a fixed rate), so they're handy in the short term. A cash ISA doesn't have any management charges. Cash ISAs operate in a similar way to a savings account in that your money is at no risk whatsoever. The big difference from the average savings account though is that returns are tax-free, so you earn more interest on your investment.

A range of providers, such as banks, building societies, and even supermarkets, offer cash ISAs. Indeed, supermarkets often come near the top of the 'best buy' tables with their mini cash ISAs, so don't be a snob and feel you have to plump for a traditional provider.

As with standard savings accounts, you can opt for a variable-rate cash ISA (where the rate of interest goes up and down in line with the Bank of England base rate) or you can choose a fixed-rate ISA, which remains at the same rate for a set period of time. Watch out for restrictions on withdrawals from fixed-rate ISAs, as you may not be allowed to get hold of your money ahead of the maturity date.

You must be at least 16 years old to open a cash ISA.

Shopping around for a cash ISA is relatively straightforward as these products are extremely simple to compare. Log onto comparison websites such as www.moneyextra.com, www.moneyfacts.co.uk, or www.moneysupermarket.com for the best deals. If you don't have access to the Internet, check out the best buy tables in the national press.

Saving on friendly terms

One way of not paying tax on your savings is to opt for a friendly society savings account (these are not related to ISAs). Friendly societies, which often have strange-sounding names, are mutual societies, like building societies, run on behalf of members. They also offer investments in the same way as life insurance companies.

You can invest up to a maximum of £25 a month (£300 a year) or a lump sum of £270 a year tax-free with a friendly society. You are only allowed to open one plan. These generally have a term, such as ten years, and the penalties for encashing your policy early can be heavy.

You may also decide that you're limited to investing such a small amount that it really isn't worth your while. You should also be aware that some of these accounts invest your cash in the stock market so there is an element of risk involved. Research the account carefully before committing your cash.

Stocking up on equities

If you can afford to tie your money up for the medium to long term (anything from five years upwards), you might want to consider equity ISAs. Over time, these tend to produce better returns than cash, along with a greater degree of risk. You must be at least 18 years old to open an equity ISA.

With an equity ISA your capital is at risk – unlike with a cash ISA – so don't invest money you can't afford to lose or that you need in the short term.

Equity ISAs are a little misleading because you aren't restricted to investing just in managed funds, such as unit or investment trusts. You can also include Government bonds or gilts and corporate bonds in an equity ISA. You can invest in individual shares as well within this ISA wrapper, so if you've got a few hundred shares you can stash them here and not pay capital gains tax on any profits you make.

Equity ISAs are not quite as attractive from a tax-planning perspective as they used to be. The tax credit on dividends was withdrawn in April 2004 so whereas a basic-rate taxpayer with an ISA would have received a 10 per cent tax credit (32.5 per cent for higher-rate taxpayers), this is no longer the case.

All other income and capital gains are still free of tax but nevertheless, keeping stocks and shares within an ISA is far less attractive than it was in the past.

Changing Tessa to Toisa

If you owned a Tessa (tax-exempt special savings account), you probably now own a Toisa (Tessa-only ISA). From 6 April 1999, Tessas were gradually phased out and replaced by mini cash ISAs. I say gradually because Tessas, unlike mini cash ISAs, had five-year investment terms during which you couldn't get your hands on your money. The last of the Tessas matured in April 2004.

Sensible investors converted maturing Tessas into Toisas so that they didn't lose the tax-free status of their invested cash. But once you've got your Toisa, you should continue to monitor it on a regular basis – just as you would a mini cash ISA. Many providers offer Toisas, so plenty of choice is available out there with no need to plump for low rates.

If the rate of interest on your Toisa starts to appear uncompetitive, you can switch your cash to another Toisa (although make sure you do this according to the rule-book or you could lose your tax-free allowance: See 'Transferring your ISA' later in this chapter for more details on this).

There is no penalty for making withdrawals from an equity ISA as there is no fixed period or maturity date: You can cash in all or part of your account whenever you wish.

You can invest a monthly amount – usually around £50 – although you can also invest a lump sum if you wish. Spreading your payments over the year in order to minimise risk is a worthwhile move (see sidebar: 'Drip feeding produces the best results').

You have to pay an initial charge when you deposit money in an equity ISA, which can be as high as 5 per cent of the sum you're investing. You also have to pay an annual management fee, which varies between fund managers from 0.5 to 2 per cent of the total amount invested. But ways exist of saving on this initial cost: See the nearby sidebar 'Saving money down the supermarket' for more details.

You don't have to invest in the same ISA each year: In fact, if you want to build a balanced portfolio (which should be your goal), you can spread your risk by investing in different assets. Then, if something happens to a particular stock market or sector, you can take comfort from the fact that you don't have all your money invested there.

Because equity ISAs are more complicated than cash ISAs, you may wish to seek advice before taking the plunge. Consult an independent financial adviser who'll be able to help you choose the best investment for your needs. For details of IFAs in your area, contact IFA Promotion on 0800 085 3250 or go to www.unbiased.co.uk.

Drip feeding produces the best results

If you have a choice between investing a lump sum or a regular monthly amount into an equity ISA, the latter is often the better way forward. By staggering your contributions throughout the tax year, you minimise the risk of buying at the top of the market, only to see it crash immediately afterwards, leaving you sitting on significant losses.

The danger of piling in with a lump sum is that you buy at the wrong time, whereas if you drip feed your money in over the year, there is no chance of doing this. You are hedging your bets: Some months your money will buy more shares or units in the fund than at other times, but you take the rough with the smooth.

The Financial Services Authority has a comparative table on its website (www.fsa.gov.uk/tables), enabling you to compare charges and other basic information on unit trust ISAs (see Chapter 12 for more on unit trusts). You're asked to input details such as whether you're investing for income or growth (see Chapter 11 for more on the difference between the two), how much you've got to invest, how long you want to invest for, and the amount of risk you are willing to take on.

Selecting your own ISA

If you're fairly experienced when it comes to investing and want more of a say on where your ISA cash is invested, you could opt for a *self-select ISA*. This enables you to pick and mix the investments within your ISA wrapper. Contact the fund management house directly to set one up, or use an execution-only broker.

Each plan has certain restrictions as to what you can include in it. You can't have any life insurance: Most plans only let you invest in stocks and shares. Most providers also insist that you invest a lump sum of at least £250 a time.

The main thing to watch with a self-select ISA is the charges. You may think you won't have to pay an annual fee because you've selected your investments, but you will be charged a percentage of the value of your portfolio – anything from 0.5 to 1.5 per cent. There isn't usually an initial or set-up charge, but you will be charged dealing costs when buying shares: This may cost a minimum of anything from £9 to £45 a time. If you buy a unit trust, you may have to pay an initial charge of up to 5 per cent.

Saving money down the supermarket

If you apply for an equity ISA direct from the fund manager, you're likely to have to pay an initial charge of 5 per cent of the sum you're investing. But you can pay much less (and sometimes nothing at all) if you shop around. This sounds the wrong way round, as applying direct usually means you get a discount. But in the era of fund supermarkets, this isn't the case.

You can get a hefty discount on the initial fee if you apply for your ISA via a fund supermarket on the Internet. Fund supermarkets enable you to choose your ISA from a range of hundreds of funds. You can also mix and match unit trusts from different providers within a single ISA. Thus you can increase your exposure to a wider range of investments and reduce your risk.

You can choose from lots of fund supermarkets. The first and best established with access to over 1,000 funds from 55 investment companies is investment house Fidelity's FundsNetwork (www.fundsnetwork.co.uk). Also worth trying is broker FundChoice (www.fundchoice.co.uk). Some brokers charge you a fee for this service, so read the small print before committing yourself.

Transferring your ISA

You don't have to put up with a poorly performing ISA. Review the rate of interest (if it's cash) or performance (stocks and shares) annually to see whether your ISA is still competitive.

If you decide to switch your ISA, whatever you do, don't withdraw the cash from your current provider and then try to deposit it in a new ISA. Even if your intention is to transfer it straight away to a new ISA, you lose your ISA allowance if you handle it this way. And when you open the new ISA, it will count as this year's allowance so you effectively lose out. What's more, if you've already used up this year's allowance, you'll be in breach of the rules and have to close the second one.

When making a transfer, you must get your new ISA provider to handle it on your behalf so you don't see the money at all. Ask your new provider for a transfer form, complete this, and return it. The new provider will then contact your existing ISA provider and arrange the transfer. You will be notified when this is completed: It can take up to a month, so be patient.

Handled this way, the transfer doesn't affect your ISA allowance for the current year, which you can invest as normal.

Choosing National Savings Certificates

If you want security and tax-free returns, consider National Savings and Investments (NS&I) products, which are backed by the Treasury and available from your local post office. You can find out more details by calling 0845 964 5000 or logging onto www.nsandi.co.uk.

National Savings Certificates are available for two- or five-year terms and the rate of interest is fixed for the term. You can invest a lump sum of between £100 and £15,000 in each issue.

When National Savings decides to change the rate of interest on the certificate, it brings out another issue with the new fixed rate. Your existing rate is guaranteed, but you can invest up to £15,000 in the new issue as well if you wish.

All returns are free from income and capital gains tax. But if you withdraw cash before the end of the two- or five-year term, you will be penalised. If you cash in your investment within the first year, for example, you won't receive any interest at all.

If you want to reduce the risk of inflation on your investment, you can buy an index-linked savings certificate, which is inflation proofed for three or five years. These pay a fixed percentage above the annual rate of inflation (also known as the retail price index).

Don't be seduced by the tax breaks. Although National Savings has made efforts to improve the rates on its products, they are unlikely to top any best buy tables anytime soon. You can nearly always get a better deal elsewhere, so consider National Savings only as part of a broad market search.

National Savings trumpets its premium bonds as a great way of earning tax-free cash, but you must hit the £1 million jackpot to get a return (all the numbers are entered into a draw each month). Otherwise, your money simply sits there, doing nothing. You can invest up to £30,000 in premium bonds but you won't make any returns unless you're lucky enough to hit the jackpot.

Exploring Venture Capital Trusts

Another way of earning generous tax breaks on your investments is via a *venture capital trust (VCT)*. A VCT is an investment company quoted on the London Stock Exchange that invests in young, growth-orientated British companies with a potential for high returns over the medium to long term.

VCTs invest in a range of unquoted and AIM (Alternative Investment Market) companies (which are also expected to deliver rapid growth), with a team of professional managers selecting a portfolio of stocks. This enables you to invest in companies, which, by their very nature, are more risky than those quoted on the London Stock Exchange, but which have the potential for faster growth and higher returns. Investing in a VCT gets you exposure to the sort of stocks that most private equity investors wouldn't achieve by any other means. Plus, you spread your risk because you're invest-ing in a selection of such companies – not just one or two.

You can invest up to £200,000 in a VCT in the 2008–9 tax year – much higher than your annual ISA allowance. In return you get:

- ✔ Income tax relief of 30 per cent.
- ✔ No CGT payable on profits when you sell your VCT shares provided you remain invested for at least five years.
- ✔ Dividends also free of tax.

In effect, this means that for every £1,000 you invest in a VCT, you can offset £300 against your tax liability for 2008–9.

To qualify for the full income tax relief, you must leave your money invested for at least five years. If you sell your VCT shares during this time, the up-front income tax relief will be withdrawn.

 While you may be attracted by the generous tax breaks, you should be wary of investing in any product purely for this reason. You must ensure that the underlying investments are right for you and shop around carefully, as the difference between the perform-ance of the best VCTs and the worst is significant.

It is also worth bearing in mind that:

- ✔ VCTs are riskier than investing in the main equity markets, so be certain about what you're getting yourself into and make sure it fits in with your overall investment portfolio. A VCT shouldn't be the mainstay of your portfolio (you should-n't have all your funds committed to it); instead, it's a useful addition to a well-diversified portfolio.
- ✔ Your money is effectively tied up for at least five years so don't invest cash that you will need to get your hands on during this time. If you withdraw your money early, you miss out on the valuable tax breaks that may have attracted you to this investment in the first instance.

✔ You may have to wait much longer than five years to make a profit, so you should only invest money that you don't need in the long term if you want a chance of making a decent return on your investment.

✔ VCT shares are not always easy to sell when you finally get round to doing so because trading isn't active. It may take a while to find a buyer and therefore get your hands on your cash.

VCTs vary greatly in terms of what they invest in and choosing the right one can be a complicated task, involving much more work than researching a unit or investment trust. You should always seek help from a financial adviser.

Chapter 11

Building Up an Investment Portfolio

In This Chapter

▶ Setting your investment aims

▶ Calculating how much risk you're comfortable with

▶ Understanding gilts and corporate bonds

▶ Getting started in equities

*W*hen you've got savings put by to tide you over in an emergency and have cleared short-term expensive debt (see Chapters 9 and 5, respectively) you can start building up your investments.

Successful investors tend to be those who build a balanced portfolio of investments containing a mixture of cash, bonds, equities, and property. With a balanced portfolio, if the property market crashes or shares in a particular company plummet, you will be protected to a certain extent because you have spread your assets (and risk) across several funds, companies, or sectors. There will be losses but they'll be limited. There's nothing worse than ploughing all your cash into the shares of one company or fund. If that company or sector crashes, you'll be left horribly exposed.

In this chapter, I help you establish your investment aims, work out how much risk you're happy to take on, and decide which products you require to answer these needs.

Planning Your Strategy

Before you invest any money, you must work out an investment strategy. Successful investing requires plenty of planning, taking into account the following factors:

✔ **Your attitude to risk:** Three main types of investor exist: cautious, balanced, or adventurous. If you aren't happy taking on a lot of risk you need to take a cautious approach and steer clear of high-risk, volatile products, such as specialist unit trusts that invest in the Far East, for example. If you're young, you can afford to take on more risk than an older investor as you've got more time to make good any losses. And if you're fairly wealthy, you can afford to be more adventurous as you can cover any losses.

✔ **How long you plan to stay invested:** The longer you can leave your money untouched, the riskier the investments you can opt for as you have longer to make good any losses. If there's a chance that you'll need your money back within the next five years, for example, or at very short notice, avoid shares and stick to cash or bonds instead. Otherwise, you may find that when you have to sell your investments at short notice, the market is in the doldrums so you don't get the optimum price for them.

✔ **Your purpose in investing:** Is your aim to generate a lump sum at some specific date in the future for a particular purpose – to pay for a wedding, children's school fees, or a deposit on a house? If so, you need to invest for growth and the type of investments you use depends on how long it is until you want to access the cash. Alternatively, you may hope to generate an income, perhaps to supplement your pension, so capital appreciation – ending up with a bigger sum of money than you invested initially – may not be as important to you. In this instance, government or corporate bonds might suit because you get a payout twice a year while capital growth is minimum (see 'Getting to grips with bonds' later in this chapter).

✔ **How much you have to invest:** Most savings and investments require you to put down a minimum amount to get started, so if you haven't got much cash – at least initially – this could affect where you invest it. If you have only £50 to invest, for example, it won't be enough to buy shares direct in a company but you'll be able to invest in a stocks and shares individual savings account (see Chapter 10 for more on these).

✔ **How regularly you can invest:** Some investments require you to invest a certain amount each month; others happily take a one-off lump sum.

Instead of committing yourself to a fund that forces you to invest a set amount each month, get into the investing habit by opening a regular fund and setting up a direct debit from your bank account so that £50 or £100 – whatever you can afford – is paid into the fund each month. If the cash is paid the day after you receive your salary you won't even notice it leaving your account.

Understanding Charges

When it comes to investing in stocks and shares, you usually face several different charges: If you invest in a collective fund, you could face an initial charge of up to 5 per cent and an annual management fee of 1 or 1.5 per cent. You may also face a charge for switching to another fund: The amount depends on the provider. You can save on charges by investing via a fund supermarket (explained in Chapter 10). If you invest directly in shares, you have to pay a stockbroker to buy and sell them (some brokers charge a flat fee of around £10) and may have to pay a further charge for maintaining your account (often a percentage of your fund). Chapter 13 has more details on finding and using a stockbroker.

Evaluating Your Risk Level

Risk is the most important consideration when taking on any form of investment. If you don't establish how much risk there is to your capital before you commit it to an investment, you could be in for a nasty shock.

Many cases of financial mis-selling boil down to the investor thinking she was buying a low-risk product – perhaps because her financial adviser implied this was the case – when it turns out not to be low risk at all.

Be wary of products that promise suspiciously high returns, particularly if these are much greater than anything else available on the market. There's likely to be a reason for this – it involves you taking on far more risk than you might normally be happy with. Treat all investments with suspicion: Look at the underlying fund and assess whether you're happy with where your money is being invested. And remember the old adage: If it looks too good to be true, it probably is.

Taking a cautious approach

Everyone should have some investments that are low risk or carry no risk at all. If you really don't want to risk your capital at all, stick to bank and building society savings accounts, cash ISAs, and National Savings & Investment products.

The money you build up for a rainy day (see Chapter 9) should be at no risk at all so you know exactly how much cash is there at any time and can get your hands on it at short notice.

The problem with cautious investing is that returns tend to be unimpressive. Even if you shop around for the best rate on your savings account or cash ISA, you could still do better, in the long run, if you invest your money in equities.

Returns on savings can be so low that your capital might actually be at risk – from inflation. If your savings are earning a particularly poor rate of interest, say 1 per cent, while inflation is 2 per cent, you're losing money in real terms in that your money won't buy as much. Opting for the highest rate of return you can find is extremely important so you can try and counter the threat from inflation.

Taking the middle road

If you have a balanced approach to risk, cash plays a role in your investment portfolio but to generate greater returns you must be more daring. When you've established your emergency savings you should aim to build up a core of investments that involve taking on a little more risk.

Investments that may suit a balanced investor include:

- **Gilts or government bonds:** See 'Getting to grips with bonds' later in this chapter.

- **Corporate bonds:** Aim for investment-grade rather than high-yield or junk bonds, which are extremely risky. I talk about these in 'Opting for corporate bonds' later in this chapter.

- **National Savings & Investments:** Turn to Chapter 10 for information on these.

- **Stocks and shares ISAs:** Chapter 10 talks about these and about investing in unit trusts.

- **Unit trusts, open-ended investment companies (Oeics), and investment trusts:** Go to Chapter 12 for details on these.

While these investments are generally lower risk than if you invest directly in shares or hedge funds (see the next section, 'Getting adventurous' for more on these investment types), some of these products are riskier than others. For example, gilts are extremely low risk in terms of the chances of the Government defaulting on repayment (although they can fluctuate in value unless they are held to maturity), whereas some specialist unit trusts can be high risk. Start with the lower-risk investments first and make sure you know exactly what you're getting into before taking the plunge as you move up to riskier funds.

When you move away from cash and into medium-risk investments, your capital is at risk. This means there is a chance you won't get back all the money you invest if the price of your investment falls during the time you own it. If you really can't afford for this to happen, steer clear.

As you move into medium-risk investments, you should aim to leave your money untouched for at least five years: The longer, the better. Shares in particular can be volatile and you can lose, as well as make, money.

Getting adventurous

The attraction of investments that put your capital at risk is the potential for higher returns, though keep in mind that these investments can be extremely volatile. Many investors look at the possible performance and disregard the risk they are taking on, forgetting that they might even lose all their capital in the pursuit of greater returns.

An adventurous approach may include:

- ✔ **Investing directly in shares:** Unlike a *pooled investment*, in which many people invest in a spread of companies, you are placing a lot of faith in one company by investing directly. If the company does well, you could make significant profits. If it doesn't, you could lose a lot of money. (Chapter 13 has more on investing in shares directly.)

- ✔ **Opting for specialist unit trusts:** Anything that narrows the scope of your investment horizon, such as investments in the Far East, emerging markets, or technology stocks, rather than a much more general and widespread UK or European fund, is risky. If you invest in a healthcare fund and a cure is found for cancer you could be onto a small fortune but if, as is far more likely, another drug fails its trials, you'll see very little in the way of returns (see Chapter 12).

✔ **Choosing junk bonds:** These are explained in more detail in 'Opting for corporate bonds' later in this chapter, but involve lending money to companies that are so high risk they don't even have an investment rating. Consider junk bonds only if you're an extremely wealthy and sophisticated investor who can afford to lose money and know what you're doing.

✔ **Hedging your bets:** Hedge funds are almost a form of gambling as they let you take a punt on what's going to happen to anything from the future performance of the stock market to the price of frozen concentrated orange juice and pork bellies. You can make a lot of money if you're a sophisticated investor who understands hedging and makes the right bets. Otherwise, steer well clear, particularly if you're a novice investor.

Any of the investments in the preceding list may form part of an already well-balanced portfolio but shouldn't be regarded as core holdings or the first products you should opt for before building up at least a spread of general unit trusts. They are far too risky for that.

Balancing Your Investment Portfolio

Your target should be to build a considered *portfolio* of investments, rather than making a series of random investment choices. The overall picture is very important to ensure you don't take on more risk than you realise or are comfortable with, and that you have a broad spread of investments.

Covering the basics

A broad portfolio contains a mix of cash, bonds, equities, and property. To pool risk further, opt for collective investment vehicles before you start opting for shares in individual companies. And concentrate on unit trusts investing in UK equities before branching out into other countries or more specialist sectors.

You may feel that you've got property covered because you own your home, but considering investing in a property fund as well would be worthwhile. Property funds invest in commercial property, such as factories and offices, rather than domestic homes, increasing your exposure to the sector and spreading your risk.

Understanding the underlying investments

Quite often, investors are over-exposed to a sector or country without even realising it. That's because they don't understand exactly what they are investing in. For example, if you're invested in a technology fund and also have an ISA investing in US stocks and shares, you're likely to have doubled up on American technology stocks so if Microsoft experiences problems, you could lose money in both funds.

Closely monitor where your funds are invested. Check the fund manager's update of performance, which you should receive twice a year. If you discover that she has left you over-exposed to a company, sector, or country, you may have to sell some of your holdings to rectify the situation.

Reviewing your holdings

The longer you leave your money invested the better, but this doesn't mean you can forget about it. Successful investing requires constantly reviewing your holdings to ensure they are performing as well as they could be.

When you've established a portfolio, review it on a regular basis to ensure it still meets your aims and remains balanced. If one stock has dramatically increased in value, for example, it may unbalance your overall portfolio so you may need to sell some shares and reinvest the money elsewhere.

Ditching poorly performing funds

Sticking with a poorly performing fund in the hope that it will recover does you no favours in the long run. If performance starts to slip, be prepared to cut your losses and switch to shares or funds with better prospects.

Find out why your investments aren't doing well, rather than panicking and selling up immediately. If all the funds in the same sector are struggling, you can hardly blame your fund manager. Selling up and shifting to another fund in the same sector won't improve matters and will just cost you extra in charges.

You may discover that your fund has performed badly while others in the sector have done well. Even the best fund managers can go through bad periods and if your manager has a good track record and a habit of getting funds back on track, it is worth sticking with her. But if you aren't confident that the situation will improve, you may have to sell up.

If you buy shares directly in a company, keep up to date with the news in case anything happens that will affect the value of your investment. For example, if you've got shares in a supermarket that issues a prof-its warning, your investment could well plummet in value. You'll need to decide whether the shares will recover or not – otherwise, you could sell at a loss only to see their value climb back up to their previous level and beyond, which would be very frustrating.

If you invest in pooled or managed funds, the decision whether to sell shares in a particular company is down to your fund manager. She is far more experienced than you in such matters and is able to assess rationally whether it's worth hanging onto the shares in the hope of recovery or cutting her losses.

Inexperienced investors should stick to managed funds as some-one else makes the difficult decisions for you.

Getting to Grips with Bonds

If you're looking for income rather than growth, but want a better return than you can get from cash, you may want to consider gov-ernment or corporate bonds. These can be bought from a stock-broker, bank, or the Bank of England.

Understanding how bonds work

A *bond* is a form of debt issued by a government or company. Bonds are a bit like IOUs: As a bond purchaser, you lend an amount of money to the government or company for a set period of time. In return, you are guaranteed a fixed income, known as the *coupon*, payable twice a year. When the bond matures, you should get your initial investment – your *capital* – back, though this isn't guaran-teed as bonds aren't free of risk. You may get back more than your original capital or less.

Bonds return little in the way of capital growth so they are best suited for investors looking for income rather than high returns. They are ideal for the retired, although younger investors should-n't write them off as they are less volatile than shares and provide

more protection (bondholders are higher in the pecking order th
shareholders if a company goes bust). It is worth including bon
in a balanced investment portfolio.

The amount you invest in government or corporate bonds depends
on your attitude to risk. As a general guide, most experts suggest
you use your age to determine the proportion of bonds in your
portfolio. For example, if you're 30 years old, around 30 per cent of
your portfolio should be in bonds.

Although bonds are issued for a specified period of time, you don't
have to keep the bond until maturity. In fact, most investors buy
and sell them ahead of the maturity date, trading them like shares.
So while they have a fixed price when they are issued, this can fluctuate up and down according to demand from investors.

Bonds are issued in bundles of £100. So if a company agrees to pay
you a set income of £10 per year, the yield is 10 per cent. If you
trade the bond in the open market and sell it for £110, the income
is still £10 per year but the yield has dropped to approximately 9
per cent. But if demand for the bond is low, so the price falls to
£90, the yield rises to approximately 11 per cent.

Demand for bonds, and therefore the price they fetch, is influenced
by the yield and rate of return investors can earn elsewhere. If
interest rates are high, for example, savings accounts pay more
and bonds become less attractive.

Working out government bonds

Governments issue bonds to help fund their spending. Bonds issued
by the British Government are known as *gilts* and are listed on the
London Stock Exchange. They are safer than corporate bonds
because it is highly unlikely that the Government will go bust or
default on the loan. The British Government has never failed to
make interest payments on gilts or to pay back investors' capital at
maturity.

Because gilts are rated more highly than bonds issued by companies,
they also produce lower returns. Some gilts pay high rates of interest with a low capital return; others pay low interest but you get a
higher capital return. The type you opt for will depend on whether
your priority is income or growth.

There are two ways to deal in gilts:

- ✔ You can buy gilts by auction direct from the Debt Management Office when they are newly issued. You don't pay any dealing charges but you must invest a minimum of £1,000. Go to www. dmo.gov.uk for details and application forms.

- ✔ You can buy or sell gilts via a stockbroker or bank, or the Bank of England Brokerage Service (contact 01452 398 3333). There is no minimum investment but there are dealing charges, so to spend less than, say, £1,000 is uneconomic.

Using Computershare's service tends to work out cheaper than buying or selling through a stockbroker or bank (see Table 11-1). Complete the relevant form, available on the website (www. computershare.com/uk/investor/gilts), and send it with the appropriate payment to Computershare Investor Services, PO Box 2411, The Pavilions, Bridgwater Road, Bristol, BS3 9WX.

Table 11-1	Gilt Commission Rates via the Bank of England	
Deal type	*Commission rate*	*Minimum Charge*
Buy up to £5,000	0.7%	£12.50
Buy over £5,000	£35 plus 0.375% of the amount in excess of £5,000	£35
Sell up to £5,000	0.7%	None
Sell over £5,000	£35 plus 0.375% of the amount in excess of £5,000	£35

Source: Bank of England

You can invest an unlimited amount in gilts. Returns are normally paid gross of tax but tax is still payable on them. Higher-rate tax-payers must do this via their self-assessment tax return, while basic-rate taxpayers can ask for returns to be paid after tax has been deducted. Capital gains are tax-free.

The several different types of gilts are described in more detail in the following sections.

Conventional gilts

The simplest and most common form of government bond is the *conventional gilt*. Conventional gilts mature on a specific date, on which you get the final coupon payment and return of your capital. They can be short (under five years), medium (five to 15 years), or long (over 15 years).

Conventional gilts are denoted by their coupon rate and maturity – for example, 4 per cent Treasury Gilt 2016. The coupon rate usually reflects the market interest rate at the time of the first issue of the gilt, so a wide range of coupon levels is available in the market at any one time.

The coupon indicates the cash payment per £100 that the holder will receive per year. So if you have £1,000 nominal of 4 per cent Treasury Gilt 2016, you'll get two coupon payments of £20 each (4 per cent of £1,000 is £40, divided into two payments of £20 each) paid six months apart.

Double-dated conventional gilts

Double-dated conventional gilts have a band of maturity dates. For example, the first maturity date may be three years and the final maturity date five years. The Government can choose to redeem these gilts on any day between these maturity dates, subject to three months' notice. When the coupon is higher than the prevailing market rate, it is in the Government's interest to redeem on the first maturity date and refinance the gilt at the prevailing rate. Double-dated gilts are fairly rare but may work out to be a good investment if you can find them.

Index-linked gilts

Index-linked gilts account for around a quarter of the Government's gilt portfolio. Coupon payments and your capital investment are adjusted in line with the UK Retail Price Index (RPI), which means inflation is taken into account, unlike conventional gilts.

Undated gilts

Eight undated gilts are still in issue – the oldest remaining gilts in the Government's portfolio. Some date back as far as the nineteenth century. The redemption of these bonds is at the Government's discretion but they have low coupons (because of their age) so there is little incentive for the Government to redeem them.

Gilt strips

Strips are Separately Traded and Registered Interest and Principal
Securities. By *stripping* a gilt, you break it down to its individual cash
flows – for example, a three-year gilt has seven individual cash flows:
six coupon payments and the payment of the original capital – and
then trade the coupons and repayment of capital as zero-coupon
bonds (a bond that pays no interest and matures at face value;
investors get a return because the bond is sold at a big discount).
Strips are very flexible and can be used to design an income flow
tailored to your needs. Gilts can also be reconstituted from all of
the individual strips, but not all gilts are strippable.

Opting for corporate bonds

Returns on corporate bonds, also called *fixed-interest securities*,
tend to be higher than on Government-issued gilts because you
take on a greater degree of risk in buying them. A company stands
a greater chance of going bust than the Government does.

Corporate bonds are split into different types according to their
credit rating:

- ✓ **Investment-grade bonds:** These have high ratings (BBB or
  higher) because the chance of the company going bust and
  defaulting on its debt is considered by the ratings agency to
  be reasonably low.

- ✓ **High-yield bonds:** These have low ratings (BB and below).
  They promise higher payouts than investment-grade bonds to
  attract investors. However, you're taking on a greater degree
  of risk and a greater chance exists that the company will
  default on its bonds.

- ✓ **Junk bonds:** These companies don't get a rating at all because
  they are extremely risky. Approach with extreme caution.

Companies also issue different types of bonds. These include:

- ✓ **Debenture stocks,** which are secured against specific company
  assets.

- ✓ **Unsecured loan stocks,** which pay higher yields than debenture
  stocks but aren't secured against the company's assets.

- ✓ **Convertible bonds,** which give holders the right to swap them
  for shares in a company at a set price or before a specified date.

Corporate bonds pay a fixed amount of interest, known as the *yield*,
and they can only be bought through a stockbroker. Expect to pay
commission of 1 per cent or so of the amount you're investing.

You can pool your risk when it comes to corporate bonds. Investment companies offer *bond funds* that invest in a series of individual company bonds. Expect to pay an annual management fee for a professional manager to run the fund. Several types of bond fund are available, specialising in investment-grade, high-yield, and overseas bonds. Some also specialise in emerging market bonds. (See Chapter 12 for more details on these types of investment.)

Building Up a Share Portfolio

Even though the stock market has performed disappointingly over the past few years, in the long run it tends to produce greater returns than cash or bonds. Thus, the remainder of your portfolio should be invested in shares.

Only commit cash that you know you won't need to get your hands on for at least five or more years – the longer the better. If you can't guarantee to leave your money invested this long, steer clear of equities. Investing for the long term gives you time to ride out the ups and downs of the market and make good any losses.

Minimising risk

The stock market goes through ups and downs, and there are no guarantees. You could lose all your money or make a bundle. Be prepared for volatility and a rollercoaster ride.

When it comes to shares, diversification is vital. If you buy shares in only one company, you take on a huge amount of risk because if that company issues a profits warning or goes bust, you could lose a lot, if not all, of your money. The sensible investor puts her money in various companies and different countries.

If you've only got a small sum of cash to invest, diversify and reduce risk by putting your money into a collective investment, such as a unit or investment trust (see Chapter 12 for more details). A professional fund manager will invest your cash along with that of thousands of other investors in as many as 50 companies. The chances of all these crashing at the same time are extremely small.

Maximising returns

Many investors concentrate on buying shares and don't give much thought to when to sell them. But knowing when to offload your equities helps you get the maximum return on your investment.

The easiest way to maximise your investment is to establish a price target. This is what you believe to be a fair price for your shares. When your shares hit this target, sell all or some of your holding. If you don't really need the money or feel loath to unload for some reason, consider whether your shares are really worth more than the price they reached. If not, you should sell.

If you don't sell at this price, you may find that when you finally offload your shares you get a much lower price for them. Don't be greedy or you may miss out.

Chapter 12

Finding Safety in Numbers with Collective Funds

In This Chapter

▶ Minimising risk by pooling your investments

▶ Dealing in unit trusts

▶ Opting for open-ended investment companies

▶ Getting to grips with investment trusts

*I*f you're new to investing or don't have much cash to spare, opting for a collective fund or pooled investment rather than buying stocks and shares directly is the easiest – and safest – way of gaining exposure to the market. Pooled investments, such as unit and investment trusts, enable you to spread your risk by gaining exposure to as many as 50 companies for as little as £50.

With several types of collective funds to choose from, and many more sectors and countries to invest in, selecting the most suitable investments can be tricky. To make matters worse, investors are often tempted by funds that have done well in the past or are flavour of the month – usually because they have a good track record. But neither reason is a sound basis for choosing an investment.

This chapter explains what collective funds are available and helps you decide what products suit you and your risk profile.

Pooling Your Investments

The greater the proportion of shares in your investment portfolio, the higher your potential return – as long as you invest for the long term, say ten years or more. Shares expose you to increased risk but by investing via a *pooled* or *collective* investment – a ready-made portfolio of shares in a particular group of companies, a sector, or a country – you can spread your risk. Collective funds enable you to reduce the damage if one of your investments suffers a downturn, while at the same time you can keep your costs low.

If you're happy to manage your own money, you can build up a portfolio of individual shares or bonds in different companies and across different sectors. But building up a portfolio in this way can be very expensive. Unless you have a serious amount of cash, you won't be able to spread your exposure beyond one or two companies at most. Also, gaining exposure to companies outside the UK, which is important for a truly diversified portfolio, can be difficult. Managing your own investment portfolio can be very painstaking and time consuming as you have to keep an eye on your investments and be prepared to make important decisions such as when you buy or sell your holdings. With a managed fund, you pay a professional fund manager to take care of this for you. (Chapter 13 talks about buying shares directly.)

Looking at the advantages of pooled investments

Pooling your investments has several advantages:

- ✔ **Reduced risk:** Your money is spread across tens of companies, rather than one or two.

- ✔ **Cheaper costs:** Buying and selling collective funds is cheaper than buying and selling individual shares. By pooling your resources with lots of other investors, you can buy in bulk. If you invest in lots of individual shares, on the other hand, costs can be prohibitive.

- ✔ **Professional management:** A full-time professional manager looks after your money. Fund managers are well regulated, so if the fund manager breaches the rules, leading to you suffer financial loss, you get compensation.

- ✔ **Reduced paperwork:** Owning lots of shares directly involves plenty of administration whenever you buy and sell your holdings. With a pooled investment, your fund manager takes care of this and you don't have to make investment decisions yourself either.

Losing out by pooling

You must weigh the advantages of a pooled investment against the disadvantages:

- ✔ **Paying for a fund manager:** If you invest in shares directly, you simply pay the share price when you buy them and a commission to a broker. You usually have to pay commission when you sell and you may have to pay a small fee to a stock-broker to have an account with him. But with a managed fund you pay an initial (or exit) charge and an annual management fee, which is taken directly from the fund. These tend to be far higher.

- ✔ **Lack of choice:** The fund manager makes the investment decisions, which you may not always agree with. Ensure that the fund you invest in matches your investment priorities.

- ✔ **No owner's rights:** If you hold shares directly, you often get shareholder perks, such as discounts on the company's products. You also have the option of attending the annual general meeting and voting on important matters, such as mergers. If you invest in a collective fund, you don't get any of the rights connected with the individual investments in a fund.

Working out the cost

The big advantage of collective funds is that as well as spreading risk, you reduce the cost of investing. To invest in the same number of companies on your own would be prohibitive in terms of charges and the minimum investment required for each share. Because a collective fund deals in large sums, transaction costs are far lower than an individual's.

You can start investing in a collective fund for as little as £30 to £50 a month or a lump sum of £250 to £500.

Jumping into Different Pools

Several different types of pooled funds are available, which invest in similar areas, although there are subtle differences in their structure – these are unit and investment trusts and open-ended investment companies (Oeics). Table 12-1 shows the variety of investment focuses available when choosing one of these funds, which I explain in more detail in the following sections.

Table 12-1	Focus of Unit and Investment Trusts and Oeics
Fund	*Investment Focus*
UK all companies	UK company shares. Aims to produce income and growth
UK growth	UK companies expected to produce capital gains rather than income (thus dividends will be low but the emphasis is on the share price rising in the long term)
UK equity income	Shares that produce high dividends
Index/tracker	Follows movement of a stock market index
UK gilt/fixed interest	Gilts, corporate bonds, preference shares (offering fixed dividend payments so appeal to people looking for regular income)
Convertibles	Convertible corporate bonds (pay a regular income and can be converted into ordinary shares at redemption)
Balanced	Mixture of shares and fixed interest (that is, bonds)
International	Invests in shares from a wide range of markets around the world
Smaller companies	Chooses smaller, and thus riskier, companies over those with a larger market capitalisation
Countries	European countries, the US, emerging markets, or the Far East
Fund of funds*	Other unit trusts
Specialist	A single sector, such as technology or healthcare

*Not Oeics or investment trusts

Understanding unit trusts

Unit trusts are the most straightforward type of pooled investment. A unit trust enables investors to buy units of equal value in a fund run by a professional manager. Because you are pooling your money with other investors', you get exposure to a broad range of shares – far broader than if you bought shares directly in various companies. Thus a unit trust enables you to reduce your investment risk.

The *trust* in the name refers to the fact that these assets are held by an independent authorised firm, known as a *trustee*, that oversees the running of the fund. The trustee provides comprehensive investor protection.

Most UK funds are authorised by the Financial Services Authority (FSA) and covered by the Financial Services Compensation Scheme. Some funds are authorised elsewhere in the European Union however: Check that a fund is authorised before you invest in it and where that regulator is based (see 'Checking authorisation' later in this chapter).

Unit trusts are *open-ended*, which means the fund gets bigger as more people invest and smaller as people withdraw their cash. There is no limit to the size of the trust. Units move up and down in value, depending on how well the fund manager invests this money in bulk in cash, bonds, and equities.

You can invest on a regular monthly basis or a lump sum and you can buy or sell your investment through a fund manager on any working day. The daily price of your units reflects the value of the shares, bonds, and/or cash the fund is invested in. There are no lock-in periods, so you can sell your holding whenever you wish, but you should aim to leave your money invested for the medium to long term – at least five years.

Choosing the best fund

Investors are spoilt for choice when it comes to unit trusts because hundreds are available. Trusts are grouped in sectors, depending on how the manager picks stocks, the level of risk of the fund, and what it invests in. Generally speaking, unit trusts are considered to be medium risk but some of the more specialist ones are riskier than others. Some funds are actively managed while others are index trackers (see 'Discovering tracked or actively managed funds' later in this chapter).

Unit trusts are sold directly by an investment house or through an independent financial adviser (IFA), stockbroker, or private client investment manager.

If you're happy to make your own investment decisions, so don't need advice, you can buy *execution only*. This means you use an online fund supermarket, which usually offers a substantial discount off the initial charge. But you don't receive any advice so you need to choose the right investment for you.

Managing with caution or aggression?

Understanding the fund manager's investment style is important to ensuring you know what you are investing in. If the manager is said to have an *aggressive* style, it doesn't mean that he is argumentative and strong-willed but instead refers to the fact that he is aiming for superior returns by investing in a small number of companies he feels will do well.

Risk is much higher with an aggressive style than a *cautious managed* fund, where the manager aims for more modest returns, opting for a greater number of underlying investments so risks are lower. This is the type of fund you need if you want to sleep at night.

However, even if you don't need advice, avoid buying the fund directly from the provider. You may think buying directly will work out cheaper, but the opposite is the case. You'll have to pay the full initial charge, which can be as high as 5 per cent. Use a discount broker instead to cut costs.

If you can't decide which fund is right for you, consulting an IFA would be a good move. You may have to pay a fee for this so ensure you understand exactly how much you'll be charged – before you receive the advice. You won't necessarily have to pay a fee, however, as many advisers are paid by commission from the provider whose product they end up recommending. See Chapter 2 for more information on choosing an adviser.

Paying for advice could save you hundreds of pounds in the long run if the adviser helps you avoid making the wrong investment decision. Only buy without advice if you are confident of making the right investment decision and choosing a product that is suitable for you.

Working out charges

When you invest in a unit trust, you usually pay an initial charge – a percentage of the amount you're investing – that can be as much as 5 per cent of the value of your investment. There is no charge to pay when you sell your holding, so it costs more to buy units than it does to sell them. The difference between the price you pay (the *offer*) and what you get when you sell (the *bid*) is referred to as a *spread*.

The spread is typically 5 to 6 per cent in most unit trusts, so if you invest £1,000 in units with a bid–offer spread of 5 per cent, the value of your investment is immediately reduced to £950.

To avoid paying an initial charge – or to pay a much reduced one – buy your fund through a discount broker or fund supermarket operated over the Internet. See Chapter 10 for more on these.

Some unit trusts don't have an initial charge; instead, they have an exit charge when you withdraw your cash. As well as an initial charge (or exit fee), you must also pay an annual management fee, which is deducted from the fund. The charge varies between investment houses but expect to pay in the region of 1.5 per cent.

Charges can eat into the performance of your fund, so make sure you know exactly what you have to pay and that you aren't being charged over the odds before committing your money.

Discovering tracker or actively managed funds

Most unit trusts are run by a professional manager who makes all the investment decisions. But this isn't always the case: Some funds are run by a computer that simply follows a specific index, such as the FTSE 100. This type of fund is known as a *passive* or *index tracker* fund.

If you opt for a tracker fund, your money is invested in the companies that make up the components of the index the fund tracks. When the index moves up or down, your investment reacts accordingly. Be aware that the fund's performance never matches the chosen index precisely. In fact, it is almost certain to do slightly worse. This is due to tracking error and charges, which mean your fund will lag the index by a small percentage.

Avoiding the investment herd

Unfortunately, when it comes to investment, many people have a herd mentality. They invest in a sector or fund because it has performed well, only to find that they invest at the top of the market right before the fund crashes.

This happened to the technology sector in 2000. The bull market at the end of the 1990s was led by technology stocks, creating a buying frenzy as investors bought specialist funds. The sector then crashed, wiping billions of pounds off the value of technology shares. Many investors lost not only their shirts but a lot more and some have yet to recover their losses. It was not an easy lesson to learn.

To avoid such a scenario happening to you, make investment decisions on the basis of what suits you and your investment risk. Don't be dictated to by past performance.

The advantage of tracker funds is that charges are much cheaper than on managed funds. Tracker funds have no initial charge and the annual fee is no higher than 1 per cent. This compares with an initial charge of up to 5 per cent on an actively managed unit trust and annual management fees of around 1.5 per cent.

Tracker funds have their disadvantages. They are often marketed as low risk but this isn't the case: Your capital is not guaranteed and you can lose money. If the stock market falls, your investment will follow. At least with a managed fund, the manager has the ability to choose investments, and so has a chance of bucking the market. With a tracker fund you've got no chance of beating the stock market because your fund simply mirrors it.

Many indices are heavily weighted in favour of a small handful of stocks, and it may be argued that tracker funds are even riskier than managed funds because of their limited investment range.

If a fund manager adds value, paying the extra fees for better performance is a good move. If you're considering a tracker because you want a low-risk investment, it's worth asking yourself whether you should be investing in the stock market at all.

For more information on unit trusts, contact the Investment Management Association (IMA), the trade body for unit trusts and similar funds at www.investmentfunds.org.uk or 020 7269 4639. IMA has a range of fact sheets, booklets, and general information about unit trusts and Oeics.

Getting to grips with Oeics

An open-ended investment company (Oeic) is similar to a unit trust (see the previous section) but is structured as a company rather than a trust. You can invest in a single fund or an umbrella company containing several sub-funds. The latter enables you to switch easily between investments.

To gain a stake in the fund, you buy shares in the Oeic. Because it's open-ended, the Oeic gets bigger and more shares are created as more people invest in the fund. When investors withdraw their cash, the fund shrinks and shares are cancelled.

Oeics have only been around since 1997 but are gradually replacing unit trusts, which have very complex legal terms. An Oeic has a single price, instead of a bid–offer spread, so the price is directly linked to the value of the fund's underlying investments. All shares are bought and sold at this price via the Oeic manager.

You pay an initial charge when investing in an Oeic and this is shown as a separate item on your transaction statement. With unit trusts, charges are included in the buying and selling prices so it is more difficult to understand what you are paying for.

Some Oeics have no initial charge – they have an exit charge instead, which you pay when you withdraw cash from the fund. As with unit and investment trusts, you pay an annual management fee, which is taken directly from the fund.

Knowing how investment trusts work

Investment trusts work in a similar way to unit trusts and Oeics in that they pool investors' money and are professionally managed. The big difference is that the price or market value of an investment trust's shares may not be the same as the value of its assets. This is because the fund is *closed-ended* rather than open-ended, so a fixed number of shares are available at any one time.

Investment trusts are quoted on the stock market and investors can buy shares in them as they would in any other company. However, because the number of shares in the trust remains the same, regardless of the number of investors interested in purchasing them, the value of a share rises and falls accordingly. If more people want to sell than want to buy, the price falls, so shares are at a *discount*. But if more people are buying than selling, the share price rises and trades at a *premium*.

Many investment trusts trade at a discount so the value of the shares is less than the value of the assets. These discounts can widen, making investment trusts riskier than unit trusts. There are no specific investment restrictions so some are heavily invested in unquoted securities or emerging markets and can be risky. They can also borrow money to buy more investments, boosting returns when investments perform well but magnifying losses when they don't.

When you buy and sell shares in an investment trust, you pay dealing charges. The difference between the prices at which you can buy and sell is, in effect, another charge. You also pay an annual management fee, which is deducted from the trust. However, this tends to be cheaper than with a unit trust – 0.5 per cent compared with 1 or 1.5 per cent on a unit trust.

You also have to pay 0.5 per cent stamp duty on the purchase of all shares in an investment trust, the same as you do when you buy shares directly.

Different types of shares are available. Some suit investors looking for income, others suit those wanting growth. For more information on investment trusts, including fact sheets and a directory of available funds, contact the Association of Investment Companies (AIC) on www.aitc.co.uk or 020 7782 5555.

Making Sense of With-Profits Investment Bonds

You can gain access to pooled investments via insurance products. A *with-profits* bond allows you to invest in the with-profits fund of an insurance company via an investment bond. The fund invests in a range of shares, gilts, and property so you get exposure to a broad spread of investments.

You get a share in the return of the insurer's with-profits fund via a *reversionary* or *annual* bonus, which is added to your fund and can't be taken away, provided you keep the policy going until its term. When the policy matures, you may get a *terminal* bonus, the size of which depends on the performance of the fund. It is not guaranteed.

Being socially responsible

Ethical or socially responsible investment (SRI) is growing in popularity, with more than 50 ethical investment funds now available. These funds apply environmental, social, and/or other ethical criteria to the selection of their investments, so companies involved in tobacco, gambling, alcohol, military sales, and pornography are excluded. Because they have diverse policies, you should check that the fund fits your own personal concerns before investing.

There is a belief that you have to sacrifice performance for your ethical beliefs because SRI funds exclude so many sectors that produce superior performance. But EIRIS, the Ethical Investment Research Service, says that five of its ethical indices have produced financial returns roughly equivalent to the returns of the FTSE All-Share Index.

The Investment Management Association has produced a fact sheet, *A Guide to Ethical and Socially Responsible Investment Funds,* which can be downloaded from its website (www.investmentfunds.org.uk). Or contact EIRIS for more information on www.eiris.org or 020 7840 5700.

To minimise fluctuating returns in bonuses each year, the insurer *smoothes* the payments. As a result, you don't see sharp variations in returns from year to year, in line with stock market movements, because part of your bonus is held back in the good years so you still get a payment in years when performance is poor. When markets are performing strongly, with-profits funds don't look that attractive as you could be making better returns elsewhere. But in bear markets, when everyone else is suffering, they come into their own because you should still see some bonuses.

With-profits funds have fallen out of favour in recent years. As the stock market has been in the doldrums, with-profits bonds have also fallen in value. Bonuses have been poor and show no signs of recovering anytime soon. However, policyholders are trapped in their funds because insurers are imposing a surrender penalty on investors who try to cash in ahead of the maturity date. This penalty is known as a *market value reduction (MVR)* and is meant to stop policyholders cashing in their policies to the detriment of those left behind in the fund. The MVR can be as high as 20 per cent of the value of your investment.

In light of this, some advisers have stopped recommending with-profits bonds to investors. But others still recommend them to clients looking for some security but who want a higher income than they can get from cash. However, if you're thinking of investing in with-profits, check the insurer's financial strength very carefully before investing. You should take into account the level of its reserves and the nature of its assets.

For more information on with-profits funds or other insurance-based products, contact the Association of British Insurers (ABI) on 020 7600 3333 or go to www.abi.org.uk.

Buying Corporate Bond Funds

A corporate bond is an IOU from a company. In buying a corporate bond, you are, in effect, lending the company money. In return, you get a set rate of interest and a return of your initial investment after a specified number of years. Chapter 11 has more details on buying individual bonds.

Investing directly in corporate bonds can be high risk, particularly if you opt for high-yield bonds. But you can minimise risk by pooling your investment via a corporate bond fund. A professional manager will invest your money, along with that of thousands of other investors, across a range of companies, reducing your investment risk and maximising your potential returns.

Not all bonds are safe investments. Generally speaking, the higher the return you are promised, the riskier the company issuing the bond and the more likelihood there is that the company could go bust and you end up losing your money. The capital value of bonds can go down because they are traded – bought and sold. They may be lower risk than shares but an element of risk still exists.

Choosing Exchange Traded Funds

An *exchange traded fund (ETF)* is structured in a similar way to an open-ended investment company but offers you exposure to an entire index, such as the FTSE 100, or to a market sector, such as European technology, in just one share – in the same way as a unit trust. But unlike unit trusts, ETFs trade in the same way as normal shares and are quoted on the stock exchange. These funds are open-ended, so the size of the fund can fluctuate according to how many people are invested. The share price reflects the value of the investments in the fund: Shares don't trade at a premium or a discount.

Most ETFs pay you dividends while your money is invested. When you sell up, you could make a capital gain or loss, depending on how your investment has performed. ETF shares have a bid–offer spread, so there is a difference between the buying and the selling price, although this tends to be very small – just 0.1 or 0.2 per cent for an ETF tracking the FTSE 100, for example.

Guarantees come at a price

If you want your capital to be secure, but still get exposure to shares, you can opt for an equity fund with a guarantee or element of protection. These are fixed-term investments with returns linked to the performance of an index. Investors like these funds because it is usually guaranteed that you'll get your capital back at the end of the term, as long as certain conditions are met. You also get some of the upside of the market. But this is key: Returns are restricted to a percentage of the growth of the index during this period, say 60 per cent of the performance of the FTSE 100. If the market falls, you still get your capital back. But if it rockets, you lose out because you're limited to just 60 per cent of the growth.

If you're worried about losing money on the stock market, steer clear completely, rather than opting for one of these half-hearted measures.

You pay an annual management charge of around 0.5 per cent or less, which is deducted from the fund, as well as a commission to the stockbroker when you buy and sell. You do not, however, pay stamp duty on purchases – as is the case with other shares.

ETF shares are bought and sold through stockbrokers or private client investment managers. These professionals can also provide you with advice, although you have to pay for it. See Chapter 13 for more details on choosing a stockbroker.

Joining a Pool

Pooled investments are available to suit all risks and investment aims. But to enable you to opt for one fund over another you should bear certain factors in mind. I go through these in the following sections.

Putting past performance in its place

If a fund has performed particularly well in the past, you'll soon hear about it. Investment houses like to draw attention to stunning past performance, and before the rules on advertising were tightened up, they often manipulated the data so that even an average fund appeared as though it was particularly impressive.

While past performance should be taken into account when choosing a fund, it is exactly that – in the past and no guide as to what is going to happen in the future. If you choose a fund because it has produced good returns before, there's a chance it won't do the same again.

While you shouldn't rely on past performance when choosing an investment – you should take plenty of other things into account – it is worth checking out. Investing in a real dog of a fund that's languished at the bottom of the performance tables for the past 15 years is pointless. It's highly unlikely that it will suddenly improve. Likewise, a fund that has done consistently well for the past several years could have a good chance of continuing this performance if certain conditions remain the same, such as the fund manager remains in place.

Cutting costs

Just as past performance isn't the be-all and end-all when choosing a fund, neither should charges be your sole focus. Most collective funds have an initial (or exit) charge and an annual management fee. Check these aren't excessive compared with similar funds, because charges do eat into investment performance, and ensure you know exactly what you have to pay.

Don't get too hung up on charges. If you pay a bit more than average but get superior investment returns, you won't be complaining. Try reducing the initial charge as far as possible by investing via a fund supermarket or discount broker rather than directly with the investment house.

Being certain of your investment aims

Before signing up for any investment fund, ensure that it suits your risk profile, fits in with your other investments, and enhances your portfolio. Check how much the fund is going to cost you and make sure you can afford that amount. You should be supplied with a key features document before you sign up, which contains all this information.

If you don't understand anything, seek advice. Use an independent financial adviser where possible: If you don't have one, contact IFA Promotion (IFAP) on 0800 085 3250 or www.unbiased.co.uk for details of IFAs in your area.

Checking authorisation

Before you invest with a firm, check that it is authorised. All firms must have a licence to carry on investment business and must prove to the Financial Services Authority, the City regulator, that they are financially sound and conduct their business fairly. If they break the rules, you may be able to get compensation, so it's important to ensure the firm is authorised.

Big, well-known firms, such as high-street banks and insurance companies, are all authorised. But smaller companies may not be, so check with the FSA before trusting them with your money. Go to the FSA's Firm and Person Check Service at www.fsa.gov.uk.

Drip-feeding your contributions

Although most investment houses accept regular monthly payments or a one-off lump sum, drip-feeding the cash into a fund over time makes sense. Although you may be tempted to get it all in there at once so it can start working for you, the danger is that you'll buy at the top of the market: If it then crashes, you could lose a lot of money, which will take time to recover.

 If you drip-feed your money into a fund, you spread the risk because you invest throughout the year rather than in one hit. Some months you'll buy more units or shares for the same amount of money than others. But in the long run, you should be better off.

Monitoring your investments

You need to do more than just research carefully, buy a fund, and then forget about it. You need to monitor its progress to ensure it continues to meet your objectives. Get into the habit of doing this at least twice a year; many fund managers or brokers send out a report every six months detailing the progress of the fund.

To check investment fund prices, go to the IMA's website at www.investmentfunds.org.uk.

 If you aren't happy with the way your fund is performing, or your objectives have changed, consider selling and switching your investment to another company. You'll have to pay a charge for this but to keep costs low, use a discount broker or fund supermarket to do this.

Taxing your returns

 You may have to pay tax on your investment returns, unless you keep them within an individual savings account (ISA), which acts like a tax-free wrapper. The other advantage to wrapping your investments in an ISA is that you don't have to declare this income on your tax return. See Chapter 10 for more on tax-free investing.

If you don't keep your unit trusts or Oeics within an ISA, the tax you pay depends on the type of fund you've invested in. If your fund invests in shares, you usually receive dividend *distributions*. These are paid net of tax at 10 per cent. If you don't pay tax, you can't claim this back. If you're a basic-rate taxpayer, you don't have to pay any further tax. But if you're a higher-rate taxpayer you are taxed at 32.5 per cent on the grossed-up dividend. You will have to pay the difference via your tax return.

If you invest in non-equity unit trusts or Oeics (those investing in gilts, bonds, or cash), you receive interest distributions, rather than dividend distributions. The interest is paid when your investment matures and 20 per cent tax is deducted at source. Non-taxpayers can reclaim the full 20 per cent, lower-rate taxpayers can claim 10 per cent, basic-rate taxpayers don't have to pay any more tax, but higher-rate taxpayers must pay a further 20 per cent.

When you are paid a distribution, you should receive a tax voucher from the fund manager. This shows how much distribution you received and any tax paid by the fund manager. You must keep these vouchers safe, as you'll need the information they provide when completing your tax return.

You may have to pay capital gains tax (CGT) when you sell your shares if the gains exceed your annual CGT allowance, which is £9,600 per person in 2008–9. To minimise your CGT liability, stagger the sale of your shares over more than one tax year.

For more information on the tax treatment of investments, check out the fact sheets available on HM Revenue & Customs' website at www.hmrc.gov.uk.

Chapter 13

DIY Investing: Opting for Shares

In This Chapter

▶ Establishing a share portfolio

▶ Deciding whether you need advice

▶ Finding a broker

▶ Trading your shares

▶ Earning returns

▶ Tracking your shares

Although share trading has been around for centuries, technology has changed it beyond recognition. It has sped up the process of buying and selling stocks, as well as reducing the cost. Hence, share trading is now far more accessible, enabling even those who aren't fabulously wealthy to dabble with direct ownership of several companies.

While share dealing has become more accessible, it's not for everyone. Stock market investing is a volatile business as your capital is at risk, so it's not for those who can't afford to lose money. It's vital to put enough cash aside to cover emergencies, and build up a spread of bonds and low-risk investments, along with a stake in a collective investment or two (see Chapter 12 for more on these), before you even contemplate buying shares in a company directly.

Despite the risk and cost of trading shares, the stock market is the place to be in the long term if you want to generate superior investment returns. This chapter shows you how – without losing your shirt in the process.

Investing Basics

More than 12 million people in the UK own *shares* – also known as *equities* – directly in a company. As a shareholder you own part of the company in which you're invested. Your investment buys you a direct share in the company's assets and future profits. If the company performs well, you may receive a slice of the profits in the form of a *dividend*, paid out twice a year. You may also make a profit if your shares increase in value while you hold them: You realise this profit (or loss) when you sell up. The *share price* refers to the value of your investment. (See 'Looking forward to returns' later in this chapter for more on this.)

The vast majority of shareholders are not sophisticated, wealthy people: Many of them fell into share ownership by accident by receiving a handful of windfall (free) shares when their building society demutualised and became a bank. Others snapped up shares in former public utilities, such as BT and British Gas, when they were privatised.

Understanding the process

The price of a share in a company rises or falls until it arrives at a price at which one person is prepared to buy and another is prepared to sell. When demand is high, share prices rise. When demand is low, share prices fall. Demand increases when a company has performed well or is rumoured to be the target of a takeover by another company (which could be good for business and hence more profits).

Planning to leave your money invested for several years to maximise your gains is vital. As individual shares tend to be more volatile than collective funds, you need time to ride out the ups and downs of the market and make good any losses.

Being aware of the risks involved

One of the most important factors to remember about shares is that they can go down in value as well as up. Although you're investing in the hope of making a tidy profit, a possibility exists that you won't even get back your initial stake. That's why it's so important to invest only money that you can afford to lose. Nobody likes losing money but as long as doing so won't leave you destitute, it's not the end of the world – just highly irritating. But if you're gambling away next month's mortgage payment, for example, the implications of making the wrong investment decision are far more serious.

Stock markets move up and down on a daily basis, so try not to worry about short-term falls in the value of your shares. Don't panic and think about selling as soon as things get difficult: Sometimes you need to brace yourself and sit it out. In the long term your shares will probably recover – if you let them – as long as you do your research carefully before choosing the shares in the first place. If you aren't prepared to put up with short-term falls, the stock market isn't for you.

Selecting Your Shares

The advantage of buying shares directly – rather than via a collective investment vehicle – is that you can tailor your investment strategy to your own needs. With a fund, the manager makes the investment decisions for you and, while this relieves some of the pressure, she could make choices that are at odds with your risk profile.

Deciding on growth or income

Choosing the right shares for you depends on your situation and attitude to risk. First you must decide what you want from your shares. Two different types of shares are available, suiting different types of investor:

- ✔ **Growth** stocks are for investors looking for significant capital gains – a good return on their initial investment – and substantial income in the long term, rather than short term. These companies may have excellent growth prospects but low *dividend yields* because demand for shares in the company has already pushed the price to a high level relative to the dividend payout. These companies may hold onto any profits to finance future growth rather than pay out to investors.

- ✔ Other stocks offer high immediate **income** with big dividends, which suits investors in or near retirement. These are likely to be companies that are less impressive than growth stocks and likely to provide more steady returns. If you invest in such stocks it doesn't mean that you aren't interested in capital growth – you want this as well as income – but it isn't your priority.

Many investors aim for a mix of growth and income, and it should be possible to tailor a share portfolio to achieve such objectives. If you're wary about doing this yourself, find a stockbroker or independent financial adviser (IFA) to advise you. (See 'Choosing a broker' later in this chapter, contact IFA Promotion on 0800 085 3250, or go to www.unbiased.co.uk for details of the IFAs in your area.)

Spreading your risk

The more speculative your investments, the greater the potential reward. But you'll also be taking on a lot more risk in order to try and achieve this. Weigh up whether you are happy with this before investing and do your research carefully so you know exactly how much risk you're taking on.

Although buying shares directly is usually more risky than investing in collective funds, it doesn't have to be. Be sure you *diversify* by buying shares in lots of different companies and various sectors of the market rather than stick all your cash in the shares of a single company. By diversifying, you significantly minimise your risk. If one stock performs badly, you can hope to be making gains elsewhere so it won't be a disaster.

One way of reducing risk is to buy shares in *blue-chip companies*. These are large-cap stocks, listed on the FTSE 100 (in other words, the biggest 100 companies in the UK). Large, well-established companies such as these should maintain their value over the longer term although you're likely to see steady returns rather than impressive ones (and don't forget they can fall in value as well, no matter how big or well-established the company is).

Picking more exotic investments

The real reason why many investors buy shares directly is to gain exposure to smaller companies that they can't access via a collective fund.

Be aware that the following investments are high risk and can be volatile.

If you buy direct, you can invest in:

- ✔ Shares traded on *AIM*, the Alternative Investment Market. AIM is a global market for smaller companies who are growing but do not wish to have a full stock exchange listing just yet. AIM is run by the London Stock Exchange (LSE) but places fewer restrictions on the type of company that can be listed than does the FTSE 100.

- ✔ Companies traded on *OFEX* (Off Exchange). These are the newest and most inexperienced of UK companies. OFEX is a quarter of the size of AIM, with 200 companies listed so there isn't much share trading. OFEX is good for experienced and more adventurous investors with good stock-picking skills. Unlike AIM, OFEX isn't run by the LSE.

> ✔ *Derivatives*, which include futures, options, warrants, and convertible bonds. Derivatives enable investors to speculate and hedge their bets, but are really only for experienced investors – not novices. Derivatives are traded on the London International Financial Futures Exchange (Liffe). Go to www.liffe.com for more details.

Choosing a Broker

The only way you can deal in shares is via a specialist stockbroker based in the City of London, a high-street bank or building society, or an online trading service such as Selftrade (www.selftrade.co.uk). The cost and type of service on offer differ widely so choose a broker carefully.

To ensure that costs don't eat into your profits, shop around for the cheapest fees. Plenty of competition exists and prices are far lower than in the past, mainly down to the growth of trading over the Internet. Many online brokers charge a flat fee of around £10 for a trade, for example. Remember: The higher the commission and fees a broker charges, the higher the profits you have to make to cover these costs. Make sure the charges are explained to you in advance: If you don't understand anything, ask. (See 'Looking forward to returns' later in this chapter.)

For a free list of stockbrokers and information about the services they offer, contact the Association of Private Client Investment Managers and Stockbrokers (APCIMS) on 020 7247 7080 or go to www.apcims.co.uk. Or try the London Stock Exchange on 020 7797 1000 or www.londonstockexchange.com.

Knowing you're protected

All APCIMS members are truly independent and aren't tied to any one company. APCIMS members are fully regulated by the Financial Services Authority (FSA). Non-UK APCIMS members are regulated by the relevant authority in their own country. Members are subjected to demanding tests of their financial resources and are obliged to meet rigorous standards in terms of operating procedures and management controls. Only those registered as being 'fit and proper' are authorised to give investment advice.

As long as the firm you use is regulated by the FSA, you get access to the Financial Services Compensation Scheme (FSCS). This guarantees to cover losses of up to £48,000 (100 per cent of the first £30,000 and 90 per cent of the next £20,000) if the advice you received was misleading or the adviser was negligent, and as a result you've lost money that the firm can't repay. (You can't claim compensation if you simply lose money on your investments, otherwise the scheme would be inundated!) Many UK APCIMS members also have their own insurance, which protects clients against theft, fraud, and professional negligence.

Deciding what service you need

You can choose from three types of services: discretionary, advisory, or execution only. The type you choose depends on your level of knowledge, confidence, and skill as an investor. Cost is also a factor: If you opt for anything other than execution only, you end up paying for the stockbroker's skill. The different types of service on offer are explained in more detail in the following sections.

Discretionary services

If you opt for a *discretionary service*, also known as a *portfolio management service*, you give an investment manager authority to buy and sell shares on your behalf, without seeking your approval first. It's a bit like being invested in a unit trust where the manager doesn't consult you every time she makes an investment decision. The only difference is that rather than pooling your risk with thousands of investors, you are the only one.

The advantage of a discretionary service is speed: Your manager can act straight away, without having to track you down first to ask your opinion. This could make the difference between a tidy profit and more average returns.

When a manager makes a transaction on your behalf, she issues you with a contract note. Your manager should also send you detailed reports on a regular basis so you can keep track of what she is up to.

If you're worried about giving somebody total free rein over your investments, you can impose some conditions in the initial contract you draw up with your broker. You could specify that your manager can't sell stocks in your portfolio, or prevent her from investing in certain companies if you'd prefer not to. You can also set limits on the maximum she can invest in a single stock.

Too many conditions and you might as well not have a discretionary service at all. It's important to find a balance that you feel comfortable with yet gives your manager enough freedom to do her job properly.

Advisory services

As the name suggests, your broker advises you on what you should buy or sell, based on your risk profile and investment objectives. She doesn't take any action on your behalf without asking first. This is the best type of service for a novice or first-time investor.

You don't have to follow your investment manager's advice or recommendations but seeing as you're paying for it, you'd be daft not to pay some attention.

Some advisory services allow you to run your own portfolio of shares and make your own investment decisions, but you also have an adviser you can contact when you need information on a particular share. You can call them and ask whether you should buy or sell. If you have some experience of investing, this may be more useful to you than a more comprehensive service: Work out what suits you best.

Execution-only services

The cheapest way of buying and selling shares is via an *execution-only service*. This service works exactly as its name suggests: When you want to buy or sell a share, you contact your broker and instruct her to execute your order. The broker offers no advice and does not manage your portfolio at all.

You're charged dealing costs, which are usually 1 to 1.75 per cent of the value of each deal, or around £15 per deal.

You can access execution-only services over the telephone or Internet, but remember that a growing number of traditional brokers also now offer this service in response to increasing demand. You should shop around for the cheapest price, as you require an extremely basic, straightforward service – there is no added value. All you get is access to the stock market.

Even if you don't buy and sell shares online, checking out the Internet is definitely worthwhile, particularly if you're trading execution-only, because thousands of free pages of research notes and information about stocks are available there. These can be useful in helping you make your investment decisions.

Execution only may be the cheapest way of buying and selling shares, but it is only for the sophisticated investor who knows what she is doing and what she wants. Otherwise, you could make an expensive mistake. If you're inexperienced, steer clear and opt for a discretionary or advisory service instead.

If you opt for discretionary or advisory services, assessing the risk of particular shares is the responsibility of your investment manager – after all, that's what you pay her for. But if you opt for execution only, you'll have to assess your own level of risk and decide whether a particular share fits in with that – or not. Any mistakes are down to you.

Buying and Selling Shares

When you've decided to buy or sell a share, you call your broker and instruct her to carry out the transaction on your behalf. You can do this over the telephone or Internet.

As well as telling your broker how many shares you want to buy or sell in a particular company, you also state the price you are willing to accept (if you are selling) or pay (if you are buying). If this price isn't available in the current market, your broker waits until it is reached.

When your broker has concluded the deal, you receive a contract note with details of the transaction. This includes the share price that you bought or sold at and the cost of the transaction.

What happens next depends on whether you are buying or selling shares:

- ✔ If you're buying, you've got three days to pay the necessary money to your broker so that she can complete the deal.
- ✔ If you're selling, you must ensure your broker has access to your share certificate(s) so that she can hand these over to the buyer's broker and receive the cash you are due within three days.

Holding Your Shares

When you've bought your shares, you can hold them in one of two ways. The method you choose depends on how frequently you trade, how much you want to retain formal legal rights in the companies you've invested in, the choice of services on offer by your broker or bank, and the cost.

The choices are:

- ✔ **Paper:** If you hold share certificates, you receive dividends, annual reports, and all other communications directly from the company. When you sell, you must send your certificate to the stockbroker or bank who undertakes the transaction. Check how much your broker charges you for holding your shares as certificates because dealing charges may be higher for such transactions than a nominee account or CREST, the electronic system.

✔ **Nominee account:** Your shares are registered in a nominee company's name, rather than yours. This is set up by your broker or bank to administer the holdings and transfer of shares for lots of investors. It cuts down on paperwork and the administration involved in owning shares in lots of companies. You remain the beneficial owner of the shares although your name doesn't appear on the company shares register and dividends are paid to the nominee company, which pays them to you. Important documents are sent to the nominee company rather than you, such as the Annual Report and Interim Statement: You will have to make arrangements to receive these. For further information on the regulatory aspects of nominee accounts and the rules they must abide by, contact the Financial Services Authority, the City watchdog, on 020 7676 1000 or go to www.fsa.gov.uk.

Proving your identity

The transfer of the proceeds of criminal activity into the financial system – known as *money laundering* – is big business and the Financial Services Authority, the City watchdog, is working hard to stamp it out. Criminals try to hide the origins of their cash by using a false name and address to set up a bank or building society account, and to buy or sell shares, amongst other things.

To crack down on this, you'll be asked to provide proof of identification when trading in shares. When you sign up with a stockbroker, you'll be asked for proof of your name and address by a recent utility bill or council tax bill. To prove your name, you'll usually be asked for your passport, driving licence, or a tax notification from HM Revenue & Customs. Because a passport or driving licence usually has a photograph, it's not easy to forge them.

If you're applying to buy or sell shares via the post or Internet, rather than face to face from a broker, you should send certified copies of your passport or driving licence, rather than posting the originals – as they could get lost. Certified copies are photocopies which a person of professional standing – a solicitor, bank manager, accountant, independent financial adviser, teacher, or doctor – has stated to be genuine copies of the originals. She should have seen the original and should write on the copy 'I hereby certify this to be a true copy of the original'. She should then write her name, address, and profession on each copy and sign and date it.

Looking Forward to Returns

Owning shares, or equities, is an excellent way of building up investments for the future. They produce superior returns to cash or bonds over the long term. As a shareholder, you're entitled to a share of any profits the company you are invested in makes.

Equities produce two types of return:

- ✔ **Capital growth:** When you sell your shares, you will hopefully realise a substantial profit, although there is a risk that this may actually be a loss, depending on market conditions.

- ✔ **Income:** Shares pay out dividends if the company performs well. When the company doesn't perform well, dividends will fall or may not be paid at all. There are no guarantees.

 Compounding your investment by reinvesting your dividends will enable the value of your portfolio to grow more quickly.

Generating dividends

As well as the increase in value of shares over time, you may also receive an income in the form of dividends. This is the company's profits or *earnings* that shareholders receive as a thank-you for investing in the business. Dividends are usually stated as an amount in pence per share.

Tracking down unclaimed dividends

If you move house and forget to notify your stockbroker or the company in which you own shares, you may miss out on some dividends because your new address isn't on the share register. If this happens to you, you can contact the Unclaimed Assets Register to find your missing dividends. Write to Leconfield House, Curzon Street, London W1J 5JA, call 0870 241 1713, or go to www.uar.co.uk.

To avoid dividend cheques going missing in the first place, arrange to have them paid by direct transfer to your bank account. Not only is this safer, it saves the hassle of having to pay a cheque into your account and then waiting for it to clear, which can take several working days.

Dividends are usually paid every six months so you get an *interim* dividend and the *final* dividend each year. If you're a registered shareholder, you'll get a cheque for your dividend or it is paid directly into your bank account, if you request this. This is usually easier as it saves it going missing (see the sidebar 'Tracking down unclaimed dividends').

You also get a voucher showing details of your holding, the dividend per share, and the tax that has been deducted and paid to HM Revenue & Customs. You need to hang onto this voucher to prove the tax you've paid and to work out how much more you need to pay if you're a higher-rate taxpayer (see 'Paying duty' later in this chapter for more details).

If you hold *preference shares* you get a fixed rate of dividend paid in bi-annual instalments. You get preference over *ordinary* shareholders – hence the name – so when the company is short of cash, you are more likely to get a dividend than ordinary shareholders. Preference shares provide more security than ordinary shares.

If the company you have invested in goes bankrupt, preference shareholders also have more rights than ordinary shareholders.

Understanding charges

Although transaction costs are higher if you invest in shares directly rather than through a unit or investment trust, competition among brokers and from online share dealing services has dramatically reduced the cost. It's a competitive marketplace so shop around for the best deal.

There are various types of charge you need to budget for:

- ✓ **Commission:** Brokers charge commission when you buy or sell shares. The commission is usually a percentage of the amount you are investing or receiving or it may be a flat fee.
- ✓ **Fixed fees:** Brokers offering investment management services often recoup their costs via an ongoing annual administration fee. Even if you don't make any transactions during the year, you still have to pay this fee. Some brokers charge higher commission on each trade they advise you on, rather than a fixed annual fee.
- ✓ **Commission plus fees:** Some firms have a tariff that combines both charges.

Don't let charges be your only, or even main, consideration when choosing a broker (unless you are opting for an execution-only service). Otherwise, they should be considered to be important but only as part of the overall picture. Remember, you often get what you pay for.

Paying duty

On top of brokers' charges and dealing costs, you must also pay stamp duty to the Government on all share purchases. This is 0.5 per cent of the value of each purchase, with a minimum payment of £5, and is rounded up to the nearest £5. So if you are buying £1,000 worth of shares, you'll have to pay stamp duty to the Government of £5.

You don't always have to pay stamp duty: For example, it isn't charged if you're buying shares in Germany, Luxembourg, the Netherlands, or Sweden. You also don't pay stamp duty if you're selling your shares.

Capital gains tax (CGT) is payable on any profit you make when selling your shares. But everyone has an annual allowance of £9,600 (for the 2008–9 tax year), so you only pay CGT on any profit above your allowance. In the unlikely event that your profit exceeds this, stagger the sale of your shares over more than one year (so you can take advantage of more than one annual allowance), or transfer shares to your spouse to enjoy double the allowance.

You also pay income tax on dividends. All dividends carry a *tax credit* of 10 per cent, which means this much tax is deducted before you receive your payment. You may have to pay further tax, depending on what sort of taxpayer you are:

- **Non-taxpayers:** Don't have to pay any more tax but can't claim back the 10 per cent they've paid either.

- **Basic-rate taxpayers:** There is no more tax to pay.

- **Higher-rate taxpayers**: You must pay a total of 32.5 per cent tax on dividend income. As you are taxed 10 per cent at source, the remaining 22.5 per cent must be paid via your tax return. Go to www.hmrc.gov.uk for more details.

Keeping Track of Your Shares

Knowledge is power and this is particularly true when it comes to deciding when to buy and sell your shares. If you are inexperienced, you should pay a stockbroker or investment manager to provide advice, while more experienced investors can get away with an execution-only service.

Whether you pay for advice or not, you should do your own research into the market. This will enable you to evaluate your broker's advice (if you get it) and decide whether it's right for you, or simply make the right decisions if you're choosing your own shares.

The first place to start your research is a national newspaper. The *Financial Times* is still the bible on share price information, as it's dedicated to business and investment. In addition, all of the broadsheets and most of the tabloids have business and City pages, with plenty of rumours, share prices, company information, and tips. You can also find plenty of investment magazines and papers: These provide more in-depth coverage but won't carry the latest share prices as a daily newspaper can. Try *Investors Chronicle*, *Money Observer*, *Moneywise*, or *Bloomberg Money* for plenty of information on shares. You could also listen to Radio 4's *Money Box* programme.

Working out employee share ownership

Part of the reason for the growth in share ownership is the introduction of employee share-ownership plans: These enable you to own shares in the company you work for. Plenty of tax advantages are available, with some schemes allowing you to buy shares at greatly reduced rates.

The Save As You Earn (SAYE) or Sharesave scheme enables you to save between £5 and £250 a month (which is deducted from your salary) with your employer for three, five, or seven years in order to buy shares in the company at the end of this period. The price is set at the start of the scheme and can be as much as 20 per cent off the market price at the time.

Alternatively, there are profit-sharing schemes, enabling your employer to give you shares free of tax and National Insurance Contributions. You aren't able to receive shares to the value of more than £3,000. Your employer sets up a trust in which you must keep your shares for at least two years. If you leave them in there for at least three years, you can retain or dispose of them without paying any income tax or National Insurance.

The other way of owning shares in your employer is via a company share option plan. This offers the option to buy a set number of shares at a stated price and at least three years in the future.

For more details on these schemes, go to www.hmrc.gov.uk/shareschemes.

The Internet is the most useful resource for private investors. Several sites specialise in private investment and personal finance matters, such as Interactive Investor (www.iii.co.uk), Hemscott (www.hemscott.com), Motley Fool (www.fool.co.uk), and Digital Look (www.digitallook.com). Also, several news services are available with the latest information that might affect your share price: Bloomberg (www.bloomberg.co.uk), Citywire (www.citywire.co.uk), and Reuters (www.reuters.co.uk).

All listed companies must issue an Annual Report and accounts. As a shareholder, you are legally entitled to receive a copy, unless you hold your shares through a nominee company. You can arrange with your nominee account holder to get you a copy.

Chapter 14

Safe as Houses: Choosing a Mortgage

- -

In This Chapter

▶ Figuring out how much money you need

▶ Looking at the different types of home loans

▶ Getting a grasp on rates

▶ Searching for the right deal

▶ Steering clear of unnecessary expenses

- -

*P*roperty is an excellent investment, enabling you to kiss good-bye to grotty rental accommodation and throwing money down the drain on rent, while at the same time investing in something that is likely to increase in value over the years.

But you can't escape the fact that getting on the property ladder for the first time is hard. Many people have to delay their first property purchase because they simply can't afford to buy any younger. The average age of a first-time buyer is 34, according to the Halifax, the UK's biggest mortgage lender, as would-be buyers spend their twenties trying to clear student debts and struggling on low incomes. (*Buying a Home on a Budget For Dummies* by yours truly offers valuable advice on creative ways to get on the property ladder.)

This chapter helps you work out how much cash you need to get on the property ladder and what you can realistically afford.

Working Out How Much You Can Afford to Borrow

Before you can actually buy a property, you need to work out whether you can afford to do so. Affordability can be a big problem, most notably for first-time buyers. Most people need a *mortgage* to buy a property – a loan from a bank or building society. Lenders calculate the maximum you can borrow based on how much you earn. But what the lender is prepared to lend you and what you should borrow are two different things.

Mortgage lenders have relaxed their borrowing criteria over the past couple of decades, with much bigger home loans now available. But that doesn't mean you should take on the biggest mortgage you can. Keep in mind that you have to repay it. Even if you can cope initially, you may struggle if you lose your job, for example. If you're overstretched, even a small change in circumstances can prove catastrophic.

Even if you can't afford to buy on your own, other ways may exist of realising your goal by buying with friends, a sibling, or persuading your parents to help out. See *Buying a Home on a Budget For Dummies* by yours truly for loads more useful advice.

Multiplying your income

Many lenders let you borrow a simple multiple of your income: Either four or five times if you buy on your own, or three and a half times your joint income if you hook up with someone else. So if you earn £30,000, you should be able to get a mortgage for £120,000 to £150,000, depending on the lender, if you buy on your own. If you buy with your spouse, who earns the same as you, you could borrow up to £210,000.

Unfortunately, these income multiples won't get you very far. Unless you have a large deposit – perhaps an inheritance from a relative – you won't be able to bridge the gap between property prices and how much you can raise.

More recently, lenders have moved away from strict income multiples towards affordability calculations. Instead of deciding how much you can borrow based solely on income, lenders are looking at the bigger picture, taking into account your outgoings as well. This way of lending is more responsible as it works out what you can really afford to pay.

No matter what size loan you're offered, think carefully before you take on a mortgage of that size. Make sure you're happy with the repayments and can cope if interest rates rise. Don't overstretch yourself.

Coping without a deposit

Even if you don't have a deposit, all is not necessarily lost. Several 100 per cent mortgages are available, so even if you haven't got a deposit, it doesn't necessarily mean you can't get a mortgage.

Realistically, saving up a 5 or 10 per cent deposit could take you several years, depending on how good a saver you are and how fast property prices climb. It might make sense to borrow a greater proportion of the purchase price now, rather than put off buying for a few years while you save up several thousand pounds for a deposit. If you delay your purchase in a rising property market, you could find prices increasing to such an extent that you're priced out of the market yet again.

The problem with not having a deposit (or having a very small one) is that you won't get the cheapest mortgage rate. You qualify for the best deals if you've a sizeable deposit because lenders regard you as being lower risk than someone without a deposit. You also have less choice of mortgages available if you don't have much of a deposit. A number of lenders also charge a *higher lending charge* (HLC) – a one-off insurance premium typically charged if you borrow more than 90 per cent of the value of the property. See the 'Watching out for HLC' section later in this chapter for tips on how to avoid paying this charge.

Calculating How Much Cash You Need Beyond the Price

The cost of buying a property largely depends on the purchase price, which reflects its location, size, features, age, and condition. The price is also partly dictated by demand: The more interest among prospective purchasers for that property, generally speaking, the higher the price.

As well as the purchase price, you need to consider several other extras that bump up the final bill. I discuss these in more detail in the following sections.

Looking out for the lender's fee

Most mortgage lenders charge a fee of some kind when you take out a home loan. This charge may be referred to as one of several things, such as an application, arrangement, or completion fee. Typically, this is around £1,000 but some lenders charge a percentage of the mortgage amount – such as 1 or 2 per cent – which can push the cost up. This fee can be added to the loan rather than paid for up front. If you add the fee to the loan, you pay more in the long run as you're charged interest on the amount.

 Mortgages with the lowest interest rates tend to carry the highest arrangement fees. However, this may still work out cheaper in the long run than paying a lower arrangement fee and higher rate of interest. Ask an independent mortgage broker to do the sums for you: See 'Seeking advice' later in this chapter for more details on finding a broker.

Paying a mortgage broker

The best way of finding the right mortgage for you is to use an independent mortgage broker. This saves you time and money, because as long as the broker is truly independent he has access to all the deals on the market so is able to source the most competitive one for your needs. He can also handle the application form for you and liaise with the lender to ensure your application is processed quickly.

 Brokers are paid by commission, a fee, or both. Those who are paid by commission receive several hundred pounds from the lender who provides your mortgage. This is known as a *procuration fee*. If the broker charges a fee, you have to pay: Prices vary but expect to pay up to 1 per cent of the mortgage amount for this advice. Whether you choose to pay a fee or use a broker who receives commission depends on personal preference and what you can afford. But make sure you're clear which you're opting for at the start of your relationship.

Commissioning a lender's valuation and survey

Lenders insist on a valuation of the property to confirm that the property is worth the amount you're borrowing. If you default on your repayments, the lender can cover its costs by selling your property. The cost of the valuation depends on the purchase price:

Expect to pay around £300 for the lender's valuation on a £200,000 property, for example.

The valuation tells you nothing about the condition of the property: To ascertain this, you must pay for a survey. A basic survey – the *homebuyer's report* – costs between £250 and £400 but is money well spent because it tells you whether the property has problems such as subsidence or dry rot. If so, you can either pull out of the purchase or try to negotiate a lower purchase price with the seller. Either way, you make an informed decision, which isn't the case if you don't know the full extent of the problem.

A more detailed (and expensive) survey is the *full structural survey*. This costs between £500 and £1,000 but if you're buying a very old or unusual property it is worth considering. If a problem emerges later on that the surveyor didn't pick up, you may have grounds for compensation.

Settling legal fees

A lot of complicated legal work is involved in the transfer of property from seller to buyer and using a solicitor to represent you is advisable, particularly if you're purchasing a leasehold property, because this is much more complicated than buying a freehold property.

Some people take on their own *conveyancing* or legal work but it is complicated and time-consuming. If you get it wrong the consequences can be great, so save yourself time and money in the long run and use a solicitor.

Solicitors don't come cheap: Fees vary, so shop around and get a couple of quotes. Expect to pay £550 plus VAT (17.5 per cent) if you're purchasing a £100,000 property. If the property is leasehold, expect to pay another £75 plus VAT to cover the extra work involved in checking the lease.

Legal fees cover the cost of instructing a solicitor to check the property's home information pack (HIP), and are payable upon completion. It is compulsory for sellers in England and Wales to provide a HIP when marketing their properties. The HIP includes information such as whether the property had planning permission before it was built and that the seller is in a position to sell the property to you, for example, as well as details of the lease where relevant. You must ask a solicitor to check these documents, however. They may want to conduct further investigations, which you have to pay for, if they're not happy about any of the information.

Sending in your stamp duty

Stamp duty is an unavoidable tax payable to the Government on completion of your property purchase. How much you pay depends on the price of the property:

✔ Nothing if it costs less than £125,000 (or £150,000 in certain disadvantaged areas)

✔ 1 per cent on properties between £125,000 and £250,000

✔ 3 per cent on properties costing more than £250,000 and less than £500,000

✔ 4 per cent on properties costing more than £500,000

Your mortgage doesn't cover the stamp duty: You need to raise these funds yourself, so remember to budget for it.

Eenie, Meenie, Miney, Mo: Choosing the Right Mortgage

The first step to choosing a mortgage is to understand the different types available and how they work.

Whether you opt for a *repayment* or *interest-only* mortgage (explained in more detail in the following sections) depends on your attitude to risk and what you can afford. Monthly payments are higher with a repayment loan but you get peace of mind because you're guaranteed to pay the capital back in full by the end of the mortgage term (as long as you keep up your repayments). With an interest-only mortgage you should set up an investment vehicle which you contribute to monthly or aim to switch to repayment within a few years: This type of mortgage usually means lower monthly repayments but you have no guarantee that the investment vehicle will raise enough cash to pay off the capital. You must decide whether you're happy to take a gamble on the roof over your head – in effect, this is what you're doing with an interest-only home loan.

Before taking out this type of mortgage, definitely seek professional advice.

Understanding repayment loans

The only way you can guarantee that all the capital is paid back at the end of the mortgage term is to opt for a *repayment* loan. You pay back a slice of the capital (the amount you borrow) each month, plus interest – what the lender is charging you for borrowing this cash. If you keep up the repayments, at the end of the term you've paid off all the capital and the property is yours.

Going interest-only

With an *interest-only* mortgage you pay just the interest on your mortgage each month. You repay none of the capital until the end of the mortgage term. If you don't have enough cash to pay back all the capital in one hit, your lender could repossess your home and sell it to recoup its outlay.

You should set up some sort of investment vehicle to raise enough cash to clear the capital due at the end of the mortgage term. You can use individual savings accounts (ISAs) as repayment vehicles to back interest-only mortgages. Chapter 10 has more details on how these work, but the main advantage is that returns are tax-free so your money grows more quickly.

For the purpose of repaying your mortgage capital, you need an equity ISA. Cash won't produce good enough returns to pay off your mortgage. The problem with using an ISA is that you have a maximum allowance of £7,200 per annum so you also need to invest in other collective investment funds (go to Chapter 12 for more details on these) to raise enough cash to clear the capital on your home loan.

You can invest monthly into an ISA offered by a fund manager, building up a personal portfolio of ISA investments over the years, which you choose yourself.

The advantage of an ISA is that you know exactly how much your investment is worth. You may have to pay an initial charge of up to 5 per cent and annual management fees of around 1.5 per cent. ISAs are also flexible: Switching investments, if your fund is under-performing, and stopping or re-starting payments is easy to do. You also have some say over where your money is invested.

When it comes to repaying a mortgage, too much flexibility is a bad thing as there's a risk you could end up with less money than you need. Plus, equity ISAs are vulnerable to stock market fluctuations so you have no guarantee that they'll raise enough cash to pay off your mortgage. Relying on ISAs to repay your mortgage is high risk and may only suit experienced investors and higher-rate taxpayers, who can make the most of the tax breaks.

Combining repayment with interest-only

You can combine interest-only and repayment deals. Mortgages that let you pay just the interest on your loan in the early years before switching to a repayment deal (to ensure you pay back all the capital by the end of the term) are particularly useful for first-time buyers who struggle with lack of funds in the early years of their mortgage. You get cheaper payments for the first two years or so because you only pay interest – none of the capital.

Watch out for a big jump in your monthly repayments when you start paying back the capital as well as the interest because the change could be considerable. Get an idea of how much the jump in your repayments will be from your lender or broker and budget accordingly.

Understanding Rates

When you decide on the type of mortgage you want, you must choose what rate to go for. Your choice depends on your circumstances and attitude to risk. I explain the various rates in the following sections.

Avoiding the standard variable rate

Each mortgage lender has a *standard variable rate* (SVR). This is the lender's benchmark, which it uses to calculate its variable-rate mortgage deals. The SVR can move up and down with no notice at all: When the Bank of England raises or cuts the base rate – the base interest rate, which it increases or decreases when it thinks this is necessary to keep inflation in check – most lenders adjust their SVR accordingly, sometimes within a matter of minutes.

You can take out a mortgage on your lender's SVR but it won't be the cheapest deal. Opt for a fixed or discounted rate instead – they're usually a couple of percentage points below the SVR.

Even if you opt for a fixed or discounted rate, don't forget about the SVR as your mortgage reverts to this when the offer period comes to an end – unless you switch to another deal. If you stay put, your mortgage repayments could dramatically increase so shop around for another deal or ask your lender if it has a cheaper mortgage to offer you.

Opting for a fix

With a *fixed-rate mortgage* your repayments are guaranteed for a set period of time, no matter what happens to the base rate. A fixed rate provides certainty: Most people opt for a 2-, 3-, or 5-year fix but you can also fix for 1, 10, 15, 20, 25, or even 30 years. Make sure you're comfortable with the length of your fix, because if you want to move house and switch your mortgage before the term is up, you could pay a penalty.

With a fixed rate, if the base rate rises you're laughing but if it falls you don't benefit. And if the base rate falls several times during your fixed term, you could end up paying a lot more than you would have done if you'd opted for a shorter fix.

The longer the fixed rate, the higher the rate of interest: 2-year fixes tend to be cheaper than 5-year deals because the lender is taking on less risk.

Tracking the base rate

A *base rate tracker mortgage* follows movements in the base rate, tracking a margin of, say, 0.5 per cent above it. So if the base rate is 5.25 per cent, the interest rate on such a tracker is 5.75 per cent – until the base rate changes. The big advantage here is that your lender can't widen the margin and charge you more than this set margin above the base rate, so you know where you stand.

Many lenders offer substantial discounts on tracker deals for the first couple of years as an incentive. A lender could offer you 1 per cent off the base rate, giving you a very attractive payable rate of 3.75 per cent if the base rate is 4.75 per cent. Some trackers let you switch without penalty at any time so you can move to another mortgage without charge when the discount period comes to an end.

Tracker mortgages have no certainty to them, and go up and down. They tend to be cheaper than fixed-rate mortgages, at least initially, because taking one on involves more risk. Only opt for a tracker if you can afford to be wrong: That is, you're still able to afford your mortgage if interest rates rise.

Plumping for a discount

Discount rates tend to be a couple of percentage points below the lender's SVR. Lenders usually offer discount rates over two, three, or five years: As with fixed rates, generally the shorter the term, the lower the rate. The big advantage of discounts is that they're also usually lower than the lender's fixed-rate deals – at least initially. You also benefit from any cut in the base rate if interest is calculated daily on your mortgage because it is directly linked to your lender's SVR. However, the lender is not obliged to pass on any reduction in full so you may be better off with a base-rate tracker because these are more transparent, so you know exactly where you stand.

If the Bank of England increases the base rate, your mortgage payments increase. And if the base rate is volatile, your mortgage payments could fluctuate dramatically from month to month, making budgeting difficult. Opt for a discount rate only if you could cope with an increase in your mortgage repayments. If you can, you get a better deal than on a fixed rate – at least initially – plus you benefit from rate reductions during the discounted period.

Checking out capped rates

With a capped rate, you know the absolute maximum you have to pay each month, just as you do with a fixed rate. However, as there is no lower cap, you could end up paying less interest than you would on a fixed-rate deal, depending on what happens to the base rate. Your initial mortgage rate is set lower than the cap: Your rate can rise but only as high as the cap. If the base rate is raised again after the cap has been reached, your mortgage repayments won't be affected. Capped rate deals are usually offered over 3, 5, or 10 years.

Because the rate is capped rather than fixed, it can fall, allowing you to take advantage of cuts in the base rate. This makes a capped rate attractive because you can benefit from the best of both worlds.

Capped rates tend to be higher than fixed-rate deals because you have to pay for having the best of both worlds. There is also less choice as fewer lenders offer them.

Flexibly does it

A number of mortgages have *flexible features*. This means you can vary your monthly repayments, overpaying if you've got spare cash and thereby paying your mortgage back more quickly, reducing the interest you pay. You can also underpay if you're short of cash, or even pay nothing at all, as long as you have built up funds in your mortgage 'account'. If you've overpaid by several hundred pounds you can take payment holidays, but you can't miss a payment completely if you haven't built up anything in reserve.

Interest is calculated daily, rather than monthly or annually, which makes a huge difference to the total amount you pay over the term of your loan. As soon as you make a payment, the money gets to work reducing your mortgage debt and the interest you pay.

Flexible mortgages are handy if you're self-employed or your income fluctuates. When you are flush you can pay more than you need to so that when finances are tight you can miss a payment or two – and not incur a penalty.

Watch out for the rate of interest on flexible deals as it can be higher than on fixed or discounted offers. If you don't use all the flexible facilities, you might want to avoid a flexible deal: Most borrowers are only interested in the ability to overpay. Many standard mortgages allow you to overpay up to 10 per cent of your outstanding loan each year without penalty. Such a mortgage may work out cheaper than a fully flexible deal.

Offsetting your mortgage

One way of reducing your mortgage interest is to opt for an offset or current account mortgage (CAM). An *offset mortgage* lets you use your savings to reduce the interest you pay on your mortgage. You open a savings account and/or current account with your mortgage lender. Although your savings and current account are kept separate from your mortgage debt, the amount you have on deposit is offset against the amount you owe on your mortgage to reduce the interest you pay. So if you owe £100,000 on your mortgage, for example, but have £20,000 in savings and, say, £1,000 in your current account, you're charged interest at your mortgage rate on £79,000 (your £100,000 mortgage minus the sum of your deposits of £20,000 and £1,000). You can also offset your family and friends' savings against your mortgage.

A CAM lumps your mortgage, current account, savings, and even credit cards and personal loans together in one account rather than keeping everything separate. Even a small amount of money can make a big difference to the interest you pay: For example, if you take out a £100,000 mortgage over 25 years at 7.5 per cent interest, and spend all your salary each month except £100, which stays in your account, you pay off your mortgage six years and nine months early, saving £40,263 in interest. The residue of money left in the account every month might not seem much but the key thing is that it eats away at your debt.

Because the interest on offset mortgages and CAMs is calculated daily, you pay what you owe on that day. So if you have just been paid, it doesn't matter that you will soon spend all that cash; for several days, your entire pay packet is offset against your mortgage. In the long run, this enables you to repay your loan more quickly.

Critics of offset mortgages and CAMs argue that they are so flexible there is a danger that undisciplined borrowers won't pay their mortgages off on time. For example, some CAM providers will lend you the difference between your mortgage (say, for example, £62,000) and the value of your house (say, £150,000). So, in this example you could get your hands on a further £88,000 to spend how you wish. Other CAM providers limit the amount you can borrow. If you're not disciplined and are likely to give in to temptation, steer clear of a CAM and opt for a fixed or discounted deal instead.

Offset mortgages and CAMs are a great way of reducing your interest payments but rates can be higher than on standard residential deals. So unless you've several thousand pounds in savings to offset, you won't save money in the long run.

Cashing in on a cashback mortgage

When you take out a *cashback mortgage*, you get a cash lump sum from your lender. The amount varies from a flat fee of a couple of hundred pounds to a percentage of the amount you borrow (as high as 6 per cent of the mortgage). You can do what you want with this cash – buy a new sofa, pay off your credit card, or even take a holiday if you need a break from the stress of moving.

You don't get something for nothing, and this is particularly true with cashback mortgages. They tend to be expensive in the long run because the cashback is an advance that you pay back over the mortgage term. So £6,000 cashback on a £100,000 mortgage is the equivalent of borrowing £106,000 because you pay interest on this additional loan over the entire mortgage term. The rate of interest also tends to be higher on a cashback mortgage than on a standard fixed or discounted deal.

Early redemption penalties are common on cashback mortgages, which could effectively lock you in for five to seven years. Check the small print before signing up.

Instead of taking out a cashback mortgage, choose a competitive standard fixed or discounted home loan and get hold of the cash another way. You could opt for a personal loan with the lowest rate of interest you can find, extend your overdraft, or apply for a credit card with a 0 per cent introductory period. Not only will you get access to a few hundred or thousand pounds, you can pay it back over a couple of years, rather than 25, and so pay less interest. You can also choose from a wider range of mortgages, rather than limiting yourself to just those offering cash back.

Finding the Best Mortgage

The bank you have your current account with may offer you a mortgage, but think twice before automatically applying for it. It is unlikely to be the best deal. You need to shop around and find the mortgage that best suits your needs and circumstances. So much competition is out there, with thousands of loans offered by scores of lenders, that there's no room for misplaced loyalty.

Seeking advice

The easiest and most foolproof way of finding the best mortgage rate is to use an independent mortgage broker. Three types of brokers exist:

- ✔ Brokers who can only sell products from one provider.

- ✔ Brokers who can advise on products from a handful of lenders.

- ✔ Brokers who can advise on the best deal available from the entire marketplace.

Before choosing a broker, ask how many lenders he can draw on. Brokers are obliged to disclose this information. Avoid brokers who work strictly for one company – or even a handful of companies. Instead, opt for a broker who has access to the whole of the market, so that you increase your chances of getting the best deal.

Any broker giving mortgage advice must be authorised by the Financial Services Authority (FSA), the City watchdog. This should reassure borrowers that he has passed certain standards of training and that you can take any dispute you have with him to the Ombudsman. Check that your broker is authorised by visiting the FSA's website at www.fsa.gov.uk or calling its consumer helpline on 0845 606 1234.

Going online

The Internet provides a wealth of information on mortgages. Even if you don't actually apply for your mortgage online, researching the various deals available before contacting a lender or broker is a good move. That way, you know whether you're getting a good deal or not.

Researching online

Several websites (see the following list) provide free calculators that enable you to work out how much you can borrow and what your monthly repayments will be. This is only a general guide – you have no guarantee that a lender will let you borrow the cash – but it's a great place to start.

Understanding how your adviser is paid

Mortgage brokers are paid by fees, commission, or both. The broker must tell you which applies: If you're happy with paying a fee or for your broker to receive commission from the lender whose mortgage he recommends, there is little between the two. Much debate goes on about which form of payment makes for the most independent broker, but the most important thing is that you're happy with the method of payment – that's what matters.

If your broker only receives commission, you pay nothing for the advice. Your mortgage provider will pay several hundred pounds to the broker for arranging the sale. Critics of commission argue that such brokers aren't truly independent, but a good, reputable broker has a lot to lose by recommending mortgages simply on the back of the commission he receives.

If you pay a fee, you should expect to pay anything up to 1 per cent of the mortgage amount – £700 on a £70,000 loan, for example. For this, you usually get a more comprehensive service than you would if you opted for a fee-free broker. If you can't afford this, use a broker who receives commission but make sure you do your research carefully when choosing him in the first place to ensure he is reputable and independent.

Many brokers also have best buy tables on their websites so you can see the best available deals at a glance. When you're ready to sign on the dotted line on your mortgage application form, double-checking these tables to ensure that you're getting the best deal is a worthwhile move.

Here are some of the best sites, all from independent brokers:

- ✔ **Charcol:** www.charcolonline.co.uk
- ✔ **London & Country:** www.lcplc.co.uk
- ✔ **Savills Private Finance:** www.spf.co.uk

The Internet is a great way of saving money. By doing your own research using brokers' websites and applying online – if you feel confident enough – you increase your chances of getting the best deal. Brokers often have access to exclusive deals not available direct, so even if you require a mainstream mortgage, a broker may still get you the best deal. If you require a non-standard mortgage, perhaps because you have an adverse credit record or an unusual property, a broker can really come into his own.

Applying for a mortgage online

Going through mortgage applications online has never really taken off. The Internet is useful as a research tool but most people still prefer to speak to someone in the lender's call centre or a broker for assistance in completing the application.

Filling in a mortgage application form online is not for everyone, particularly if you're a first-time buyer and don't understand the mortgage process. Forms can be complicated and many homebuyers prefer to be guided through them by a lender or broker.

Avoiding Unnecessary Costs

If you don't understand all the terms and conditions, your mortgage could end up costing you more than you thought it would. In the following sections, I run through where you might get caught out.

Watching out for HLC

If you don't have a deposit, or much of one, some lenders still insist on some guarantee that you won't default on your mortgage repayments, leaving them having to pursue you for the balance – which could lead to the sale of your home to cover the costs. This is why some lenders charge a *higher lending charge* (HLC) if you borrow more than, say, 90 per cent of the purchase price. The level at which lenders charge HLC varies: Some charge HLC on loans greater than 80 per cent, others 95 per cent. HLC is insurance, paid for by you even though it protects the lender. It's a one-off fee worked out as a percentage of your mortgage and usually costs a few thousand pounds.

Try to avoid paying HLC. Generate as big a deposit as possible by asking relatives to chip in or simply use a lender that doesn't charge HLC – there are plenty who don't.

Escaping early redemption penalties

Most mortgage deals carry redemption penalties if you remortgage during a set period of time. If you take out a two-year fixed-rate deal, for example, the only way the lender can offer those terms is if you stick with it for at least two years. If you switch your mortgage sooner, the lender loses out. The lender imposes a penalty to dissuade you from doing this and to cover its losses if you switch regardless. The penalty is a percentage of the interest on the loan. Most lenders charge redemption penalties during offer periods on fixed or discounted deals, although not all do.

Never take out a mortgage with an *extended redemption penalty*, or *overhang*. The rate on offer will undoubtedly be more attractive than loans without overhangs, but this is because you will be stuck on a higher, uncompetitive rate for what can seem forever. For example, a lender might offer a market-leading two-year discount, but the payback is you're tied to that mortgage for not two but maybe five years, or longer. Although you no longer benefit from a cheap deal because you are on your lender's SVR once the offer ends, remortgaging could cost you thousands of pounds in redemption penalty. To make matters worse, these lenders often have the highest SVRs. Any of the earlier savings you made tend to be lost because you pay higher interest for years after the offer has ended.

Plenty of loans are available with no tie-ins or lock-ins after the offer period, and some lenders don't impose a penalty at any time. Such deals are cheaper in the long run. Don't be dazzled by the headline rate: Look beyond it and think longer term.

Sidestepping compulsory insurance

Some lenders force you to buy their buildings insurance when you take out a mortgage. Even though some lenders offer competitive insurance, don't assume this is the case. Usually this insurance tends to be a rip-off and should be avoided at all costs. Certain forms of insurance are unavoidable, including buildings insurance (see Chapter 4 for more on this), but you are entitled to shop around in order to get the best deal.

Some lenders, particularly building societies, offer two mortgage rates: a really cheap deal and a pricier one. The catch with the cheap deal is that you have to take out the lender's buildings insurance (and in some cases contents cover as well). The higher rate comes with no such restrictions. In the long term you're better off opting for the higher rate and shopping around for cover; this enables you to find cheaper insurance and to change insurer when your premium is up for renewal (not so easy if cover is linked to your mortgage).

Some lenders don't have compulsory insurance but make it as easy as possible for you to take out their cover. Often, the mortgage application form includes a box you can tick if you want buildings cover alongside a reminder that it is compulsory to have such insurance. Lenders count on the fact that you're stressed by the whole home-buying process so will welcome one less thing to worry about. Some lenders charge you a fee – around £25 – if you don't take out their buildings cover. Even if you have to pay, doing so is nearly always worthwhile as you're likely to find more competitively priced insurance elsewhere.

Part IV
Taking Care of the Future

'Tell me, Miss Pimley, why can't our employees announce their early retirement in a normal way?'

In this part . . .

This part demystifies pensions and contains suggestions on how to go about providing for your retirement. I cover all the options, from joining your employer's pension scheme to providing for yourself in a personal plan. And once you reach retirement, you need to know how to make the most of your money (but you won't find anything on blue rinses and bingo).

Chapter 15

Planning for Retirement and Beyond

. . . .

In This Chapter

▶ Anticipating retirement

▶ Covering all your bases

▶ Making your own retirement provision

▶ Evaluating investment tools

▶ Planning for the future: wills and inheritance tax

. . . .

*I*f you're like most people, you don't like to think about getting older. But the sooner you start thinking about retirement – and start planning for it – the better. As people live longer and healthier lives, with a bit of luck, you'll be a long time retired. Relying solely on the state pension to see you through this golden age will only mean a miserable retirement.

Workplace pensions and personal or stakeholder plans aren't the only answers. Spreading risk via several types of investment is worthwhile, so that if your employer goes bust and takes your final salary scheme with her or your pension doesn't perform as well as you'd hoped, it's not the end of the world. Spreading risk cushions you against stock market volatility or the property market collapsing just as you sell up the house whose proceeds you were relying on in old age.

In this chapter, I look at the various options available when saving for retirement.

Making Some Vital Decisions about Retirement

How you save for retirement depends on four factors:

✔ What age you plan to retire

✔ How much cash you need in retirement

✔ When you start saving

✔ What you can afford to save

Plucking numbers out of the air is futile: Each of these factors needs examining in detail. Only then will you discover whether your lofty aims are unreasonable given the limitations of your wallet and the time you have left. You may have to revise your expectations or start saving a lot more than you are doing.

Planning your retirement age

The first step is to decide when you're going to retire. If you're in your twenties you may feel this is ridiculous: How on earth can you possibly predict how you'll feel about working in 40 years or so? Or it may be one of the easiest questions in the world to answer if you have long had no intention of working past the age of 50. Whichever type of person you are, thinking about the age you plan to give up work is crucial because it has an impact on your retirement planning – how much you need to save and where you invest it.

Retiring at 50 or indeed anytime before the official state retirement age of 65 for men and 60 for women (until 2020, when it becomes 65 for both) is an impossible dream for the majority. Realistically, you'll probably have to work until your seventies because you simply can't save enough to retire before then. Retiring at 50 requires a huge pension pot, supplemented with additional investments. If you're in a well-paid job and start saving a significant percentage of your salary from your early twenties, it might just be possible. Otherwise, it won't be. Doing the sums could make you appreciate that your dream is unrealistic. Either you invest more cash to make it possible or get used to the fact that you'll have to stay in the rat race for longer.

Calculating how much income you need to live (and play)

Working out what you'll need to live on some 20 or 30 years in the future isn't easy, particularly as price levels will be very different by the time you retire. But establishing a ballpark figure is useful. Think in terms of today's prices and make a rough estimate of day-to-day expenses (see Table 15-1).

Your outgoings should fall in retirement. For one thing, your mortgage will ideally be paid off so you can live rent-free. You don't need to buy smart suits to wear to the office; pay train and bus fares for your daily commute; or fork out a fiver for lunch at an over-priced sandwich shop either.

Don't underestimate your financial needs. Certain outgoings cease but you have more free time on your hands. Filling this costs money: You may want to travel several months of the year, take up golf, dine at fancy restaurants twice a month, or spoil the grandchildren. A retirement spent watching television all day is no fun: Plan carefully so that you've got enough cash to enjoy yourself.

Table 15-1 Everyday Outgoings in Retirement

Expense	Yearly Cost
Gas/electricity/water	£..........
Telephone/mobile	£..........
Council tax	£..........
Television licence	£..........
Satellite TV	£..........
Travel: bus/train	£..........
Buildings and contents insurance	£..........
Pet costs: food/insurance/vet	£..........
Running a car: insurance/ petrol/road tax/breakdown cover	£..........
Dentist/optician	£..........
Private medical insurance	£..........

(continued)

Table 15-1 *(continued)*

Expense	Yearly Cost
Food	£...........
Clothing	£...........
Dining out/cinema/theatre/concerts	£...........
Other	£...........
TOTAL OUTGOINGS	£...........

After you work out the cost of everyday essentials, start dreaming. Make a list of what you'd like to do and the cost. Your list might look something like the one in Table 15-2.

Table 15-2   Retirement Wish List

Expense	Yearly Cost
Three holidays a year at £1,000 each	£3,000
Three weekend breaks a year	£900
Dinner out once a week (for two)	£5,200
Day trips with grandchildren	£600
Golf membership	£5,000
TOTAL OUTGOINGS	£14,700

Working out your current position

Add together the total outgoings from Table 15-1 and your own version of Table 15-2: This is the yearly income you need in retirement. The next step is to work out what you're actually likely to retire on, taking into account your current saving levels. If a shortfall exists between what you're saving and what you need – which is more than likely – you can start planning to bridge this gap.

If you plan ahead, you should be able to rely on several sources of income in retirement:

- ✔ The basic state pension
- ✔ The state second pension (S2P)

✔ A private pension (occupational, personal, or stakeholder plan)

✔ Other investments, such as individual savings accounts (ISAs) and property

To get a rough idea of how much of an income you'll get in retirement based on your current pension contributions, use the pension calculator on the Trades Union Congress (TUC) website (www. pensioncalculator.org). Be prepared to be horrified by what you discover, but try not to be too disheartened – you may have time to rectify the situation.

The size of your pension also depends on annuity rates at the time you transform your private pot into a yearly income for the rest of your life. Three-quarters of your pension pot must be used to purchase an annuity by the age of 75. See Chapter 18 for the low-down on annuities.

Starting saving

The earlier you save for retirement, the better. Investing early gives your money longer to grow, which means you can opt for riskier investments, such as stocks and shares, which have historically produced higher returns in the long run. You will also end up investing more over the years than if you start your pension in your forties.

It's not worth having sleepless nights over your lack of pension. Save what you can afford to, when you can do so. Stakeholder pensions (see Chapter 17) are ideal because they require a minimum investment of no more than £20 a time. Then, when you can afford to invest more, make sure you increase your contributions.

If your employer offers an occupational scheme, she will contribute to your pension: If so, join immediately. You may not have to make a contribution but you still benefit from money going towards your pension. See Chapter 16 for more on occupational pensions.

Reviewing your plan

Review your pension planning on a regular basis – yearly at least. Pension providers are required by law to send you an annual statement detailing how much you have contributed, your fund's value, and a forecast of how much you could get on retirement. This is not a guaranteed amount but should give a good indication as to whether you need to put more cash aside for retirement.

If a fund isn't performing well, consider shifting your money else-where. If you leave your cash in badly performing investments for many years, you'll end up with a much lower income in retirement than you would have done if you'd ditched the dog funds. (This is not possible with final salary schemes.)

Looking at the Big Pension Picture

Everyone receives a basic state pension (as long as you have made enough National Insurance contributions (NICs) during your working life) and sometimes the state second pension, and the pension credit. But this is only a start: You need to make additional provision.

Coping on the state pension – forget about it!

The basic state pension is a flat rate payable once you reach state pension age: 65 for men and 60 for women. The retirement age for women is gradually being raised to 65 from 2010 and will be in place by 2020.

The full state pension, as of April 2008, is:

- ✔ £90.70 a week for a single person
- ✔ £145.05 a week for a married couple

These benefits are uprated every April. Details of the rates are available in leaflet GL23 *Social security benefit rates*, available from your pension centre or social security office.

The amount of pension you get depends on your National Insurance Contribution (NIC) record during your working life. Your working life is usually calculated from the beginning of the tax year in which you are 16 years old to the one before you reach state pension age. This is taken to be 49 years for a man and 44 years for a woman born on or before 5 October 1950, rising to 49 years for women born on 6 October 1954 or later.

To qualify for the full state pension, you must have paid full-rate NICs for approximately 90 per cent of your working life: These are known as *qualifying years*. Men need 44 qualifying years and women 39 to get a full state pension. From 2020, women will also need 44 years.

If you don't have a full contributions record, you won't get the full state pension; you get a reduced amount, based on the number of qualifying years instead. And if you retire with less than 25 per cent of your qualifying years, you won't get any basic state pension at all. You won't have your NICs refunded either. You can make voluntary contributions to top up your NICs but make sure you contribute enough to cover at least 25 per cent of your qualifying years or you still won't get a pension.

You may be *credited* with NICs, with the Government adding contributions to your NIC record, if you receive state benefits such as Incapacity Benefit or Jobseeker's Allowance.

You can't stop contributing to the basic state pension like you can with the state second pension (S2P). But you don't have to claim it once you reach state pension age. If you can afford to put it off, your state pension will be increased by 10.4 per cent for every year you delay. This translates to a higher weekly payment when you finally claim it but you won't be paid for the weeks you gave up. You can delay receiving your state pension for as long as you want. When you pass state retirement age, you no longer have to make NICs, although your employer will continue to do so. You will be sent a Certificate of Age Exception to give to your employer to prove that you no longer have to pay NICs.

If you retire before state pension age, you may have to make extra Class 3 NICs to qualify for the full basic pension once you reach the age of 65. Get hold of leaflet CA08 *Voluntary National Insurance Contributions* from HM Revenue & Customs for more details. Go to www.hmrc.gov.uk.

Find out how much state pension you've earned so far and how much you can expect to get in retirement. This will make you appreciate just how much you need to save in addition for a comfortable retirement. Ask your pension centre or social security office for form BR19, fill it in, and send it to the address on the form. Alternatively, complete a copy by telephone (0845 300 0168) or write to The Retirement Pension Forecasting Team, The Pension Service, Tyneview Park, Whitley Road, Newcastle upon Tyne, NE98 1BA. You can also download a form at www.thepensionservice.gov.uk. The nearer you are to retirement the more accurate this projection will be as it is based on current circumstances, which may change. But you shouldn't be dissuaded from finding out, even if you're a long way off retirement.

Building up the state second pension

The basic state pension isn't enough on its own for a comfortable retirement so an additional state second pension (S2P) is available to employees – particularly those on low or moderate incomes – to top up their pension income. It replaced the State Earnings-Related Pension Scheme (SERPS) in April 2002. S2P is paid at the same time as the basic state pension but you can get S2P even if you don't get a basic state pension.

S2P is based on your earnings above a certain level on which you have paid Class 1 NICs. If you earn at least £4,524 (in 2008–9), you are entitled to S2P unless you have *contracted out* of the scheme. This means you pay lower NICs (if you're a member of an occupational scheme; see Chapter 16 for more on this) or have your NI rebates paid into your personal or stakeholder plan instead.

You should contract out if you think you'll build up a bigger pension outside the S2P. This is an individual call but generally speaking, the more money you earn, the longer you have to invest, and the more positive your outlook for the stock market, the more reason there is to contract out. If you are nearing retirement, don't like to take on a lot of risk, and are on a fairly low salary, you may be better off staying contracted in. If you belong to an occupational scheme, the decision to contract out may have been made for you. If so, you can't do anything about it.

If you do have a choice, seek advice from your pension scheme adviser or independent financial adviser before taking action.

The amount of S2P you get is based on the level of earnings between the *lower earnings limit* of £4,524 and the *upper earnings limit* of £40,040 a year (2008–9). The Government is changing this to a flat-rate top-up rather than an earnings-related one when you have earnings above a certain amount. To do this, it is introducing an *upper accrual point,* set at £770 per week, in April 2009 to replace the upper earnings limit.

If you're self-employed, you aren't entitled to S2P. The Class 2 NICs you pay only count towards the basic state pension. You can top this up via a personal or stakeholder scheme. See Chapter 17 for more on these options.

Getting credit for your pension and other benefits

The pension credit replaces the minimum income guarantee and provides extra money from the state if you are 60 or over and on a low income. You are guaranteed to receive at least:

- ✔ £119.05 a week if you are single
- ✔ £181.70 a week between you and your partner

If you're 65 or over and have some pension savings, you'll be rewarded for making this provision. You can get up to £9.05 a week if you're single or £25.26 for you and your partner. The amount is calculated at £1 a week income for every £500 or part of £500 over £6,000 that you have in savings. So if you've saved £8,000, you'll get £4 a week pension credit.

The Pension Service has produced leaflet PC1L *Pension Credit, Do I qualify and how much could I get?*, with more details on what you can claim. This is available from your local JobCentre or social security office.

As well as pension credit, there are several other benefits available:

- ✔ **Christmas bonus:** If you get a state pension or pension credit, you also get a tax-free Christmas bonus every year.
- ✔ **Cold weather payments:** If you receive pension credit, you automatically get a cold weather payment when the average temperature is 0 degrees centigrade or below for seven consecutive days.
- ✔ **Winter fuel payments:** One-off payments of up to £200, depending on circumstances. You don't have to be receiving benefits to qualify but you must be 60 or over.
- ✔ **80+ annual payment:** If you are 80 or over and entitled to a winter fuel payment, you get an extra annual sum of up to £100, depending on circumstances.
- ✔ **Council tax and housing benefit:** If you are on a low income, you can claim council tax benefit. If you are paying rent, you can also claim housing benefit. Contact the Pension Service for more information: www.thepensionservice.gov.uk.

Supplementing the State Scheme with a Personal Pension

With the state pension declining in value relative to earnings during the past couple of decades, the Government wants everyone to save for our own retirement via a private pension. This can be an occupational or company scheme from your employer (see Chapter 16), or a personal pension or stakeholder plan (see Chapter 17).

Saving for retirement via a pension, as opposed to other investments such as property, has several advantages. I go through those benefits in the following sections.

Taking advantage of the tax breaks

The biggest selling point of private pensions is the generous tax relief on contributions:

- ✓ For **basic-rate** taxpayers (paying 20 per cent tax), every 80p you invest in your pension fund is topped up to £1 by the Government (in 2008–9).

- ✓ For **higher-rate** taxpayers (paying 40 per cent tax), every £1 that goes into your pension pot costs you 60p.

You aren't taxed on your contributions but are taxed on your pension income. Most people tend to be on a lower rate of tax in retirement, so you may have tax relief at 40 per cent on your contributions but be taxed at 20 per cent when you draw your pension.

Locking away your cash

When you've made a contribution to your pension, you won't see that money again until the age of 50 at least (and possibly much later, depending on when you retire). This ensures that you have a chance of accruing a reasonable sum of money. If, instead, you invest in equities or savings accounts, you can withdraw cash to buy a car, pay for your daughter's wedding, or go on a cruise. Without restrictions on withdrawing your pension money, you could run out of cash by the time you get to retirement age – particularly if you aren't disciplined when it comes to saving.

The whole point about pensions is that they give you an income in retirement. To do that they have to be inflexible: If you want flexibility, supplement your pension with other investments that can be cashed in when the need arises.

Pensions aren't for teenagers

While working on a national newspaper, I interviewed a mother who had taken out a stakeholder pension for each of her two children (both under the age of 5). I asked her why she considered it important to give them a headstart. She answered: 'So that they have some cash to pay their way through university.'

I then had the unfortunate task of telling her that they wouldn't be able to access the cash until they were at least 50. She was horrified; she had been so impressed by the tax breaks that she hadn't read the small print. That was the last contribution she made to their stakeholder pensions; she opened a savings account in each child's name instead.

Guaranteeing an income

A pension guarantees you an income for life. Whether you live 30 years after retirement or just three doesn't matter; when you purchase an annuity (see Chapter 18 for more on these) you get an income for as long as you live. You have no chance of running out of cash – an extremely comforting thought.

Mixing and Matching –
Alternatives to Pensions

One of the best ways of ensuring a comfortable retirement is to build up a portfolio of investments. This ensures you make the most of the tax breaks on offer via a private pension but also get flexibility from other investments. In this section I look at other investments you may want to use to save for retirement.

Investing in bricks and mortar

Property has become one of the most popular ways of saving for retirement. The growth of buy to let – whereby you let property to tenants – is seen by many as the sensible alternative to a private pension. Rocketing property prices and demand for rental accommodation mean many landlords not only enjoy an income that covers their expenses but also benefit from capital appreciation in the long term.

I discuss some of the reasons for the growth in popularity of property as a retirement planning tool in Table 15-3.

Table 15-3	Property versus Pensions
Property	**Pension**
Property is more concrete: Well, bricks and mortar, but you get my drift. You can see and touch it. It isn't going to disappear over night.	A pension is just figures on a piece of paper: Your pension may under perform so you end up with less growth than was forecast or your employer could go bust taking your final salary scheme with them.
Your children benefit: Property is easily passed on in a will.	Not so easy to pass on depending on the type of pension and whether you're retired when you die: Your beneficiaries may get the majority of your pension savings or they may not.
More liquidity: If you need cash, you can sell up. Finding a buyer may take time (depending on market conditions) but there aren't restrictions on when you sell (apart from avoiding a slump).	You have to wait until you're at least 50 to draw any money. You cannot withdraw cash before then, even in a dire emergency.
You can do what you want with it: Keep it or sell it, the choice and timing are yours.	You must buy an annuity: Up to 25 per cent of your pot can be taken as a tax-free lump sum, with the remainder used to purchase an income for life.
You get income from the rent to supplement your pension *and* capital appreciation.	You get a guaranteed income for life once you purchase your annuity: With property, the proceeds of a sale can run out.
Property is more fun: You can manage the property yourself and enjoy dealing with tenants.	There isn't much fun at all: Pensions are rather boring investments.

You don't get the same tax relief on property as you do with pensions. But you can offset your rental income against an interest-only mortgage (or the interest portion of a repayment home loan).

Managing property can be time-consuming and a lot of hassle. You also need a tidy sum of money to get started: Usually around 15 to 20 per cent of the property purchase price to put down as a deposit. You should also have enough savings to cover the mortgage for several months if you can't find suitable tenants. That's why buying the property in the right area in the first place is so important – so you don't struggle to find tenants.

Even if you can't imagine yourself managing your property on a day-to-day basis, it doesn't mean that buy to let isn't for you; you can pay a managing agent to screen tenants, collect rent, and deal with problems that arise. See *Renting Out Your Property For Dummies* for more information.

Utilising individual savings accounts

Some people use individual savings accounts (ISAs) as an alternative to saving in a pension. ISAs, like pensions, offer tax breaks, although these aren't as good as the tax breaks for pensions.

With an ISA, your returns are free of tax. You can invest in cash or equities. When saving for retirement, you should concentrate your ISA on equities so that your money can grow as quickly as possible. Cash ISAs are a waste of time because the returns aren't good enough to generate much of an income. So, unless you're extremely close to retirement and want to avoid taking on stock market risk, don't invest your ISA in cash.

You can invest up to £7,200 per person in an equity ISA each tax year (6 April to following 5 April) or £3,600 in a cash ISA.

Rather than use ISAs *instead* of a pension to save for retirement, it's worth using them *in addition*. You can cash in an ISA as and when you need extra cash so they offer more flexibility, but you won't be missing out on the tax relief you get with a pension. See Chapter 10 for more on ISAs.

Where There's a Will, the Family Know Where They Stand

While you're thinking about the future, spare a thought for what will happen after you die. It can be devastating for your loved ones if you haven't left a will and die *intestate*. There is also a chance that your wishes won't be carried out.

Your heirs are also likely to end up paying more inheritance tax than they would have done if you'd written a will (see the following section 'Protecting your estate from an unnecessary tax bill'). Also, sorting out the financial affairs of people who die intestate takes much longer.

Delaying writing a will is unwise

To encourage people to start a pension is hard, but persuading them to think about death is even more difficult. Yet, for your family's sake, writing a will is crucial. If you don't, your assets are divided according to intestacy rules, which aim to be fair to all beneficiaries. But your wishes may have been different: Perhaps you would like to leave money to charity, for example. This won't happen if you die intestate.

Getting down to business

Writing a will can be simple. If your affairs are straightforward, you can do it yourself with a will-writing kit from a stationer's, which costs about £10. But if your affairs are more complicated, or maybe just for peace of mind, consult a solicitor or specialist will-writing agency.

Follow these several steps for making a will:

1. **Name two people as executors.**

   The *executors* deal with your affairs after you die, assembling your property, obtaining probate from the courts, paying any inheritance tax, and distributing your assets in line with your will. You should opt for two executors in case one of them dies before you do. You can appoint your solicitor to act as executor but there will be a charge. Your executors may also be beneficiaries.

2. **Be specific.**

   Make a list of all your possessions and leave no doubt as to who gets what.

3. **Sign the will.**

   Get two people to witness your signature. The witnesses must not be beneficiaries nor have spouses who benefit from your will. You don't have to show them the contents of your will, they just have to see you sign it, then sign it themselves.

4. **Keep it somewhere safe.**

   Inform your executors where you stash your will. You could leave it with your bank or solicitor but there is a charge. Alternatively, you can keep it at the local probate registry for £15 (see the Yellow Pages for details of the one nearest to you).

5. Review your will every few years.

If you remarry, your will is invalid so you should make a new one. Otherwise, your new spouse will automatically inherit your estate and children from a previous relationship won't get a look-in.

Protecting Your Estate from an Unnecessary Tax Bill

While you're writing your will, think about inheritance tax (IHT) as you can include provisions to mitigate against it. IHT is paid after your death on any belongings above the *nil-rate band* – £312,000 for the 2008–9 tax year. If the total value of your cash, investments, property, and belongings is less than the nil-rate band, your heirs don't pay IHT. But if the value exceeds this, IHT is charged at 40 per cent on the surplus.

IHT is payable before your beneficiaries can gain probate, although if it is due on land, property, or shares in a family firm (which isn't listed on the stock exchange), it can be paid in 10 annual instalments.

Price inflation in bricks and mortar means IHT is no longer only for the super-rich. There are ways of minimising your IHT liability – completely legitimately. Assets passed between husband and wife are not liable for IHT, whether the gift is made during life or after death.

Changes to IHT rules mean that married couples can combine their individual £300,000 allowances. This means that most families will avoid paying any IHT on the first £600,000 of the estate.

You can also give away a certain amount tax-free:

- ✔ Up to £3,000 a year to anyone you like.

- ✔ No more than £250 a year to as many people as you wish.

- ✔ *Regular* amounts from income, as long as you leave a sufficient amount to maintain your standard of living.

- ✔ Up to £5,000 to your son or daughter on marriage. Grandparents can give up to £2,500 and other relatives £1,000.

✔ Potentially exempt transfers: If you live for seven years after making a gift, it becomes wholly exempt from IHT. If you die before then, IHT may be payable as these gifts are set against your nil-rate band. There is taper relief depending on how long you live after making the gift: If you live three years, for example, IHT is payable at 80 per cent of the full rate (40 per cent), which is 32 per cent.

✔ Setting up a trust enables you to transfer assets out of your estate while still maintaining a degree of control over them. Most people opt for a *discretionary* trust as this gives the trustee absolute discretion over who benefits from the assets from among a number of beneficiaries you specify when setting it up. Gifts into these vehicles are taxable at 20 per cent if they exceed your nil-rate band.

Tax planning can be complicated so seek professional advice from a tax specialist, particularly if you think a trust might be best for you.

Chapter 16

Getting to Grips with Company Pensions

In This Chapter

▶ Realising the benefits of a company pension

▶ Understanding the various types of pension

▶ Knowing what your contribution limits are

▶ Making moving jobs work with your company pension

*A*long with a monthly salary and private health cover, many employers offer some form of pension plan to provide employees with retirement income on top of the basic state pension. Indeed, if a company employs five or more people, providing a pension scheme is compulsory, although making contributions into the scheme isn't.

In this chapter I explain the different types of pension available via the workplace to help you decide whether you should join your employer's scheme. I also guide you through the process of making extra contributions to ensure you build up a big enough pension to get the retirement you're hoping for.

Being Smart by Joining the Company Scheme

When you start a new job, your employer should give you details about any pension scheme you are eligible to join. You may be invited to join the company scheme straight away or may have to work a probationary period of six months or a year before you are allowed to do so.

If you're allowed to join the company pension scheme only after you've worked there for a certain length of time, make a note in your diary of when you're eligible to join and ensure you sign up at that point, if it's in your interest to do so.

Joining the company pension has several advantages, particularly if your employer contributes money to your retirement fund. Your employer may also cover the running costs of the scheme, saving you money. There is an annual management fee, for example, to cover the cost of the manager investing your pension money. And if you have to retire early as a result of ill health, you should be able to start drawing your pension, providing you with useful income.

I discuss these major benefits in more detail in the following subsections.

Benefiting from employer contributions

If your employer offers an *occupational scheme*, he has to make a contribution to your pension pot. From your perspective, this is getting something for nothing. It also means that you should end up with a much bigger pension pot than you would've done if only you contributed to it. Some occupational schemes require no contribution from you, while others enable you and your employer to contribute to them.

If your employer doesn't offer an occupational scheme, he may instead offer a *group personal pension* (GPP) or *stakeholder scheme*. These schemes work slightly differently to an occupational pension: The main thing to remember is that your employer doesn't have to contribute to your pension pot if he offers a GPP or stakeholder scheme (see 'Exploring the types of workplace pensions' later in this chapter for more details on these schemes).

If a prospective employer offers an occupational pension scheme, make sure you ask at interview what percentage of your salary the employer contribution is. Prior to 6 April 2006, the maximum amount that could be invested in your pension was 15 per cent of your annual salary – whether you invested this or your employer did. Your employer may contribute a set percentage of your salary, or he may match your contributions each month. From 6 April 2006, restrictions on contributions were removed but tax relief is restricted to the annual allowance. You can obtain tax relief on your contributions up to £3,600 or 100 per cent of your earnings if greater. The annual allowance in 2008–9 is £235,000.

You don't *have* to join your occupational scheme, and it may not be suitable for you, depending on your personal circumstances, such as your working patterns, and existing pension arrangements. If you aren't planning on staying with the company for longer than a couple of years, say, you might decide not to join the company pension: If you leave within two years your contributions are refunded to you. (See 'Changing jobs – and your pension' later in this chapter for more information.) In such a situation you may be better off taking out a personal pension that you can take with you when you move jobs.

Ask your employer for details of the scheme and check it out carefully when considering your pension options. But while membership is voluntary, it is nearly always worth joining. Many employers contribute more to their employees' occupational schemes than the employees do themselves.

Some employers run schemes in which their employees don't have to make any payments at all. This can be useful if you're on a low salary and simply can't afford to contribute at this point. Joining the scheme is still worthwhile because your employer's contributions will build up in the meantime and you can start contributing when you get a pay rise, for example. There is no point in delaying joining until you can afford to contribute as well.

Your contribution is shown on your monthly pay slip. At the end of each tax year you should receive an annual statement detailing how much has been invested in your pension, what share of the fund this has bought, and how much it is worth. The statement should also provide a projection of how much you stand to retire on if you continue making contributions at that amount and retire at state retirement age.

Protecting your family with life cover

Rather depressingly, this is also known as *death in service benefit*, but then that is exactly what it is. If you die at any time while you're employed by the company providing your occupational scheme, your beneficiary receives a lump sum payout. The value of the lump sum is normally calculated as a multiple of your final earnings and can be paid free of tax if it is less than your available lifetime allowance.

The beneficiary is either a person nominated by you or selected by the trustees of the occupational scheme. Make sure that you nominate somebody to be your beneficiary; you usually receive a form enabling you to do this from the administrator of the scheme. But no matter whether you nominate someone or not, the trustees have the final say as to who receives the money. There are two reasons for this:

- ✓ The money is not technically your property on your death so is not liable for inheritance tax.

- ✓ The trustees can take other circumstances into account. For example, suppose you have not changed your beneficiary for 20 years. During that time you got divorced and had children with someone else, yet your ex-wife is still named as beneficiary. The trustees are likely to determine that your second family has a greater need and award them the death benefit. Also, if you've asked for something that the trustees deem unreasonable, they can veto it.

To ensure your wishes are followed, keep your nomination form up to date. If your circumstances change – and you get married or have children, for example – contact your pension administrator to complete a new nomination form.

Your beneficiaries are no longer entitled to this death benefit when you retire.

Providing pensions for surviving partners

If you die while employed your occupational scheme usually pays out a pension to your husband or wife (and in some cases to your partner if you're not married). The level of pension payable is set by the rules of the scheme: It is usually half your pension but may be as much as two-thirds.

Money purchase schemes tend to give only a pension bought out of the fund that has built up for the member by the time they die, which could be very small if you die young.

If you die after you retire, your husband or wife should still receive a pension. This is usually no more than half of your pension.

Check whether the death benefits offered by your pension, both on life cover and a pension for your spouse, are reasonable to protect those who are left behind. If not, you should raise this with your pension administrator or consider making alternative arrangements.

Exploring the Types of Workplace Pensions

Occupational pension schemes, also known as *company schemes*, are set up by employers for the benefit of their employees to provide them with an income in retirement. Your employer and/or you invest cash in this fund, which is spread across a variety of assets such as shares and property. Over a number of years, this money builds up and forms your pension pot, which you receive as income in addition to the basic state pension when you retire.

If your employer offers an occupational pension scheme, he must contribute to your pension pot on a monthly basis. In most instances you will also contribute to the scheme, but not all occupational pensions demand that you do. The size of the employer's contribution varies but the total contribution (by you and your employer) must not exceed your annual allowance (£235,000 in 2008–9).

Some employers let you join the company pension as soon as you join the workforce, while others demand that you serve a probationary period first. Find out from your employer whether it's possible to join the scheme at a later date.

The two main types of occupational or company pension scheme are *final salary* or *money purchase*. With the former you are offered a pension as a proportion of your earnings on retirement, but because the employer takes on all the investment risk, they are becoming less popular. As a result, when you start a new job you're far more likely to be invited to join a money purchase scheme. With these schemes, the contribution you make is fixed but the pension you end up with depends on how the investment fares over the years your money is invested. You can also be offered a hybrid or mixture of the two.

Your employer may offer an occupational pension but it is legally required to have a board of trustees to run the scheme: Your employer is not allowed to do this himself. However, if you work in the public sector, for the civil service or the NHS, for example, your pension is a *statutory* scheme run according to Acts of Parliament rather than trustees.

If you're a member of an occupational scheme, you may not be making the maximum contributions you could be. If you have cash to spare you may be able to increase your contributions to the occupational scheme: Ask your employer whether this is possible. If not, you can top up your pension via additional voluntary contributions (AVCs) or a stakeholder scheme. If you can afford to do so, you can contribute to all three types of pension as long as you don't exceed the annual allowance of £235,000 in 2008–9.

You can have a stakeholder pension as well as being a member of an occupational scheme as long as you are not a controlling director of your company and earn no more than £30,000 a year. You're allowed to invest up to £3,600 a year in a stakeholder plan on top of contributions to your occupational scheme – as long as you don't exceed the annual allowance. (For more on AVCs, check out 'Making additional contributions' later in this chapter.)

Figuring out final salary schemes

Final salary pension schemes are also known as *salary-related* or *defined benefit* schemes because you are promised a certain pension income once you retire. Your pension will be based on your *final pensionable salary*. The definition of this varies between schemes: Some base it on your income in the last year before retirement; others average the last three years' income, and may include overtime and bonuses in this or not. Check the scheme details to find out which applies. Your employer (and sometimes you) makes contributions to a pension fund. The amount you receive in retirement rests on three factors:

- The **length of your pensionable service,** otherwise known as the amount of time you belong to the pension scheme as an employee of the company.

- Your **earnings just before retirement** or when you leave the scheme or final pensionable salary. Your final pensionable earnings may be an average of your earnings over the past two or three years before retirement, or years further back if your earnings dropped just before retirement.

- The scheme's **accrual rate,** which is the proportion of salary that you get for each year you worked for your employer. For example, if the scheme has an accrual rate of 60, you receive 1/60 of your final pensionable salary (see previous bullet point) for each year you worked for the company. In this example, if you worked for the company for 20 years and your pensionable salary was £25,000, your pension would be £8,333 a year (20 years multiplied by £25,000 final salary divided by an accrual rate of 60).

Final salary pensions must also be protected against inflation of up to 5 per cent a year or the annual increase in the Retail Price Index – whichever is lower. This starts from the date you leave the scheme up until retirement.

Traditionally, most employers offered final salary schemes so if you've been with a company for a while, you may be lucky enough to have one.

 When you retire, most final salary schemes give you the option of taking part of your pension as a tax-free lump sum, though how big this lump sum can be is limited. Under HM Revenue & Customs rules, you can take 3/80 of your final earnings for each year of service up to a maximum of 40 years. So if your final earnings were £50,000 per annum and you worked for the company for 30 years, you could take a lump sum of £56,250 (3/80 of £50,000 final salary multiplied by 30 years). Alternatively, your scheme may let you take a lump sum that is two and a quarter times your annual pension before this amount is subtracted.

 If you move jobs frequently, signing on for a final salary scheme at an early employer may not be the best plan for you. If you leave the scheme before you retire, your pension benefits are based on completed service up to the point of leaving. These will be increased to take account of inflation up to your retirement age. But a salary-related pension derived from a short period of service early on in your career, when you weren't earning much money, may not grow as much as it would've done if you'd invested your cash in a good money purchase scheme. Money purchase schemes are also easier to switch from employer to employer (see 'Making the most of a money purchase scheme' later in this chapter).

Mourning the demise of the final salary pension

The granddaddy of all pension schemes, the final salary plan is a generous arrangement, which is why employers are abandoning it in droves. According to a report from pensions consultants Towers Perrin, barely a quarter of all companies offer final salary pensions to new staff compared to 58 per cent in 2002.

This decline is not really surprising, as final salary schemes are extremely expensive for employers who take on all the investment risk and have to fulfil the guarantee element of the scheme no matter how poorly the markets perform. If stock markets don't perform well, as was the case between 2000 and 2004, employers have to make up a large shortfall between the pensions they are obligated to provide and the low investment return they received.

As well as closing final salary schemes to new entrants, some employers have frozen them so existing members can no longer build up further pension rights.

If you're lucky enough to be offered a final salary scheme snap it up straight away – before your employer has a chance to change his mind!

Final salary schemes tend to be the best sort of pension. But if you move jobs a lot, work on short-term contracts, or have gaps in your employment, they may not be the best option for you. A good personal pension that you can take from job to job regardless may be more suitable. Seek independent advice from a pensions specialist and see Chapter 17 for more on these.

Making the most of a money purchase scheme

Money purchase schemes are also referred to as *defined contribution* schemes. Generally, both you and your employer contribute to your pension plan under a *money purchase scheme*. Often the employer matches your contributions, but in other schemes the employee contributes much more than the employer or makes no contributions at all. The contributions are invested in a range of different investment funds, with most employers offering a choice of equities, bonds, property, and cash.

How much risk you're prepared to take on and your age are factors to consider when deciding where to invest your pension. You may also have personal preferences, such as wanting to invest in ethical funds, for example. Someone in their 20s or 30s, for example, can afford to take on a lot more risk by investing in company shares than someone in their 40s or 50s because the younger person has more time to make up any losses. As you get closer to retirement, switching your money into less risky investments, such as government bonds or cash, makes sense. These produce lower returns than company shares but there is also virtually no chance of losing your money, which is important as you come closer to relying on the income from your pension. If you incur losses at this stage, you might not have any time to make these up again before retirement.

If you can't decide where to invest your pension, or don't want the responsibility of choosing, most schemes have a *default* option. This makes the investment decisions on your behalf. Initially, your contributions will be invested in riskier investments, shifting to safer havens with lower returns as you move closer to retirement.

The aim of a money purchase scheme is to build up an individual pot of money, which you then use to buy an annuity. The way an *annuity* works is that you give your pension pot to an insurance company that in return gives you a guaranteed income for the rest of your life. The amount you receive in retirement depends on several factors:

✔ The **amount of money paid into the scheme** by you and your employer. Generally speaking, the longer your payments are invested, the larger your pension will be when you retire.

> ✔ The **performance of the investment funds** your cash is invested in.
>
> ✔ The **annuity rate** when you retire. The annuity rate is calculated according to how long the provider reckons you will live in retirement: In other words, how many years you will be receiving a pension for. It may also make payments to your husband or wife if you die first. Chapter 15 has more information on annuities.

At retirement, you may be able to receive part of your pension pot as a tax-free lump sum, with the rest purchasing an annuity. If you have a very large pension fund – at least £100,000 – you can defer purchasing an annuity until the age of 75 and drawdown a limited but regular income on the fund instead. Most pension schemes provide an *open market option* so you don't have to take the annuity offered by your pension provider and can instead shop around for the best rate on the market. This is fairly straightforward and nearly always results in a better price for your annuity so it's worth doing this. (See Chapter 17 for more details on shopping around for annuities.)

The disadvantage of a money purchase scheme is that you have no idea how big a pension you're going to get. The annual projection you receive from your pension provider is just a forecast, not a guarantee. You have to make sure you put enough aside, yet you can have no idea how your investments will perform. There is an element of pot luck involved.

Going with a group personal pension or stakeholder scheme

An employer unable or unwilling to make the pension contributions required by occupational pension schemes may still offer a group personal pension or stakeholder scheme, which is cheaper for the employer to run.

Investing with a group

The *group personal pension (GPP)* is a type of personal pension that is often mistaken for an occupational scheme. It is organised by your employer with a single life insurance company. Your employer chooses the company and if you sign up to the GPP, you have a personal pension with that provider. The advantage of signing up to a personal pension via a GPP is that your employer may be able to negotiate lower charges with the provider than you would have been able to on your own. Your employer may also contribute to your scheme as well, although he is not obligated to. Contributions are limited according to a maximum amount per annum (£235,000 in 2008–9) (see 'Looking at limits on your pension' later in this chapter). When you retire, you can take up to a quarter of your pension pot as a tax-free lump sum, using the remainder to purchase an annuity by the age of 75.

A GPP offers no guarantee as to how large your pension will be. Your money is invested in equities, bonds, cash, and property, and you end up with a pension depending on how much you contribute, how well the investment performs, and the annuity rate when you retire. See 'Making the most of a money purchase scheme' earlier in this chapter for more on annuities.

Claiming a stake in your workplace

Many employers have replaced GPPs with stakeholder pensions because they have guaranteed low charges. Stakeholder pensions have been around only since April 2001 and most people between 0 and 75 may take one out. Employers with five or more employees are required by law to offer this type of pension if they don't have some alternative form of pension provision. Stakeholder pensions are straightforward, uncomplicated, and designed to encourage those who don't contribute to a personal pension to start doing so.

Stakeholder pensions have a number of advantages for you, the employee:

- ✔ **Low cost:** They have an annual management charge of a maximum of 1.5 per cent for the first ten years, reverting to 1 per cent after this time, and no other fees

- ✔ **Easy access:** You can invest just £20 a month and don't have to make regular payments

Stakeholder pensions have not been the big success the Government had hoped because while many employers are obliged to offer them, they aren't forced to contribute to their schemes. As a result, many don't bother. And this means there are few incentives for employees to join the scheme, resulting in plenty of *empty shells* – stakeholder pension schemes in the workplace with no members at all – across the country.

Looking at Limits on Your Pension

Although it may be tempting to try and build up the biggest pension possible to ensure a comfortable retirement, HM Revenue & Customs imposes a maximum limit on the amount of pension contributions that will attract tax relief. The main limit to bear in mind is the annual lifetime limit (see the following 'Bumping into the contribution ceiling' section for more details).

As a member of a money purchase scheme you receive a yearly illustration of the amount of pension you might receive when you retire. Although this is only a projection and not guaranteed – unlike with a final salary scheme – you should check that you are happy with this level of income. If you aren't you need to think about increasing your contributions – if you can afford to do so. HM Revenue & Customs also limits the contributions you can make to your pension, which has an effect on the size of your final payout. I talk about these limits in the following sections.

Bumping into the contribution ceiling

The more you invest in your pension now, the greater the amount you'll have to retire on. But you must remember the statutory lifetime allowance for the maximum amount payable from pension schemes, which is treated as tax-privileged. In 2008–9 this allowance is £1.65 million. Table 16-1 shows increases in the lifetime allowance for future years.

Table 16-1	Lifetime Allowance Limits
Tax Year	*Lifetime Allowance*
2007–8	£1.6 million
2008–9	£1.65 million
2009–10	£1.75 million
2010–11	£1.8 million

Funds in excess of the lifetime allowance are subject to a 25 per cent charge, so make sure you don't invest more than the lifetime allowance.

You also need to consider the annual allowance. Table 16-2 shows the annual limits for coming tax years. If you and/or your employer contribute more than the annual allowance to your pension fund, you don't qualify for any tax relief on the excess.

Table 16-2	Annual Allowance Limits
Tax Year	*Annual Allowance*
2007–8	£225,000
2008–9	£235,000
2009–10	£245,000
2010–11	£255,000

After 2011, the system will be subject to further review. If the value of your pension benefits from all sources exceeds the lifetime allowance, you'll have to pay a tax charge.

The rules mean you can contribute up to 100 per cent of your salary to your pension scheme each year, subject to an overall maximum of £235,000 in 2008–9.

Getting tax relief

The big attraction of pensions is that you get tax relief on any payments you make, up to a set limit. The amount of tax relief you get depends on how much tax you usually pay:

- ✔ For a basic-rate taxpayer paying tax at 20 per cent (based on the tax year 2008–9), every time you make a payment into your pension the Government tops this up by 20 per cent. So if you invest £80 into your pension, this is topped up to £100

- ✔ For a higher-rate taxpayer who pays income tax at 40 per cent, every £100 that goes into your pension costs you £60 (based on the same tax year), with the Government paying the other £40. Higher-rate taxpayers must claim back this additional 20 per cent of tax relief on their contributions via their tax return

To find out how much tax relief you get, go to HM Revenue & Customs' website (www.hmrc.gov.uk).

Increasing your contributions

Review your pension on a regular basis to ensure it is on track to provide enough cash for you in retirement. Few people invest as much as the maximum annual allowance into their pension. Your employer may allow you to increase contributions to your scheme but if not, other ways of boosting your retirement income exist, via a stakeholder pension, additional voluntary contributions (AVCs), or freestanding AVCs (FSAVCs).

Both AVCs and FSAVCs are used to boost your pension (and the size of annuity you can purchase). No portion of these can be taken as a tax-free lump sum. I explain AVCs and FSAVCs in more detail in the following sections.

Making additional contributions

If you decide to increase your contributions because your annual pension statement shows that your predicted pension income isn't enough to meet your needs or because you have received a pay rise, your employer has to arrange for you to make *additional voluntary contributions* (AVCs). You make AVCs via a separate scheme run by your employer (which all occupational schemes must offer). This additional scheme is likely to be a money purchase scheme (explained in the 'Making the most of a money purchase scheme' section earlier in this chapter) and your employer may pay all the administration costs.

Contributions made to AVCs enjoy the same tax concessions as contributions to your main scheme. However, while AVCs enable you to increase your contributions, you still can't invest a total exceeding your annual allowance of £235,000 (adding your AVCs to your regular pension contributions).

Your pension administrator or employer should be able to provide details of AVCs. Some schemes impose their own restrictions on how much you can pay in and when you can do this, so check the small print. Your choice of investment is also limited to that offered by the company scheme.

Opting for a freestanding plan

You don't have to make additional contributions to your workplace scheme: You can make these to another scheme provider. These separate plans are called *freestanding additional voluntary contributions* (FSAVCs) and have the same aim of boosting your retirement income. The advantage of using an FSAVC over an AVC is that you can choose where your funds are invested.

Charges for FSAVCs tend to be considerably higher than AVCs through your own occupational scheme – eating up as much as 20 per cent of your contributions. This is because FSAVCs are sold by independent providers, such as insurance companies or building societies, whereas your employer may be able to negotiate a low rate for in-house AVCs and be prepared to pay this cost. The in-house AVC is therefore likely to offer you better value for money, but if it is a poor-quality scheme you may want to consider an FSAVC and swallow the extra costs.

Contracting In or Out of the State Second Pension

When you join an occupational pension scheme, you may be asked whether you want to contract in or contract out of the State Second Pension (S2P) scheme. This is the additional state pension, which you may get in retirement as well as the basic state pension. S2P is based on your earnings above a certain level and your National Insurance Contributions (NICs). You are entitled to S2P unless you have contracted out. For an explanation of whether you should contract in or out, read on:

- ✔ If you **contract in,** you pay the full amount of National Insurance Contributions (NICs). When you retire you receive the basic state pension (which is unaffected whether you contract in or out), an occupational pension, and the S2P as well.

- ✔ If you **contract out,** you give up some or all of the S2P and rely on your occupational pension instead. You and your employer pay lower NICs.

- ✔ The shortfall between what you would pay if you contracted in and what you actually pay is the *rebate*. The rebate is supposed to compensate for the S2P you are giving up. The Government pays this into your occupational scheme in the autumn following the end of the tax year. When you retire you get the basic state pension plus your occupational scheme, which should be bigger than it would have been if you'd contracted in. Most members of occupational pension schemes contract out of S2P, but whether you're better off contracting out or not depends on your personal circumstances.

In a money purchase scheme the decision about opting out or not is up to you; with final salary schemes, it is usually up to your employer to decide. If the scheme is contracted out, you have no choice in the matter. If your employer's scheme is contracted in to S2P, however, you can contract out if you wish.

Traditionally, the decision to opt in or out largely depended on your age and your attitude to risk. Younger employees tended to contract out because the feeling was that over the long term they would be better off investing in the stock market, rather than relying on the Government to provide part of their pension income.

The rebate you get from contracting out depends on your age: The older you are, the more money is paid into your pension scheme from the National Insurance Fund.

Ask your pension administrator for advice as to whether you should be contracted in or out of the S2P. And after you make a decision, review it on an annual basis to see whether it is still the right choice for your circumstances. You can change your mind at a later date if you wish.

For an occupational scheme to be contracted out, it must meet certain conditions imposed by HM Revenue & Customs. For more details on these, contact the Pension Service. Contact 0845 6060265 or check out the Web site at www.thepensionservice.gov.uk.

Changing Jobs – And Your Pension

Employers pay into occupational pensions belonging only to their employees, so when you leave to work for someone else you can no longer contribute to your former employer's pension scheme and he will no longer contribute on your behalf. You may be able to transfer your pension to your new workplace and carry on contributing to it. However, you'll probably have to pay a fee for transferring and it might not be in your best interests to do so. Seek advice from a pensions specialist before making your decision. You may have to pay for this advice. The best way of finding a good independent adviser is through personal recommendation; if you don't have one, contact IFA Promotion (IFAP) on 0800 085 3250 or www.unbiased.co.uk, for details of IFAs in your area.

When you change jobs, your employer should give you an up-to-date statement of the value of your pension, known as the *transfer value*. This cash lump sum can be paid on your behalf into another occupational, stakeholder, or personal pension plan. The one you choose will depend on your circumstances: If you're moving to another job and an occupational pension is available, this is the best bet. Otherwise, check out a stakeholder or personal pension (Chapter 17 has more information on these).

If you were in a money purchase scheme this transfer value reflects the value of your fund, but if you were in a final salary scheme it reflects the value of the fixed benefits provided under the scheme. This is often 1/60 or 1/80 of the pensionable salary you were earning at the time you left the company. If you had a final salary scheme with your old employer and your new employer is offering only a money purchase scheme, it may not be worth transferring. This is because you give up the promise of a fixed level of pension income. Instead, your pension will depend on how well the invested money grows.

The transfer value doesn't take into account discretionary benefits that the scheme or your employer may choose to give you but is not obliged to provide. These could include discretionary increases to your pension once you retire, for example. If you transfer your pension to your new employer or a personal pension scheme, you may lose these benefits. Consider carefully what you could lose out on if you transfer your pension.

You may find that you aren't allowed to transfer your pension to another provider. If this is the case, you'll be told what pension benefits your money entitles you to. Or you can leave the amount you have in your present scheme and start a new one with your new employer.

If you've worked for your employer for less than two years, you'll normally receive back your contributions but not your employer's, less the tax relief you benefited from on those contributions. You are not obliged to put this cash into another pension (indeed, the limits on the amount you can invest in any one tax year may prevent you doing so) but bear in mind that you've lost some pension provision. For example, if you worked for your ex-employer for 18 months and have your contributions returned when you leave that employment, you'll be 18 months behind on your pension planning.

Chapter 17

Examining Personal Pensions and Stakeholder Schemes

In This Chapter
▶ Looking at personal pensions
▶ Investing in stakeholder schemes
▶ Deciding on the right scheme
▶ Paying into your scheme
▶ Drawing from your pension
▶ Figuring out self-invested personal pensions

A personal pension – of which stakeholder schemes are one type – is the alternative to an occupational pension when it comes to utilising the tax breaks available to you in saving for retirement.

A personal pension is more flexible than an occupational scheme because you can take it from job to job. You can pay into it when you're out of work or if you're self-employed. You can take out a personal pension even if you're employed full-time.

This chapter guides you through the maze of personal pensions so that you can decide whether one of these is the product for you.

Understanding How Personal Pensions Work

A *personal pension*, sometimes referred to as a *private pension*, is a scheme you set up yourself – rather than through an employer. You have a choice of all the personal pension schemes on the market, rather than having to opt for one because your employer happened to choose it. You make all the contributions yourself however; in most instances your employer doesn't make a contribution on your behalf.

A personal pension provides a retirement income on top of your state pension. As the state pension doesn't provide a decent retirement on its own (see Chapter 15 for more details) your aim should be to generate as much supplementary income as possible, bearing in mind that there are limits as to how much you can invest in a personal pension (see 'Making contributions' later in this chapter). Having a personal pension doesn't affect your entitlement to the state pension.

The personal pension process works something like this:

1. **Buy a personal pension or have one bought for you.**

   You can start a personal pension at any age between birth and 75, but if you already belong to an occupational scheme, you may face restrictions. These relate to the amount you can contribute. Ask the provider of your workplace pension for more details. Your parents can start a stakeholder pension on your behalf if you're under the age of 18 or you can start a pension for a lower-earning spouse.

2. **Make contributions to your pension provider.**

   How much and how often you contribute depend on the type of pension scheme. See the upcoming 'Sticking to the limits' section for more on this topic.

   Your employer may also contribute to your personal pension (see Chapter 16 for more details).

3. **Pay charges as necessary.**

   Set-up fees are usually payable with personal pensions, as is an annual management fee. These fees vary between providers, so shop around to ensure you aren't paying over the odds. Stakeholder pensions have no initial charge and a maximum annual fee of 1.5 per cent, reducing to 1 per cent after ten years.

4. **Trust that your money is invested wisely and watch your fund build up.**

   Because personal pensions are money purchase schemes (as opposed to final salary: See Chapter 16 for more on these) the amount you retire on depends on a number of factors (see 'Reap the benefits of your investment' in the next section). Unlike final-salary schemes where you're guaranteed to receive a set proportion of your salary in retirement, with a money purchase scheme no such guarantees exist, with you taking on all of the investment risk.

5. **Reap the benefits of your investment.**

   See the 'Receiving your pension' section for details on when and how you can draw your pension.

   The pension you receive depends on:

   - The amount you pay in over the years.

   - How well the invested cash performs.

   - Charges made by the provider for running the scheme.

   - The annuity rate on retirement (see Chapter 18 for more on this).

Figuring Out How Stakeholder Schemes Enter the Equation

Stakeholder pensions are a type of personal pension. They are intended to be basic, straightforward products that are fully transparent with no hidden costs or expensive charges.

Stakeholder plans were introduced in April 2001 as an alternative to the old-fashioned, incomprehensible, inflexible, and expensive schemes that prevailed until then. Stakeholder plans are designed to make saving for retirement much easier; they are primarily aimed at those on low incomes who don't belong to an occupational pension. Stakeholder pensions offer several benefits:

✔ **They have low charges.** The maximum annual charge is 1.5 per cent of your pension fund per year (for the first ten years before reverting to 1 per cent per annum), with no initial charge or other set-up fees. You can switch your stakeholder to another provider without restriction or penalty. The provider may charge extra for additional services, such as advising you on your fund, but such services are optional.

✔ **They are easily accessible.** By law, the minimum investment amount can be no more than £20, with some providers imposing no minimum amount at all. You are not required to invest every month: You can stop and re-start contributions as, and when, you can afford to do so. There are no penalties for doing this, but if you don't invest significantly more than the minimum amount you won't be able to build up a decent pension pot.

✔ **They are easy to understand.** Pensions tend to be complicated beasts, but stakeholder schemes are far more straightforward than most.

Stakeholder pensions have succeeded in bringing down charges on pensions generally. Because stakeholder providers can't charge more than 1.5 per cent of the fund's value per year for the first ten years for administering the scheme, providers of the old-style, pricier pensions are being forced to reduce their costs or risk being priced out of business. Make sure you don't pay more than 1.5 per cent a year in charges.

If you're considering a personal pension, you may as well opt for a stakeholder as charges are usually much lower than on non-stakeholder plans. However, there may be a case for taking out a non-stakeholder if the charges aren't much more than 1.5 per cent per annum and it is invested in a wider range of funds.

The cost of your pension isn't the be-all and end-all – performance is more important – but the charges eat into your investment returns. Avoid paying more than is absolutely necessary. However, don't pick the cheapest stakeholder plan just for the sake of it: It may have particularly low charges because it invests in tracker funds, which simply follow a stock market index and are unlikely to produce the best returns. Check to see exactly what you're investing in before taking the plunge. You can compare the charges imposed by pension providers on the Financial Services Authority's website (www.fsa.gov.uk).

Choosing the Best Scheme for You

You hope to contribute to your pension for many years to come, so picking the right scheme is vital. Your choice may make the difference between retiring on a decent income or on a much poorer one. You may be able to switch providers if you aren't happy with your plan's performance, but this may cost you (unless you have a stakeholder plan).

If you opt for a group personal pension or stakeholder provided by your employer, she chooses the provider, you don't have a say; but if you take out a personal pension yourself, you choose.

Even if your employer offers a pension scheme, you may decide to do your own thing with a personal pension. Your employer's occupational scheme may not be suitable for you if you're pretty certain you'll move jobs in less than two years or you're on a short-term contract so don't qualify to join. If your employer doesn't offer an occupational scheme and doesn't contribute to a stakeholder or group personal pension on your behalf, a personal pension might be a better way of supplementing the basic state pension in retirement.

Compare pension plans by asking providers for their *key features document*, which includes a breakdown of charges and how these affect your pension. This document also offers a projection of what you should receive in retirement so you can decide which plan is more likely to perform better. Providers must offer prospective policyholders their key features document.

Bear in mind the pension provider's reputation and past results. While these are no guarantee of future performance, a fund that has performed consistently well over the years is likely to be a better option than one that has done consistently badly. And make sure you pay attention to the penalties for changing schemes, in case you find yourself having to do this.

Searching for sources

You can buy a personal pension from an insurance company, high-street bank, other big financial institution, or retailer, such as a supermarket. The easiest way of finding information about the range of pensions available is to log onto the Internet, where you'll be able to do a search on various providers' websites to check the details of each pension scheme. You should also consult an independent financial adviser who can recommend the right pension for your circumstances: Unless you really understand what you're doing, this may be too big a decision to make on your own.

Some employers offer a personal pension scheme through the workplace: either a stakeholder scheme or group personal pension (GPP). Your employer chooses the provider and deducts your contributions from your pay packet, but otherwise these operate in the same way as a personal pension. Chapter 16 deals with company pensions in more detail but it is worth reiterating the benefits of a personal pension via this source:

- ✔ Your employer may contribute to your pension (although she is not obliged to do so). If she does, your fund will build up more quickly and you'll retire on a bigger pension.

- ✔ Charges for running the scheme are usually paid by your employer. Even if she doesn't foot the bill, she should be able to use her purchasing power to negotiate lower charges.

- ✔ Pensions advice should be available. With scores of employees signed up to a GPP or employer-designated stakeholder scheme, your employer may ask a financial adviser to visit the workplace and talk you through what's on offer. If you take out a personal pension yourself and require advice, you'll have to pay for it (see 'Seeking advice' later in this chapter).

However, there are downsides to a personal pension through the workplace if you quit your job or are made redundant:

- ✔ If your employer was making contributions to your GPP or stakeholder, she is likely to stop doing so. However, you can continue contributing to your scheme yourself and should consider increasing your contributions to cover the shortfall left by the cessation of your employer's contributions.

- ✔ You may have to foot the bill for belonging to a fund after you leave the company. Charges vary according to the pension provider but you may have to pay an annual fee. You may have to increase your contributions accordingly to ensure the same amount of cash goes into your fund each month.

Seeking advice

You can buy a pension in two ways: direct from the provider or via an intermediary, usually an independent financial adviser (IFA). If you know what you want, buying direct from the provider cuts costs as you don't have to pay for advice and may be able to negotiate lower charges.

However, if you aren't sure, you should seek impartial advice. Any old IFA won't do, however: You need one who specialises in pensions. You may have a perfectly good adviser you use most of the time, but you need someone who knows this specialist subject inside out.

You may have to pay a fee for this advice or your adviser will receive commission from the pension provider you end up signing up with. If you're paying a fee, you'll be told at the initial consultation how much the advice will cost. With commission, you should also be told how much your adviser is earning for recommending a particular product.

You may prefer to use a fee-based IFA to ensure that she is completely independent and supplying the best advice for you – rather than recommending a product because it pays the most commission.

If you can't afford financial advice, at least shop around for the best pension for you. Ask the provider if you don't understand the key features document and compare several deals to ensure you find the best one. Take a look at the Pension Service website, part of the Department of Work and Pensions at www.thepensionservice. gov.uk, as this has plenty of advice to bear in mind when making your decision.

To find an IFA specialising in pensions, contact IFA Promotion at www.unbiased.co.uk.

Deciding where to invest

Choosing the pension itself is just the beginning: Many providers also let you choose where your money is invested. However, not all providers offer this, so if making this choice is important to you, shop around for a provider who gives you this freedom.

When deciding where to invest your fund, bear in mind your attitude to risk and your planned retirement age: The younger you are, the more risk you can afford to take on. But make sure that you'll be able to sleep at night because if you're of a nervous disposition, plunging your life savings into high-risk hedge funds is not a good idea.

In the long run, equities produce better returns than less risky investments such as bonds and cash, so if you have some years to go before retirement, you can afford to opt for stocks and shares.

The main investment choices available are:

- ✔ **Stock market funds,** such as UK, American, or European equities. You could even opt for emerging markets or the Far East, if you're feeling more adventurous. You also have the choice of actively managed funds or *index trackers*, which simply follow the performance of a stock market index, such as the FTSE 100. These are less risky than actively managed funds and tend to produce lower returns. With some funds, you can also choose ethical investments.

✔ **Managed funds,** which can be less risky than stock market funds because they invest in a spread of assets – including shares, property, and fixed interest – via a balanced portfolio. Over the longer term they may not grow as well as stock market funds, however. (See Chapter 12 for more.)

✔ **Property funds,** investing in shares of property companies or commercial property. These can be extremely risky, depending on the number of properties you are exposed to and market conditions.

✔ **Fixed interest funds,** such as bonds and government securities, also called gilts. These are suitable for more conservative investors or those nearing retirement, as they are considered less risky than stocks and shares.

✔ **Cash,** which isn't much riskier than a building society or bank account. Your money is guaranteed but you won't generate much in the way of returns, so avoid unless you are just about to retire.

If you haven't the first clue about where to invest your pension, you can leave it to the experts. This is known as a *default* arrangement. Your money is allocated to a range of investments on your behalf and you're told where your cash is invested. All stakeholder schemes must have a default arrangement.

The default arrangement may not be the best place for your money because it doesn't take into account your particular circumstances. Look out for providers offering a *lifestyle* option instead: This is when your money is invested according to your age and risk profile, so as you move closer to retirement your money is automatically moved to lower-risk investments, such as bonds and cash, that are less volatile (and thus give potentially lower returns). This means you have less chance of experiencing significant losses as you near retirement and need to get your cash. Lifestyling often happens even if you initially choose where your money is invested, with the fund automatically switching to less risky investments as you near retirement.

If your scheme provider offers a lifestyle option, check out how flexible it is. You should be able to choose your retirement age and have the funds moved to safer investments to accommodate that.

Making Contributions

You must contribute the same amount to your pension on the same day every month – unless you have a stakeholder plan. With a stakeholder pension, the minimum investment is no more than £20 and you can make contributions as large or small as you like as often as you like.

Contributions are usually made via direct debit or standing order from your account to your pension provider's account and are made net of tax. You can also pay by debit card or cheque. If you're contributing to an employer-designated stakeholder scheme or GPP, your contributions are made from net salary.

Mostly, you'll make all the contributions to your fund, but in some instances your employer may also contribute. This usually happens where the employer would have made contributions to an occupational scheme if you'd joined but is prepared to pay into your personal pension instead.

 If your employer offers an occupational scheme, think carefully before deciding not to join it. You may not be able to join at a later date and your employer might not make the same contributions into your personal pension. Joining an occupational pension where one's on offer is nearly always in your best interests (see Chapter 16 for more on these).

 One solution worth considering is to join the occupational scheme (so you receive your employer's contributions) but instead of contributing to the plan yourself, continue to pay into your personal pension. This gives you the best of both worlds. There are no restrictions on this as long as total contributions (made by you and your employer) do not exceed your annual allowance – £235,000 in 2008–9 – or the lifetime allowance – £1.65 million in 2008–9. If total contributions to your fund exceed these amounts you'll be charged tax at 40 per cent on the surplus.

Sticking to the limits

 There are limits on the amount you can invest in a personal pension plan, unlike an occupational scheme where the restriction is on the amount you can receive in retirement. In 2008–9, the maximum limit that you can accumulate in a pension during your lifetime is £1.65 million.

Everyone can invest up to £3,600 a year, before tax relief, into a personal pension or stakeholder plan. This is regardless of earnings: You don't even need to earn anything, as a spouse or parent can contribute to your pension scheme. The provider of your pension scheme claims back the relief from HM Revenue & Customs at the basic rate of tax and adds this to your scheme. Higher-rate taxpayers can claim the extra tax relief they are due via self-assessment or pay-as-you-earn.

If you want to contribute more than £3,600 (and if you can afford to do so, you should in order to build up a decent pension) you can do this up to a maximum of 100 per cent of your annual income or the annual tax allowance, whichever is the lower. The annual allowance for 2008–9 is £235,000. So if you earn £250,000, you can invest a maximum of £235,000 in your pension (if you can afford to do so and subject to the lifetime allowance).

Your percentage contribution is calculated on your earnings for a basis tax year. When this is set, it remains the same for the next five years, regardless of whether you earn more or less. Every five years you can get the percentage revised upwards if your earnings increase, but even if your earnings decrease, or you lose your job, you can still make the maximum contribution depending on your revised earnings.

Topping up your pension

One of the main problems many people face is not saving enough for retirement. If you find you have cash to spare, consider topping up your contributions to generate a bigger income in retirement (remember that you should not exceed your contribution limits, however). Stakeholder pensions are often used by people in occupational schemes to top up their pension, as charges tend to be lower than with additional voluntary contributions (see Chapter 16). However, you can only use a stakeholder (or any personal pension) for this purpose if:

✔ You are not a company director.

✔ You earn less than £30,000 a year.

✔ You do not pay in more than 100 per cent of your earnings up to £235,000 in any tax year. Otherwise, you will not get tax relief on all your contributions.

This enables you to receive an extra pension on top of the maximum pension that HM Revenue & Customs allows.

Stopping contributions

At some stage you may stop contributing to your pension. This could be down to joining a company with an attractive occupational scheme that you've decided to join. Or you may be short of a bob or two and decide to skip your contributions.

If you have a stakeholder plan, nothing happens if you miss a payment: The fund manager continues to deduct the annual fee (no more than 1.5 per cent for ten years, before falling to 1 per cent) and your money is still invested. You can contribute again whenever you want or make no further contributions before retirement.

If your personal pension isn't a stakeholder scheme, it isn't so easy. The pension may become *paid up* once you miss three months' worth of contributions so you can't make any more contributions. Charges are deducted as normal, if this is the case, and the fund continues to grow (because it is invested in the stock market) until you're ready to draw your pension. Some schemes enable you to start paying into the pension again at a later date but your provider may charge a fee for this. However, paying the fee might be worthwhile as it's likely to be cheaper than starting a policy from scratch.

If you stop contributing to your plan, even for just a couple of years, you are likely to retire on a smaller pension than you would otherwise have done. Missing contributions for several years could leave you with a significant shortfall, which you never have a chance to make up. Think carefully before you stop contributions.

Transferring to another fund

If your circumstances change – for example, you join a company with an excellent workplace scheme – you may decide to transfer your existing pension to the new scheme.

Think twice before transferring your personal pension into an occupational scheme (unless it's a stakeholder) as you may be heavily penalised for doing so. It might be in your interests to leave the money where it is and simply allow the pension to become paid up, while you join your employer's scheme and start contributing to it from scratch.

If you have a stakeholder pension, you can transfer it at will, without charge. So you can move the cash you've saved into your employer's scheme or another stakeholder or personal pension, without penalty. This is one of the main benefits of such schemes.

Receiving Your Pension

You can receive your pension at any age between 50 and 75. From 6 April 2010, you'll only be able to take benefits from the age of 55. Your expected retirement age is usually written into the pension contract, but you can retire at a different date if you wish.

Up to 25 per cent of your fund can be taken as a tax-free lump sum when you retire. If you've been contracted out of the state second pension (see Chapter 16) this portion can't be taken as a lump sum. It must be converted into a pension along with the remainder of your pot, via the purchase of an annuity (see the following section 'Working out annuities').

If you retire early, you'll receive a smaller pension than you would've done if you'd worked up until normal retirement age (65 for men, 60 for women, 65 for women from 2020) because you'll have invested less money and it won't have had as long to grow. Check whether early retirement is feasible before taking the plunge: The Trades Union Congress (TUC) website (www.worksmart.org.uk) has a calculator that works out how big a retirement income your pension pot will purchase.

Working out annuities

An *annuity* is a guaranteed income for life, which must be purchased with at least three-quarters of your pension pot by the age of 75. This is the absolute cut-off point: You can buy it between the ages of 50 and 75, depending on when you want to retire and need an income from.

Two main types of annuity exist:

- ✔ A single-life annuity provides a pension based on your life only.

- ✔ An annuity that provides an income to your surviving spouse or dependants after you die.

When you've decided which type to opt for you must decide whether:

- ✔ To buy a non-increasing annuity or pension or one that increases each year so the real value of your retirement income doesn't fall.

- ✔ To purchase a guarantee so if you die within a certain number of years the balance of unpaid instalments goes to your dependants or spouse.

The more options you choose, the more you pay and the lower your annuity will be. So consider carefully what provision you'd like to make.

Shop around for an annuity. You're not obliged to buy the annuity offered by your pension provider: Research proves you almost certainly get a better deal if you exercise your *open market option* by going to another insurance company, unless you have a guaranteed annuity rate written into the policy. Annuity rates vary considerably among providers and the Office of the Pensions Advisory Service (Opas) reckons that you can get as much as 20 per cent more on your annuity if you shop around.

Drawing an income

You don't have to buy an annuity at the same time as you take your lump sum: You can opt for *income drawdown* instead, which provides increased flexibility and control. This enables you to draw a certain amount of income while your fund is still invested in the usual way. HM Revenue & Customs imposes a maximum limit on what you can take, which is reassessed every five years. The maximum income you can draw down is 120 per cent of the income that would be provided if you used your pension savings to buy a lifetime annuity.

Income drawdown isn't suitable for everyone: Speak to an independent financial adviser specialising in pensions for more information.

Phasing your retirement

If you aren't sure about when you want to retire, you can do so in stages, known as *phased retirement*. Your pension fund is divided into segments, with each one continuing to be invested as usual. You can encash each segment when you choose, as long as they are all encashed by the time you are 75. Each time you encash one, you can take a tax-free lump sum and use the rest of that segment to purchase an annuity.

Understanding what happens when you die

When you start contributing to a pension, it's worth finding out what happens to it after you die. When you apply for a pension, you should be given an *expression of wish* form to complete. This enables you to nominate who receives death benefits from your pension after you've gone.

Before retirement

If you die before you retire and before the age of 75, the fund is paid tax-free, together with any life assurance that has been accumulated, to whoever you nominate. The total amount can be paid out as a lump sum. However, your spouse does not have to take a lump sum: The amount can be used to provide dependants' pensions.

After retirement

If you purchase an annuity before you die, the terms of the annuity dictate the benefits payable on your death. You can set up the annuity to provide a dependant's pension: This is taxed as income. As an alternative or as a joint possibility, you can set up your annuity to pay a lump sum if you die within a set period – say, five years.

If you haven't bought an annuity but have drawn an income from the fund, the balance of any unused fund can be used to buy dependants' pensions, paid as a lump sum or a combination of both options.

If you die after retirement and are older than 75, any remaining fund must be used to buy an annuity.

Taking the Bull by the Horns: Self-Invested Personal Pensions

If you know a thing – or several – about pensions and investments, and can afford to make significant contributions to your fund, you can take more control of your money via a *self-invested personal pension (Sipp)*.

Instead of having a pension fund manager invest your money for you, a Sipp leaves you free to build up a portfolio of your own investments. An insurance company or independent financial adviser will administer a Sipp, but you decide where your contributions are invested.

Using a Sipp gives you several advantages:

✔ **Control:** You make the investment decisions, not a pension manager. So if you think you can do better than the experts, here's your chance to prove it.

✔ **A wide choice of investments:** Many things can be held within a Sipp, from unit and investment trusts to shares, gilts, and commercial property.

✔ **More fun:** Pensions are boring but deciding where your money is invested at least keeps your interest up.

However, it's not all plain sailing. Sipps have their problems too, including:

✔ **Relatively high set-up and running costs.** Sipps are only really suitable for wealthy investors because of this. Mind you, while the fees are high they're also fixed so there are no nasty surprises.

✔ **You could easily make the wrong investment decisions.** Chances are you don't invest in pensions as a career so should be at a disadvantage to a pension fund manager. If it all goes pear-shaped and you make the wrong calls, you have no one to blame but yourself.

✔ **You don't have time to track your investments.** If you have a busy full-time job and many demands on your time, you may not be able to keep up to date with your investments. You need to track them to see how things are going and if you don't do this from one year to the next, you could easily lose out.

✔ **You may panic because things are going badly.** You could make rash decisions while an experienced pension manager in the same position may decide to ride out the storm.

Chapter 18

Coping in Retirement

· ·

In This Chapter

▶ Working out the best retirement age for you

▶ Deciding how much of a lump sum you need

▶ Finding the best annuity

▶ Using your home to provide income

· ·

Saving throughout your working life towards your pension is only the beginning. How you put that money to work in retirement can play a big part in whether it generates a good income or you have to struggle to get by on a poor one.

You have to abide by certain restrictions when you draw your pension, but you also can make lots of choices. In this chapter, I guide you through the major decisions you face so that you can make them in an informed manner. When you do certain things, such as purchase an annuity, you can't undo them, so getting it right first time is crucial. This chapter shows you how.

Deciding When to Retire

I look at deciding when you'd like to retire for the purpose of pension planning in Chapter 15. Here I help you decide when it's finally time to jack in the day job and spend the rest of your life doing exactly what you please. Or at least that's the general idea, finances permitting.

When you retire isn't totally your decision: The state retirement age is 65 for men and 60 for women. This is when you receive the basic state pension and most people can't afford to retire before this because they need to live off this pension. The state retirement age is gradually being raised for women from 2010 so that by 2020, women will also officially retire at 65. The amount of basic state pension you receive depends on the amount of National Insurance Contributions made during your working life (see Chapter 15 for more on this).

You don't *have* to retire at state retirement age. You may not want to or be able to if you haven't saved much for retirement. The Government is keen for you to work longer, if this is feasible, and is offering incentives, such as a higher state pension, if you do so.

The Government is also raising the age at which you can take your private pension (if you have one). Under current rules, you must be between the ages of 50 and 75, although your particular scheme may have its own rules preventing you from retiring at 50. From 2010, the minimum age at which you can draw your private pension will be 55.

Those people with an early normal retirement date, such as professional footballers, will still be allowed to retire and draw their pension before the age of 55. But there will be a 2.5 per cent discount off the lifetime allowance for each year they don't work before the age of 55. (The lifetime allowance is the maximum amount of pension savings that can benefit from tax relief; it has initially been set at £1.65 million for 2008.)

The longer you work and put off claiming your pension, the better. Avoid retiring in your 50s if you can help it as you'll get a much smaller pension than if you pack in your job at 70. Table 18-1 shows the difference delaying your pension by a few years can make. The figures in the table assume an index-linked, single pension for a male non-smoker bought using a £100,000 pension pot. Payments are monthly in advance. You'll have to pay tax on these.

Table 18-1	Pension Amounts at Different Ages
Age	*Monthly Income*
50	£206
55	£272
60	£322
65	£335
70	£411
74	£572

Source: Financial Services Authority

If you have several pensions, you could draw one or two in your 50s or 60s and leave the others invested until later on to maximise your income.

Taking early retirement

Early retirement is beyond the means of most of us, as we won't have a big enough pension pot to enable us to give up working before 65. You can't claim the state pension until this age (60 for women until 2020) – even if you're no longer working. You may also have to carry on making National Insurance Contributions (NICs) if you retire early to ensure you get the full basic state pension. See Chapter 15 for more details on this.

If you suffer a disability so can't work, you may be able to take early retirement if you belong to an occupational scheme (see Chapter 16).

One of the questions you must consider before giving up work is whether you have enough cash to see you through a long retirement. If you've got enough savings and investments to tide you over, you may not have to draw your pension until state retirement age anyway. But if you haven't got a comfortable income to rely on, you will struggle and it won't be much fun at all.

You can take up to 25 per cent of your pension pot as a tax-free cash lump sum from the age of 50, using the remainder of your fund to buy an annuity. You must buy your annuity by the age of 75 at the latest.

Retiring at the usual age

Most people retire at the official state retirement age of 65 (60 for women until 2020 when it rises to 65). Private pension savings are usually made with this target in mind, and you can draw the basic state pension and state second pension at this age (see Chapter 15) as long as you have made enough NICs to qualify.

Working past retirement age

You may want to continue working past the official state retirement age but it's not always straightforward. New legislation means your employer can't automatically chuck you onto the scrapheap when you reach 65, but whether you can stay on depends on whether you're still competent to do your job. If you aren't, your employer doesn't have to continue employing you.

You can delay receiving the state pension until after state retirement age if you carry on working: In fact, the Government encourages you to do so (see Chapter 15 for details). Retiring at the official retirement age may not be in your best interests if you haven't built up a big enough pension pot to provide for a comfortable old age.

If you've built up enough NICs to qualify for a full basic state pension, you don't have to make any more after retirement age, saving you up to 11 per cent of your salary. However, you need to pay income tax on your earnings and if you haven't paid enough NICs, it might be a good opportunity to top them up (see Chapter 15 for details).

You can receive your pension and carry on working if you wish, although normally you can't work for an employer and receive your pension from that employer's scheme. But you could work for another employer or go self-employed in order to get over this hurdle.

Taking the Tax-Free Lump Sum

Whether you retire at 50, 65, or 70, if you have a personal or stakeholder pension, or money-purchase occupational scheme, you can take up to 25 per cent of it as a tax-free cash lump sum when you are 50. The remainder of your pension pot must be used to purchase an annuity at the same time, unless you opt for income drawdown (see 'Withdrawing income' later in this chapter).

If you have a final salary pension scheme, you should also be able to take a lump sum: This is usually a maximum of one and a half times your final salary, depending on how long you have worked for your employer.

Since 5 April 2006, all pension funds pay out up to 25 per cent of the value of your pension pot as a tax-free lump sum. However, a restriction is placed on this: The sum must be no more than a quarter of the *lifetime allowance* (the maximum amount of pension savings that can benefit from tax relief – initially set at £1.6 million in 2008). In 2008, the maximum lump sum you can take is £400,000, or a quarter of your pension pot, whichever is the lesser.

Deciding how much you should take

Although most private pensions let you take up to 25 per cent of your pot as a tax-free lump sum, you don't have to take that amount. Whether you choose to do so depends on your personal circumstances. In most cases it is worth taking the maximum you can because you don't pay tax on it, while you do pay income tax on your annuity. If you invest your lump sum rather than spend it (see 'Working out what to do with it' in the following section) you may also be able to generate a higher income in retirement than if you'd used your whole pension pot to purchase an annuity.

Whatever is left over in your pot after taking a lump sum is used to purchase an annuity, guaranteeing you income until you die. The more money you have to purchase your annuity, the bigger your pension. If you take a quarter of your pot as a lump sum, you're withdrawing a significant proportion of your fund. And if you have a small pot in the first place, you won't have much cash left to buy a meaningful annuity (see 'Explaining annuities' later in this chapter).

Working out what to do with it

You may be tempted to splash your cash, but it may be more prudent to invest it or keep it in a high-interest savings account where you can get your hands on it as, and when, you need it. You have several options for disposing of your lump sum:

- ✔ **Spend it.** You'll never get this much cash again so it's tempting to spoil yourself. But only do this if you know that you can cope without using your lump sum to provide an income.

- ✔ **Invest it.** You can do what you like with your lump sum, unlike the rest of your pension pot, which must be used to buy an annuity. You can also leave your lump sum to your beneficiaries after you've died, which isn't so easy with an annuity. Make sure you're happy with the level of risk you're taking on when investing your money.

- ✔ **Purchase a life annuity.** While you have to pay tax on your income from standard pension annuities, this is not the case with a *purchased life annuity* as the income is only partly taxable. The older you are when you buy this type of annuity, the less tax you pay. Ask a financial adviser for more details.

Explaining Annuities

If you have a money purchase pension scheme – a personal, stakeholder, or occupational pension – when you've taken your lump sum the remainder of your savings must purchase an *annuity* from an insurance company. This is a guaranteed income for the rest of your life. It is not subject to investment risk, unless you opt for an investment-linked annuity. If you choose not to buy an annuity at this point, you can opt for income drawdown instead (see 'Withdrawing income' later in this chapter).

You can buy an annuity anytime between the ages of 50 and 75, although most people do so when they actually retire because they need the replacement income.

Income tax is payable on annuities. The insurance company deducts this before you receive your money. If you were a higher-rate tax-payer during your working life, you're likely to pay only basic-rate tax in retirement because your income is lower.

Working out annuities

Your retirement income depends on two main factors:

- ✔ The size of your pension pot. The more you save, the bigger your pension.
- ✔ The annuity rate offered by the insurance company.

The value of your fund is multiplied by the annuity rate to give you your pension. So if you have £100,000 in your pot and the insurance company offers you a 7 per cent annuity rate, you get a pension of £7,000 a year (100,000 times 0.07 [7 per cent]).

When calculating your annuity rate, the insurance company predicts how long you might live and how much your declining fund will generate over the years. The insurance company's aim is that your fund runs out the same time as you die. The insurance company takes on all the investment risk, which is quite a gamble: If the insurance company gets it wrong, it is an expensive mistake. Live longer than the company predicts and it loses out because it has to pay you more than the value of your pension pot. But if you don't live as long as your insurer estimates, the insurance company is quids in because it keeps the balance of the money you invested.

Actuaries calculate annuity rates using several criteria:

- ✔ **Age and mortality rates:** The older you are, the better the rate as you'll be drawing your pension for fewer years.

- ✔ **Gender:** Women tend to live longer than men so if a woman purchases an annuity at the same age as her husband, he will get a higher rate than her.

- ✔ **Health:** Smokers and heavy drinkers or those who are ill get better annuity rates than people in good health because they aren't expected to live as long.

- ✔ **Current market conditions:** The life insurance company invests your fund in low-risk investments such as government bonds or gilts. If yields are attractive compared to interest rates, prices go up so the insurer has to pay more for gilts. This lowers the yield.

- ✔ **The type of annuity:** A standard annuity pays out the same amount each year for the rest of your life. But you can also choose one that pays out cash to your spouse after you die or increases in line with inflation each year. The more extras you opt for, the lower your pension.

Understanding different types of annuities

Choosing an annuity is a major decision. You can't change your mind and switch to another one if you decide you don't like what you chose. And if you choose wrongly you could lose out on thousands of pounds of pension income over the years. Making the right decision is crucial.

The annuity you choose depends on your attitude to risk, your circumstances, and your needs. As well as considering yourself and your situation the day you retire, don't forget the future: Whether you might need extra funds as you get older to pay for long-term care or nursing fees and how your family will cope after you die.

You must also choose when to receive your annuity payments. The state pension is paid weekly but most people receive their private pension monthly. Alternatively, you can have your pension paid quarterly, half-yearly, or yearly. You can be paid in advance or arrears. If you opt for the former, payments start immediately; the latter starts after the first month, quarter, six months, and so on. The longer the delay before receiving your payment, the greater your income – a deferred pension is bigger than one paid in advance. Table 18-2 shows annual payment amounts for a retiree with a £100,000 pension pot.

Table 18-2	Receiving Annuity Payments in Advance or Arrears	
Income Paid	*Male Aged 65*	*Female Aged 65*
Annually in arrears	£7,713	£7,034
Annually in advance	£7,152	£6,565
Monthly in arrears	£7,437	£6,802
Monthly in advance	£7,390	£6,763

Source: The Annuity Bureau

In the following sections, I run through the different types of annuity and what you should bear in mind when choosing one.

Deciding between staying level or rising

A *level annuity* – also known as a *flat* or *standard annuity* – is fixed for life so you get the same amount each year until you die. However, receiving the same amount year after year means that you'll be able to buy less with your money each year because of inflation. In real terms, the value of your pension declines each year. For example, the buying power of £1,000 after 10 years is £776 (allowing for inflation of 2.5 per cent per year). If you live 30 years after retirement, and don't inflation-proof your pension, that £1,000 will be worth £468 (if inflation grows at the same rate).

 To protect your income, opt for an *index-linked* or *rising annuity*, which increases each year rather than remaining level. You can ensure that the amount you receive increases by the same amount as inflation by opting for a *Retail Price Index-linked (RPI-linked)* annuity – or choose an *escalating annuity* to get a 3 or 5 per cent increase each year. A rising annuity safeguards the purchasing power of your pension.

Of course, if there is a period of *deflation* (in other words, retail prices fall rather than rise) your pension income declines as well if it is RPI-linked. But your purchasing power remains the same so you're no worse off in real terms.

 The increases you get under a rising annuity are attractive but expensive. The pension you get when you first retire is far lower than you would have got if you'd chosen a level annuity. But the amount you receive will rise each year, unlike the level annuity. The greater the escalation you opt for, the lower your initial income. Table 18-3 illustrates this fact. The figures in the table relate to the initial annuity a woman retiring at 60 would get with a £30,000 pension pot.

Table 18-3   Differences in Level and Rising Annuities

Annuity Type	Annual Income
Level	£1,798
Rising at 3%	£1,229
Inflation-linked	£1,222
Rising at 5%	£915

Source: The Annuity Bureau

Choosing for one or two

If you opt for a single life pension, payments stop when you die, which is fine if you're, well, single. But if you have a husband, wife, or partner, you may want a joint life annuity so that your spouse gets an income for the rest of their life. This is particularly important if they don't have their own pension, or much of one, and you aren't leaving any other savings or investments.

If you choose a joint life annuity, you receive less pension while you're alive than you would if you opt for a single life annuity. A 60-year-old male with a £30,000 pension pot who wants his wife to receive half his pension after he dies will receive around 8 per cent less for a joint life annuity than a single life.

You can usually choose how much income your partner receives after your death, depending on restrictions on your pension plan. Most couples choose between one-third and two-thirds of their pension, although you can opt for them to receive the full amount that you would've got if you'd lived. The more your partner receives, the lower your pension, so weigh this up and talk it through before making a decision.

Going for the guaranteed period

All annuities guarantee to pay out for as long as you live. But if you (and your partner, if you opt for a joint life annuity) die soon after purchasing the annuity, all that pension saving was a waste of time because you never got to see any of the proceeds. One way round this is to buy an annuity that guarantees to pay the income for a fixed number of years after you purchase it whether you live or die. Most people who choose this opt for a five-year guarantee, although you can have a guarantee of up to ten years.

The guarantee lasts for five or ten years after you purchase the annuity, not after you die. So if you die nine years after you bought the annuity, it will pay out to your partner for just one year after your death. This may not be enough to support your partner adequately. You may be better off opting for a joint life annuity – more expensive but with more valuable benefits for your partner.

Accounting for impaired life

If you have a health problem, such as diabetes, high blood pressure, a heart condition, or cancer, you should get a better annuity rate because you aren't expected to live as long as someone in excellent health. If you smoke ten or more cigarettes a day and have done for at least ten years, you could also qualify for an *impaired life* annuity. Seek advice from an independent financial adviser (IFA) before you buy, as cases are underwritten on an individual basis.

Linking your annuity to investments

Most annuities are fixed for life so you get the same rate or a set increase every year. If you want to generate a (potentially) higher income, you must opt for an investment-linked annuity.

An *investment-linked annuity* gives you flexibility and growth potential in exchange for reduced guarantees. Your pot is invested in a range of funds and your pension income moves up and down in line with their performance. The more risky the underlying investments, the more your income fluctuates.

These annuities can be of one of two types:

- **With-profits:** Your income is linked directly to the performance of the insurance company's with-profits fund. You get a minimum starting income, set at a low level, plus bonuses. The insurance company announces bonus rates once a year: They depend on stock market performance. (Chapter 12 has more on with-profits.)

- **Unit-linked:** Your retirement income is linked directly to the performance of an underlying fund of investments. You choose the type of fund from a range of medium-risk or higher-risk funds, according to how much risk you are happy to take on. Unit-linked investments are more volatile than with-profits funds so you could see more dramatic swings in the value of your annuity.

Investment-linked annuities are only suitable for wealthy retirees who can cope with wide fluctuations (and potentially big falls) in income. If you scrimp and save, rely on every penny of your pension, and don't have other investments to tide you over, this type of annuity isn't for you. If you don't want to take on risk, steer clear. But if you're happy taking on extra risk, consult an adviser before doing so.

Deciding when to buy an annuity

You must buy an annuity by the age of 75 but you have a window of around 25 years – anytime between 50 and 75 – during which you can do so. The longer you leave it, the higher the rate you get because you'll draw your pension for fewer years. But you should delay only if you can cope without an income from a pension.

If annuity rates fall just as you're about to purchase your annuity, you lose out. You can delay purchasing an annuity if rates are bad by opting for income drawdown (see 'Withdrawing income' later in this chapter) after you have taken your lump sum. Or you can reduce the impact by choosing phased retirement (see 'Retiring gradually' later in this chapter). But there is no guarantee that rates will improve (in fact, they could fall) and you have an ultimate deadline – when you hit 75 – so there's not much room for manoeuvre.

If you have several pensions, you can purchase different annuities at various times, giving you more flexibility and lowering your risk.

Shopping around

Take advice before purchasing an annuity because it is such a major decision. Consult an IFA. If you haven't got one, contact IFA Promotion (IFAP), which can give you details of IFAs in your area: Call 0800 085 3250 or go to www.ifap.org.uk. You can also download free copies of various pensions guides written by the Financial Services Authority from www.moneymadeclear.fsa.gov.uk.

Don't accept the annuity offered by your existing pension provider without shopping around to see whether you can get a better price on the open market. Make sure your pension plan includes this *open market option*. It is vital that you compare annuities because big differences exist between the best and worst annuity rates.

Four months before you're ready to purchase an annuity, ask your pension provider what price it will give you. Don't leave this until the last minute or you may rush the decision and make the wrong choice because you're desperate for income. When you know what income you'll get from the company your pension pot is invested with, see whether you can find a better deal elsewhere. If you have a pension fund of at least £20,000, an adviser such as The Annuity Bureau will do this legwork for you. Compare annuity income on a like-with-like basis to find the best deal. If another provider offers a higher income, purchase your annuity from them.

If you have a small pension pot you may not have much choice when shopping around as some insurers refuse to touch anything smaller than £20,000. If this is so, it means you are stuck with your pension provider and if it isn't offering much, there's nothing you can do about it.

Retiring Gradually

If you have a large pension pot (at least £250,000) and don't want to purchase an annuity just yet – because rates are poor or because you're cutting back on work gradually so only need a small income

– you can opt for *phased retirement*. Your pension fund is divided into segments and each one treated almost as if it were a separate pension. You can take up to a quarter of each segment as a tax-free lump sum, purchasing an annuity with the remainder.

The advantage of phased retirement is that you don't have to draw all your segments at the same time, although they must all be encashed by the age of 75. You could purchase an annuity with one segment and leave the remaining segments invested in the stock market until annuity rates (hopefully) improve.

There is no guarantee that annuity rates will improve while you are phasing retirement. They could fall instead, leaving you in a worse position than you would have been in if you'd taken your pension in the normal way instead of staying invested in the stock market.

You must convert enough segments to purchase an annuity. Some insurance companies have a minimum purchase price, so if one of your segments doesn't provide enough cash, you may have to encash several at the same time.

The benefit of phased retirement is that if you die before encashing all your segments, your spouse or other beneficiaries inherit those you haven't yet turned into an annuity. No tax is payable, as long as your funds came from a personal pension. If they come from an occupational scheme, your spouse may receive a lump sum equal to 25 per cent of the fund, with the remainder used to buy an annuity. As for the funds already placed in your phased retirement plan, your beneficiaries may receive income from these.

Withdrawing Income

If annuity rates are poor, you can delay purchasing an annuity (at least until you're 75) and still get your hands on part of your pension by opting for *income drawdown* or *income withdrawal*.

The way an income drawdown or income withdrawal scheme works is that you take part of your pension as a tax-free lump sum – if you want to. You then start taking an income from your fund: This is taxed, just as it would be on a regular pension. You don't buy an annuity at this stage.

If you opt for income drawdown, you receive an income every year, the amount of which is set by HM Revenue & Customs. The amount is roughly the same as a single life, non-increasing annuity with no guarantee. This is the maximum you can take: You have to take an income between this and a minimum amount, which is 35 per cent of the maximum. So, a 60-year-old male with a £40,000 pot can draw an income of between £1,092 and £3,120. These limits are before tax, which is deducted at source. The company you invest with must review your scheme every three years to ensure your income remains between the Revenue's limits. You can vary the amount you withdraw each year, within these limits, if you desire.

Income drawdown can be expensive so don't even think about it unless you have a pension pot of at least £250,000.

Because a portion of your savings remains invested in the stock market, the value of your fund can go down as well as up. Charges are also taken from the fund each year, whereas if you'd purchased an annuity from the outset, you wouldn't have to pay charges. And although you hope that annuity rates will rise, they may fall instead and you will be forced to purchase one by the age of 75 irrespective of this fact.

As long as you can cope with these downsides, there are several reasons why you might consider income drawdown:

✓ You can delay purchasing an annuity until rates improve while still receiving an income.

✓ If you die before purchasing an annuity, your heirs inherit the full value of your pension fund – less 35 per cent tax. Most annuities (apart from joint life and some guaranteed plans) don't pay a pension to your heirs after your death.

✓ You get flexibility. You get your cash lump sum and can choose just a small income if that's all you need to keep going. Your fund can stay invested in the stock market, hopefully giving you a bigger pension when you finally purchase an annuity.

Review your decision as to when to purchase your annuity every year. Your situation and/or stock market conditions can change.

Most personal plans and some employer schemes let you convert your pension into a drawdown plan. But not all occupational schemes let you; you may have to transfer from your employer's scheme into a personal pension beforehand. You are likely to be charged for this transfer so shop around for a good deal if this is the case.

Dealing with a Trivial Pension

If the total of all your pension funds is less than £15,000, you can take some or all of them as a cash lump sum rather than taking an income or annuity, so you get more flexibility. This is known as 'trivial commutation'. The first 25 per cent is tax-free; the remainder is taxed as income. If you're a higher-rate taxpayer you pay 40 per cent tax and a basic-rate taxpayer pays 20 per cent tax.

So if you're a basic-rate taxpayer who cashes in trivial pensions up to the maximum value of £15,000, you can take a lump sum of up to £3,750 tax-free. You then pay £2,250 tax (20 per cent) on the remainder. The total sum you would receive is £12,750.

However, bear in mind these restrictions:

- ✔ You must be aged between 60 and 75 to cash in your trivial funds.

- ✔ You must take all your trivial pensions within the same tax year (6 April to 5 April the following year). So if you have several funds that you are thinking of cashing in (up to a total value of £15,000), you must do this within 12 months.

The alternative to cashing in your pension is to buy an annuity. But cashing it in gives you more flexibility: You can keep it in cash or opt for a low-risk investment, such as gilts, to provide a fixed income.

Getting Money from Your Home

If you have a small pension there are ways of generating a bigger retirement income. Cashing in on the increase in value of property is the only answer for many: Via equity release (see 'Releasing equity' later in this chapter) or by downsizing.

Downsizing

If you have paid off your mortgage and have a lot of cash tied up in your home, you can increase your income by selling up and buying a smaller property with the profits. The surplus cash can be used to bolster your income by investing in low-risk products such as gilts or corporate bonds or be put into a savings account paying a high rate of interest.

Apart from generating extra income, there are several reasons why you might downsize:

- ✔ You simply don't need such a big property when your children have flown the nest.

- ✔ A smaller property is more manageable when it comes to cleaning, heating, and maintenance as you get older.

✔ You may become less mobile as you get older and not be able to negotiate lots of stairs.

✔ You reduce your estate's inheritance tax (IHT) liability. Under current rules, everything you leave over £312,000 (including property in the 2008–9 tax year) is taxed at 40 per cent after you die. If you downsize before death, and spend the proceeds, you'll have less to leave your family in your will. Thus the IHT liability may be greatly reduced, although you may prefer to ensure your family gets a decent inheritance instead. See Chapter 15 for more on IHT planning.

Don't downsize before you need to. You could be a long time retired and moving into a cramped one-bedroom bungalow with your spouse at the age of 65 could be a recipe for disaster. Think carefully about when it's practical to sell up.

Releasing equity

Not everyone is prepared to sell the family home. But if the majority of your assets are tied up in your property, you can still get hold of some money without selling up and downsizing by opting for *equity release*.

The two main types of equity release are:

✔ A **lifetime mortgage,** in which you borrow against the value of your home.

✔ A **home reversion scheme,** in which you sell part or all of your home while retaining the right to live in it.

I explain these in more detail in the next sections.

Opting for an equity release scheme may affect any benefits you're entitled to, such as Pension Credit and Council Tax, because they are calculated according to income and savings. Even if your benefits are cut, you may be better off overall by opting for equity release. Consider your overall position before making a decision. Take legal and financial advice before opting for equity release so that you understand all the implications of what you're getting into.

Living with a lifetime mortgage

Like a regular mortgage, a *lifetime mortgage* enables you to take out a home loan but retain full ownership of the property. You receive a lump sum, regular income, or both. You pay interest on the loan but not during your lifetime; instead, it is added onto your loan each year and rolled up. When you die, your home is sold and the debt repaid. The longer you live, the greater the debt and the less money left over for your beneficiaries to inherit.

If you opt for a lifetime mortgage, ensure you choose one that guarantees that your debt can't exceed the value of your property: Otherwise, your beneficiaries could find themselves having to make up the shortfall.

The rate of interest you pay on a lifetime mortgage is usually at least a couple of percentage points higher than on a regular home loan. However, rates vary significantly between providers so shop around for the best deal using an independent financial adviser.

Going for a home reversion scheme

Unlike a lifetime mortgage, with a *home reversion scheme* you sell your home or a share of it to a *private reversion company*. You get a cash lump sum in exchange, which can be used to buy an annuity or other investment to provide income. You continue to live in the property until you die; your home is then sold and the reversion company repaid.

The advantage of home reversion schemes is that you know exactly what proportion of your property you can leave in your will. However, there's no way of telling what this will be worth until the property is sold after your death and the reversion company has taken its portion.

Your age and sex are also taken into account when the finance company is deciding how much money to give you: The longer you live the more time it has to wait to get its money back. So if the finance company thinks you will live a long time you'll get less money than if it thinks you're going to die in a year or two. If you live with your spouse, you'll get even less money as both of you have to die before the finance company can get its cash.

Deciding whether equity release suits you

Equity release schemes don't suit everyone. You must be at least 60 or 65 (even 70 with some schemes) to be considered. At the age of 65, you can release about 25 per cent of the value of your home; this rises to 35 per cent at the age of 75 and 45 per cent at the age of 85. The longer you can hang on, the more cash you can get.

If you opt for a lifetime mortgage, try to leave it for as long as possible. Some companies offer lifetime mortgages to anyone aged 60 and above but you'll only be able to draw a small percentage of the value of the property – around 10 per cent – and there's a strong chance you'll end up paying a lot of interest. Every year you live after you release some equity is another year's interest your estate has to pay, so if you live 20-odd years after opting for equity release, it could significantly eat into the value of your estate.

Telling your family

If you opt for equity release it will have a big impact on your family's inheritance so you should talk to them about your plans. They may disagree but ultimately the decision is up to you. You'll save a lot of heartache after you've gone if they know what to expect.

Finding an equity release scheme

A number of insurance companies, banks, and building societies offer lifetime mortgages. Insurance firms tend to be the only providers of reversion schemes. Consult an independent financial adviser for more information on both types of scheme before taking the plunge.

Part V
The Part of Tens

'The taxmen never give up, do they?'

In this part . . .

This wouldn't be a *For Dummies* book without the Part of Tens. Here you find mini explosions of useful information on saving your hard-earned dough and getting out of debt, coping financially with the events life throws at you, and remembering the golden rules for sorting out your finances.

Chapter 19

Ten Tips to Get Out of Debt and Save Cash

In This Chapter

▶ Finding ways of clearing what you owe

▶ Spending less to save more

*I*n this chapter I look at ten ways to help you get a handle on your debt and develop good habits so you can kiss goodbye to it.

Taking Scissors to Your Plastic

It's all too easy to spend more than you can afford when you use credit or store cards because it doesn't feel real: It's just a piece of plastic. But when the bill arrives, you realise that you may as well have handed over cash in the first place. You end up paying for items and then some. Depending on the rate of interest on your plastic, you could get stung with high interest rates.

None of this is a problem if you clear the balance on your store or credit card each month. But if you haven't got enough income to enable you to do this, plastic really isn't for you. You are spending beyond your means and this is when debt becomes a problem.

If you aren't disciplined and can't just put your plastic away in a drawer and forget about it, there's only one thing for it – cut it up. Get a pair of scissors and chop up all your cards before returning the pieces to the card issuer with a letter stating that you wish to cancel your card. Stick to cash rather than plastic in future, which should rein in your impulse to spend as you will be able to see exactly how much you are handing over. Plus, there's the simple matter that you can't spend what you don't have in the first place.

Going Interest-Free

The easiest way of clearing the debt you've already run up is to switch your outstanding balances to a credit card charging 0 per cent interest on balance transfers for an introductory period. This is usually around six months, although some providers offer interest-free periods of up to 15 months.

Once you switch to a card charging 0 per cent interest, start chipping away at the balance. When you were being charged interest on your old cards, you may have found that any payments you made simply went towards paying that month's interest. If you don't have to pay interest, the money can go towards clearing your debt instead.

Several providers offer 0 per cent deals: Shop around on the Internet using www.moneyfacts.co.uk, www.moneysavingexpert.com, or www.moneysupermarket.com. Remember, if you haven't paid back what you owe by the time the 0 per cent offer runs out, switch to another card offering a similar deal, so you can carry on chipping away at the balance. Do this until you have paid back what you owe.

Some credit card providers charge a handling fee of around 2.9 per cent of the balance transfer. Check with the provider before you apply for the card. And don't use the card for purchases – the 0 per cent interest only applies to the balance transfer, not the £500 stereo system you've got your eye on.

Having a Night In

Okay, so it may sound boring but bear with me. You don't have to stay in every night, just try to stay in one night each week when you'd normally go out. It's one of the easiest ways of saving money, as dinner at a fancy restaurant or a visit to a club could leave you with little change, if anything, from £50. If you manage to save this much a week on going out, you could save around £2,600 a year, which can go a long way to clearing your debt or saving for something special.

You don't have to be Johnny-no-mates. Ask friends round to your place instead of meeting them in a bar, restaurant, or club and ask them to bring a bottle. All you need provide is a few snacks or a filling bowl of pasta, which is cheap and easy to make, and will stave off the hunger pangs so you won't have to order a pricey takeaway. Hire a DVD or video to keep you all amused and split the cost.

Steering Clear of Buying a Round

The pub round is a time-honoured tradition. But while a night out down the pub with your mates can be fun, it's bad news for your finances. Getting your round in can be pricey – depending on how many of you there are – particularly if others are drinking fancy cocktails or double measures while you stick to pints.

You can avoid buying a round without developing a reputation as a cheapskate and annoying all your mates. Stick to buying your own drinks: Don't get involved in a round in the first place. Then you won't feel guilty that you can't afford to buy everyone a drink – and won't feel pressurised into taking 'your turn'. Explain that you'd love to buy everyone a drink but you're short of cash so you're going to get your own drinks in.

Wearing Last Season's Threads

As the new season's collections hit the high street, you may be dreaming about the new coat you're going to buy or the must-have bag that you plan to splash out on. But clothes can be expensive, even if you don't opt for designer fare: It's easy to get carried away on the high street and purchase several 'bargains', plunging you further into debt.

Make it a rule not to buy clothes unless you really need them – at least until you have cleared your debts. Avoid window-shopping: This will only depress you because you can't afford anything. Or you may find your resolve weakening and give in to temptation, buying something you can't really afford.

You may find an excuse to go shopping – because you are going to a wedding, say, and have nothing to wear – but most of us do have something in the wardrobe already if we only look hard enough. Be creative: You may be able to jazz up last season's frock with new accessories to make it look up to date.

Once your finances are back on track, allocate a certain amount to spend on clothes each month and don't exceed this. If you'd particularly like something but it costs more than your monthly limit, don't buy anything for one or two months until you've saved up enough allowance to pay for the desirable item.

Taking on Part-Time Work

If it's taking ages to clear your debts you can speed up the process by earning extra dough, but make sure part-time work doesn't interfere with your day job (run the idea past your employer in case it is against company policy).

Taking on a bar job a couple of nights a week or at weekends should be manageable, give you extra cash, and help clear debts more quickly. But working every night of the week after a busy day in the office will leave you no time for anything else. This is really only feasible if you want to clear your debts quickly and plan to give up the part-time job once you've achieved this.

Don't forget that you may have to pay tax on your part-time earnings if you already have a full-time job. Anyone who earns more than £5,435 a year (2008–9 tax year) must pay income tax. Your new employer may tax you at source by deducting the tax from your wages before you are paid. If you take on freelance work, you are classed as being self-employed for that portion of your earnings, so you have to pay the tax you owe via a self-assessment tax return. Contact HM Revenue & Customs on 0845 900 0444 to register as self-employed or go to www.hmrc.gov.uk for more details.

Steering Clear of Lattes and Muffins

Most of us slip into debt not because we spend a fortune on large items but because we don't appreciate how much we spend on the small stuff every day. Buying a pack of cigarettes, a magazine, a posh coffee, and a muffin doesn't leave you with much change from £15. That's £75 a week (if you spend this every working day) or just over £3,900 a year on items that you could really live without.

Economise: Get up earlier in the morning and have a cup of tea or coffee and toast or cereal before leaving for work, so you aren't tempted to stop off and buy a coffee and muffin on the way. Once you get to work, put the kettle on rather than nipping out for a beverage. You will soon notice the difference in your wallet and have to make fewer visits to the cash point to get more money.

Buying Supermarket Own Brands

One of the easiest areas in which to economise is where food is concerned. This doesn't mean you can't ever dine out again and have to stay in eating beans on toast every night. But if you eat out one night less a month, and shop carefully at the supermarket, you could save a fortune.

Supermarket own brand goods can be significantly cheaper than branded items and are often the same quality. There is no room for snobbery when you've got debts to clear. Make a list of what you need before you go shopping and don't be tempted to purchase anything that's not on the list. Get into the habit of visiting your local supermarket just before closing time for reduced bargains. Freeze what you can't finish before it goes off.

Walking to Work

Train, bus, and tube fares can be expensive, while running a car is also pricey once you've bought it and paid the insurance, road tax, petrol, and allow for depreciation. Save money by walking or cycling to and from work. If that's impossible because it's too far, try car sharing with a colleague or asking your boss if you can work from home once or twice a week. You may also be able to get an interest-free train or tube season ticket from your employer: Ask whether this is the case.

Making Your Own Cards and Pressies

Christmas and birthdays can be expensive if you have lots of friends and relatives. But you can save money, and avoid getting further into debt, by making your own. When it comes to gifts and cards, it really is the thought that counts and anything homemade, with a little thought and effort gone into it, is usually appreciated. If you are good at baking, try a birthday cake or homemade biscuits, or you might be able to turn your hand to making jewellery.

Be original and give favours as gifts! Make a voucher for your mum, promising to clear her garden, or one for your friend to cook dinner one night, or do their ironing. All you need is a little imagination.

Chapter 20

Coping with Ten Events Life May Throw at You

In This Chapter

▶ Being prepared to cope with life's ups and downs

▶ Ensuring your finances don't hold you back

*M*ost of us experience certain life events at some point, such as living on your own or having kids. If you plan ahead and work out where the money is going to come from when you need it, there shouldn't be anything to hold you back. In this chapter I look at ten major life events you may encounter and how to ensure your finances can cope with them.

Leaving Home

The average age of a first-time home-buyer is now 33, according to the Halifax. But there is no need to wait that long: You don't have to buy to gain your independence. You can rent. All you need is a month's rent in advance and the equivalent of a month's rent as a deposit.

If your heart is set on buying, ideally you need savings to put down as a deposit. But this isn't compulsory: You can get a 100 per cent mortgage. An increasing number of first-time buyers also rely on their parents to help them get on the property ladder, by contributing to the deposit, acting as guarantors, offsetting their savings, or releasing equity in their home. (Chapter 14 has more on mortgages.)

Paying University Costs

Students now have to pay to attend university, with tuition fees costing up to £3,145 a year from 2008. Up-front maintenance or special support grants are available for the poorest students but, other than this, precious little financial help is out there.

Most students rely on loans from the Government-backed Student Loans Company to see them through their studies. Two types of loan are available:

- ✔ A **tuition fee loan** that allows you to borrow up to a maximum of £3,145 (in 2008–9).

- ✔ A **student loan for maintenance** that allows you to borrow up to a maximum of £6,475 for accommodation and other living costs. The amount you can borrow depends on several factors including where you're studying and your parents' incomes.

You don't have to start repaying your loan until you earn more than £15,000 a year. For more information, go to www.slc.co.uk.

Students also rely on interest-free overdrafts. The big high-street banks all offer interest-free overdrafts of up to around £1,250 in your first year, rising by around £250 a year until your final year. Check whether you can extend this overdraft and how much this will cost.

Joining the Rat Race

As money is likely to be tight when you start your first job, especially if you have university debts to clear or are saving for your first home, ensure you're getting what you're entitled to. Check on HM Revenue & Customs' website that you are on the right tax code (www.hmrc.gov.uk); if you aren't, you may be paying more income tax than you need to.

If your employer offers a pension scheme, consider joining (see Chapter 16 for more on occupational schemes). If your employer makes a contribution on your behalf money will be going towards your pension pot, even if you can't afford to contribute yourself until a later date. The earlier you start, the better your chances of a decent income in retirement.

Getting Hitched

It may sound practical and unromantic but as well as making a commitment to the love of your life, marriage can help your finances. It simplifies matters as husbands and wives can make gifts to each other without having to pay capital gains tax on them. And if one spouse dies, the other receives their share of the home on their death, without having to pay inheritance tax.

Keep your own money: By all means have a joint bank account to pay the mortgage, bills, and groceries but keep your own bank account so you retain independence. Make sure the property is in both partners' names so that you are assured of your share if things don't work out. If you contributed a bigger chunk of savings to the deposit, or pay more towards the mortgage each month, get your solicitor to put this in writing.

One of the factors that puts people off marriage is the cost, with the average wedding leaving little change from £15,000. But given that it is such an expensive day, it's worth taking out wedding insurance. A one-off premium to cover a £15,000 wedding costs about £175. There are plenty of companies offering wedding insurance over the Internet so start your search for a policy here.

Starting a Family

If you're considering having children, check out your employer's maternity entitlement beforehand. You need to have worked for your employer for at least six months to qualify for statutory maternity pay, which is paid for up to 39 weeks. You get 90 per cent of your average weekly salary for the first six weeks' leave, and £112.75 (or 90 per cent of your average weekly earnings if less than this) for the remaining 33 weeks.

The earlier you start saving to cover the cost of a child, the better. As soon as you know you're expecting, you should save as much as you can in an instant access account to pay for the immediate costs of a new baby. Then look to the longer term, perhaps starting a savings account for your newborn.

The *child trust fund* is a tax-free savings and investment account for children born on or after 1 September 2002. The Government contributes a £250 (£500 for poor families) voucher to start the account and potentially another payout of £250 at the age of 7. The money is invested to build a nest egg for your child, which they get their hands on when they are 18. You can also invest up to £1,200 a year in the fund.

Giving Up Your Day Job to Raise the Kids

One of the biggest decisions you have to make after having a baby is who's going to look after him when you return to work. You may want to give up work to look after the baby full-time but can you afford to do so? Work out whether you can cope on one salary: Write down your monthly outgoings and income if you give up work. If there is a shortfall, are there areas where you could economise, by cutting back on the number of holidays you take, for example?

If the numbers still don't add up, you will have to reassess your plans: Perhaps working part-time would raise enough extra cash for you to be at home the rest of the time. Perhaps your employer will let you work from home a couple of days a week, which will ease childcare costs, or you may have relatives or friends you could call upon to help.

Many women have to work full- or part-time just to cover the cost of childcare. A nursery place costs roughly between £130 and £200 a week, depending on where you live, says the Daycare Trust. A full-time childminder who looks after several children costs up to £145 a week, while a nanny will set you back between £230 and £400 per week before tax.

Getting Divorced

A bit of planning before you tie the knot can save a lot of pain later, no matter how unromantic it sounds. Ask your solicitor to draw up a pre-nuptial agreement: They aren't legally binding in the UK as they are in the US, but they do set out each partner's intentions. Because you bothered to take legal advice, a court may well take the agreement into account if you break up.

If you do get divorced, keep it amicable as far as possible, particularly if you have children. It will also save a fortune on legal fees. But if you simply can't negotiate with your partner, hire the best solicitor you can afford to ensure you get your rightful share.

Going Self-Employed

Fed up of the daily commute and want to be your own boss? An increasing number of people are becoming self-employed. But before you take the plunge, take stock of your financial position. You will need a buffer to keep you going until you turn a profit. Build up savings in an instant access account beforehand, enough to last several months. Consider changing your mortgage to a flexible deal and make overpayments in the months leading up to self-employment so you can take payment holidays when money is tight.

Don't forget insurance: If you work from home, you need to contact your home and contents insurer, and review your life insurance if you left a company pension. You may also need personal liability cover, depending on your line of work. You must also notify HM Revenue & Customs as you will have to fill out a self-assessment tax return within three months of becoming self-employed, or else you face a £100 fine.

Being Made Redundant

Statutory redundancy pay is pitiful: One week's pay (up to a maximum of £330 in 2008) for every complete year you've worked for your employer if you are aged between 22 and 40. Those aged between 41 and 65 get one and a half weeks' pay for each year. You must also have worked for your employer for at least two years to qualify. Go to www.berr.gov.uk for a calculator to see what you're entitled to.

The state offers no help with your mortgage if you lose your job, so saving the equivalent of three months' salary in an instant access account while you have a job should tide you over until you find alternative employment.

You can take out various types of insurance that pay out if you are made redundant, such as accident, sickness, and unemployment insurance. There is also specialist redundancy insurance, which covers only your mortgage or pays a monthly sum to cover living expenses as well, depending on the policy. Whether you need to take these out or not depends on your personal circumstances and whether your employer offers any help: Check this out before doubling up on cover.

Check out www.redundancyhelp.co.uk for more information.

Taking Early Retirement

Most people have no chance of giving up work before the state retirement age (60 for women and 65 for men, rising to 65 for women from April 2020).

However, if you are determined to retire early, check how doing so affects your pension and National Insurance Contributions (NICs): You need to have paid the latter for 90 per cent of your working life (normally 44 years for men and 39 years for women) to get a full state pension, although you can top up your NICs voluntarily at a later date if you have missed any payments. If you take early retirement you won't be able to get the state pension until retirement age so you'll need cash to keep you going until then. Get a forecast from the Retirement Pension Forecasting Team on 0845 3000 168 or go to www.thepensionservice.gov.uk.

Next calculate the income you need in retirement and from which date. The Trades Union Congress (TUC) has a calculator on its website, which works out how much you will retire on if you continue contributing to a pension fund at your current level (go to www.worksmart.org.uk). If there is a shortfall you either delay retirement or save more. Check that your pension scheme will also pay an income if you retire early: Some don't. See Part IV for loads more on pensions.

Chapter 21

Ten Golden Rules for Sorting Out Your Finances

In This Chapter

▶ Shopping around for the best deals and advice

▶ Building up your assets for the future

*S*orting out your finances may seem like an overwhelming task, particularly if you have a limited understanding of how various products such as pensions or mortgages work.

However, if you follow the golden rules I set out in this chapter, you should be able to get your finances on track.

Live within Your Means

It may sound boring, but setting a budget – and sticking to it – makes sound financial sense. Gaining control of your finances is all about living within your means. Clear your debts every month and never spend more than you can afford to repay. Do this, and you'll never have money worries. So, if you're on a high-street salary, the sooner you appreciate that designer clothes are beyond your reach, the better.

But life isn't always easy. Unexpected expenses can crop up, such as the boiler packing in or your car failing its MOT. And if you don't have savings to cover the cost, you may find yourself dipping into an overdraft or using your credit card to cover the damage. How you deal with such setbacks is key. Your best plan is to cut back on your spending a bit the following month.

Live within your means the majority of the time to make sure debt doesn't become a problem.

Start Saving from a Young Age

I have fond memories of the ceramic NatWest pigs I started collecting as a youngster (for those who don't remember this promotion, you got a piggy bank every time you paid another £25 into your NatWest savings account). I remember the competition between my brother and myself to be the first to get the next pig – spending our money on records, sweets, or magazines was the furthest thing from our minds.

We are both still pretty good at saving, proof that the younger you get in on the savings habit, the better. It really does establish good principles that can last a lifetime. Likewise, I have friends whose parents didn't teach them the benefit of saving and they are struggling in debt just like their parents did before them.

Build up an emergency savings fund (see Chapter 9 for more on this) to cover you if disaster strikes and then concentrate on building up your savings and investments.

Become a Rate Tart

The one place where it is actually worth aspiring to be a tart is when it comes to your finances. Rate tarts shop around for the best deals rather than remaining loyal to a bank or building society that doesn't offer the best rates.

If you automatically approach your current account provider every time you're after a credit card or personal loan, stop right there! One high-street bank can't possibly offer the best rates on every product so you need to develop the habit of shopping around. So many providers offer a wide variety of products that you should change provider every time you find a better deal – and don't be afraid to be called a tart.

Being a rate tart doesn't necessarily involve a lot of time and hassle. Start your search on the Internet, using sites such as www.money supermarket.com, www.moneyfacts.co.uk, and www.moneyextra. co.uk. These allow you to compare the cost of current and savings accounts, cash individual savings accounts, insurance, credit cards, mortgages, and personal loans. Check out the 'best buy' sections in the financial sections of quality newspapers too.

Avoid Store Cards at All Costs

It's very tempting to take up the salesperson's offer of a 10 per cent discount on your purchases in your favourite high-street store in return for signing up for a store card. You may wonder where the harm is. But where do I start? If you don't clear your balance when the bill arrives, you are likely to be stung with high interest charges. Most store cards have extortionate annual percentage rates of around 30 per cent, so if you do rack up interest, you could easily end up paying more than the savings you made on your new outfit in the first place.

The only people who should take out store cards are those who can afford to clear the balance when the bill arrives: That way, you benefit from the one-off discount (and can then cut the card up afterwards and send it back to the issuer). If you can't afford to do this, resist the temptation and steer clear.

Get on the Property Ladder

Buying your first home is a rite of passage that is becoming harder than ever following years of escalating property prices. The housing market has calmed down a little, with prices looking more realistic, but it is still difficult for first-time buyers to get a big enough mortgage on their salaries to buy even a poky one-bed flat.

There are ways round this – buying with parents, friends, or siblings. Or you could try asking your parents to help in other ways – by becoming a guarantor, lending you the cash for a deposit, or offsetting their savings against your mortgage debt. (For more tips on buying property, head to Chapter 14.)

It may seem like way too much effort but in the long run it's worth persevering. Historically, property increases in value over time so the longer you delay purchasing your first home, the harder it will be to climb on the ladder at a later date. Property is usually a sound investment, whereas renting is not dissimilar to throwing money down the drain.

Put Your Pay Rise towards Your Pension

Nothing gladdens the heart quite like a pay rise – finally, recognition for all that hard work! But resist the temptation to spoil yourself by splurging the extra cash on treats and indulgences. By all means treat yourself – but just the once, the first month you see the pay rise in your wage packet. The following month you should arrange to put some of your pay rise (or all of it, depending on whether you can afford to do so) into your pension. It is one of the most painless ways of increasing your contributions because you are putting more cash into your pension without even realising it.

It's a good habit to get into: Every time you get a pay rise, make sure a portion of it goes towards your pension. This way you ensure that your pension contributions increase over time. (Chapters 16 and 17 have more on occupational and personal pensions respectively, and how you can increase your contributions.)

An alternative to saving your pay rise in your pension is to put it into another investment product, such as a tax-free equity individual savings account (see Chapter 10 for more on this type of investment), which can be put towards retirement or withdrawn before then if you need the money. The key is to increase your proportion of saving to spending if you want to steer clear of debt and keep your financial picture rosy.

Take Advice before Taking the Plunge

If you're arguing all the time with your partner or have a problem with your boss, you might well approach a friend or colleague who has experience of these matters for advice as to what action to take. But when it comes to financial advice, it pays to consult an expert – not the man standing next to you down the pub.

Finances can be fiendishly complicated, so relying on mates for guidance is foolhardy. What you need is an independent financial adviser (IFA), who can make the difference between a champagne-and-oysters lifestyle and a beer-and-chip-butty one. (Chapter 2 has all the info you need on choosing an IFA.)

The sooner you arm yourself with a trusty range of reliable advisers, the better your finances will be. As well as an IFA, a mortgage broker with access to all the deals on the market can find you the right home loan, a good accountant ensures you don't pay more tax than you need to, and a solicitor can help you get your will up to date.

File Your Tax Return on Time

If you have any earnings that aren't taxed at source, you must complete a self-assessment tax return each year and return it to HM Revenue & Customs, along with the tax you owe. If you don't do so by 31 January after the tax year in question (for example, 31 January 2009 for the 2007–8 tax year) you get an automatic £100 fine and are charged interest for every day your completed return (and tax) are late.

You have to complete your return at some stage, so get into the habit of doing it on time. It saves you both stress and money!

If you can't face calculating your taxes yourself, hire an accountant to do it for you. Alternatively, return your form by 30 September following the end of the tax year (so 30 September 2008 for the 2007–8 tax year) and the Revenue will work out what tax you owe.

Provide for Your Dependants

It is easy to fall into the trap of thinking only about yourself when it comes to your finances: How much you earn each month, whether you can afford this month's mortgage/bills, and so on. But you should also think about would happen if you weren't around.

If you're single, it probably won't affect anyone else's finances adversely. But if you have children or a spouse who relies on your income, they could suffer a great deal.

If you have dependants, financial planning is vital: It's not just about the here and now but the future and how they will cope if anything happens to you. Life assurance is the obvious answer (see Chapter 4 for more on this and other types of insurance to protect your family). Writing a will so that there's no confusion after you've gone is another (see Chapter 15 for the lowdown on will writing).

Insure Yourself from Risk

Insurance covers the unknown and limits the trauma that unexpected events can cause. Nobody wants their home flooded with dirty water, but at least if you have buildings and home contents cover you can afford to get it cleaned up and replace anything that's damaged. This might not be so easy if you don't have insurance.

There is just one type of insurance that you'll be breaking the law if you don't have – and that's third-party motor cover. In addition, your mortgage lender will insist that you take out buildings insurance before it releases the funds to enable you to buy your new home.

Other than these forms of insurance, you can buy as much or as little cover as you think you need. Whether you really need other forms of insurance or not depends on whether you can cope without them: Sit down and work out the figures, and if you would struggle, pay for the cover and save yourself some heartache (and a big financial headache!). Chapter 4 has the lowdown on all the types of insurance you might need.

Appendix

Resources

• •

*T*his appendix lists some of the main organisations I refer to throughout this book. You can contact them for more help and information on sorting out your finances.

Professional and Trade Organisations

Association of British Insurers (ABI): The trade association for the UK insurance industry, the ABI represents around 400 companies. Contact: 020 7600 3333 or visit www.abi.org.uk.

Association of Investment Trust Companies (AIC): For more information on investment trusts, including fact sheets and a directory of available funds, contact the trade body on www.theaic.co.uk or 0800 085 8520.

Association of Private Client Investment Managers and Stockbrokers (APCIMS): Provides a free list of stockbrokers and information on the services they offer. Go to www.apcims.co.uk or call 020 7247 7080.

British Bankers Association: Most banks and building societies in the UK are members of this trade association. Contact 020 7216 8816 or go to www.bba.org.uk for more details.

Citizens Advice Bureau (CAB): The CAB offers free, confidential, and independent advice on a range of financial issues to those living in England and Wales. Find your nearest CAB at www.citizens advice.org.uk. For **Citizens Advice Northern Ireland**, go to www.citizensadvice.co.uk, or for **Citizens Advice Scotland** call 0131 550 1000 or visit www.cas.org.uk.

Consumer Credit Counselling Service: For free debt advice go to www.cccs.co.uk or call 0800 138 1111.

Council of Mortgage Lenders (CML): The CML is the trade association for UK mortgage lenders and promotes good lending practice. Call 020 7437 0075 or see www.cml.org.uk.

Ethical Investment Research Service (EIRIS): EIRIS provides research and information on investing ethically. Go to its website at www.eiris.org or call 020 7840 5700.

IFA Promotion (IFAP): If you want an independent financial adviser but don't know where to find one, contact IFAP. It will provide you with details of three local advisers for you to choose from. Contact 0800 085 3250 or go to www.unbiased.co.uk.

Investment Management Association (IMA): The trade body for unit trusts, the IMA has a range of brochures, fact sheets, and booklets available. Log onto www.investmentfunds.org or call 020 8207 1361.

London Stock Exchange (LSE): If you're looking for a stockbroker, the LSE can provide you with a list. Call 020 7797 1000 or go to www.londonstockexchange.com.

National Debtline: For free help and advice about sorting out your debts, call 0808 808 4000 or go to www.nationaldebtline.co.uk.

Government Agencies

Financial Ombudsman Service (FOS): If you complain to your bank, building society, or insurer about their service, and it doesn't rectify the situation to your satisfaction, the FOS will try to settle the dispute. Contact 0845 080 1800 or log onto www.financial-ombudsman.org.uk/consumer/complaints.htm.

Financial Services Authority (FSA): The City watchdog regulates the mortgage industry, providers of general insurance, and independent financial advisers. It also provides lots of information about different aspects of saving, investing, and debt. Visit www.fsa.gov.uk or call the consumer helpline on 0845 606 1234.

Financial Services Compensation Scheme (FSCS): If your bank or building society is registered by the FSA but goes bust, you can get back a portion of the cash you lose as a result via the FSCS. Visit www.fscs.org.uk or contact 020 7892 7300.

HM Revenue & Customs: For loads of information about all things tax related, from how much tax you should be paying on your savings and investments, to advice on how to claim back overpaid tax and register for self-assessment, visit www.hmrc.gov.uk.

Other Useful Websites

Insuresupermarket: Compare thousands of different insurance policies to find the best price. Visit the website at www.insure supermarket.com.

Moneysupermarket: A comprehensive service allowing users to compare the cost of a range of financial products from mortgages, credit cards, and personal loans to home insurance and life cover. Check out www.moneysupermarket.com.

Up My Street: All the local information about an area that you could possibly need to know. See www.upmystreet.com before deciding to move to a new area.

Credit Reference Agencies

Callcredit, Equifax, and Experian are the three main credit agencies that hold a copy of your credit file. Lenders contact these agencies to check your file before they decide whether to let you have credit or not, for a mortgage, for example. Your credit file contains details of your debts, and shows whether you are a good risk or not: If you have missed payments on a personal loan or previous mortgage, for example, this information is recorded on your file. With so much riding on what is contained on your file, it's worth checking that it's correct *before* you apply for a mortgage as errors can be rectified. Write to Callcredit, Equifax, or Experian, enclosing a cheque for £2 to get hold of a copy of your credit file.

Callcredit PLC

Consumer Services Team
PO Box 491
Leeds, LS3 1WZ
Phone 0870 060 1414
Website: www.callcredit.plc.uk

Equifax PLC

Credit File Advice Centre
PO Box 1140
Bradford, BD1 5US
Phone 0870 0100 583
Website: www.equifax.co.uk

Experian Ltd

Consumer Help Service
PO Box 8000
Nottingham, NG1 5GX
Phone 0870 241 6212
Website : www.experian.co.uk

Index

• *Numerics* •

80+ annual payment, 195

• *A* •

Abbey, Internet Banking, 35
ABI (Association of British Insurers), 50, 147, 273
accident, sickness, and unemployment insurance (ASU), 49
accounts. *See also* current accounts; individual savings accounts (ISAs)
  bonuses, 109
  connected, 38
  easy access, 108
  instant access, 108
  no notice, 108
  nominee, 161
  offset, 110
  packaged, 32
  savings, 107–112
  tax-exempt special savings (Tessas), 114, 117
accrual rate, final salary pension scheme, 208
acute conditions, 49
additional voluntary contributions (AVCs), 215
administration fees (overdrafts), 58–59
Advanced Financial Planning Certificate (AFPC), 25
advice
  advisory services, 159
  debt, 98–99
  fees-only, 25
  mortgage, 179–180
AER (annual equivalent rate), 108
AF3, financial adviser qualification, 25
AF4, financial adviser qualification, 25
affinity credit cards, 71

affordability, mortgage, 168–169
AFPC (Advanced Financial Planning Certificate), 25
AIC (Association of Investment Companies), 146, 273
AIM (Alternative Investment Market), 121, 156
Air Miles, 71
Alternative Investment Market (AIM), 121, 156
annual allowance limits (pensions), 214
annual bonus, 146
annual charges (credit card), 72
annual equivalent rate (AER), 108
annual percentage rate (APR)
  on cash advances, 72
  defined, 66
  loan, 81–82, 85
  store cards, 90
annual report, 166
annuities
  calculating, 240–241
  defined, 211, 230
  escalating, 242
  flat, 242
  guarantees, 243
  impaired life, 243
  index-linked, 242
  investment-linked, 244
  joint life, 243
  level, 242
  money purchase pension schemes, 210–211
  overview, 239–240
  personal pensions, 230–231
  purchased life, 239
  rising, 242
  sample payment amounts, 241
  shopping for, 245
  standard, 242
  types, 241–244
  unit-linked, 244
  when to buy, 244–245
  with-profits, 244

any occupation, income
   protection, 48
APCIMS (Association of Private Client
   Investment Managers and
   Stockbrokers), 157, 273
applications
   current account, 37–38
   loan, 81–82, 85
   mortgage, 181
   store cards, 90
APR (annual percentage rate)
   on cash advances, 72
   defined, 66
   loan, 81–82, 85
   store cards, 90
arrangement fees (overdrafts), 58–59
assessing risk, 14
asset review, 11
Association of British Insurers (ABI),
   50, 147, 273
Association of Investment Trust
   Companies (AIC), 146, 273
Association of Private Client
   Investment Managers and
   Stockbrokers (APCIMS), 157, 273
ASU (accident, sickness, and
   unemployment insurance), 49
ATMs (automated teller machines)
   credit cards, 67
   overview, 34–35
   using abroad, 73
authorised overdraft, 56–57
automated teller machines. *See* ATMs
   (automated teller machines)
available credit, 67
AVCs (additional voluntary
   contributions), 215

• *B* •

balance transfers
   credit card, 69
   store card, 92–96–97
balances, current account, 36
balancing
   investment portfolios, 128–130
   risk, 126–127

Bank of England
   Brokerage Service, 132
   gilt commission rates, 132
banking
   branch locations, 35
   branch savings accounts, 111
   Internet, 35–36
   by phone, 36
   proof of identity, 37
Banking Code
   changeover period, 39
   defined, 31
   standards of, 37
bankruptcy, 97–98
Barclays, current accounts, 33
base rate tracker mortgage, 175
basic-rate taxpayers
   dividends, 164
   pensions, 214
   private pensions, 196
   trivial pensions, 248
beneficiaries, company pensions,
   205–206
bid, 142
Bien, Melanie
   *Buying a Home on a Budget For
      Dummies,* 167–168
   *Renting Out Your Property For
      Dummies,* 199
Bloomberg Money (newspaper), 165
Bloomberg website, 166
blue-chip companies, 156
bonds
   capital, 130
   convertible, 134
   corporate, 126, 134–135, 147–148
   defined, 130
   government, 131–134
   high-yield, 134
   investment-grade, 134
   junk, 128, 134
   overview, 130–131
   risk, 131
bonuses
   accounts, 109
   annual, 146
   Christmas, 195
   reversionary, 146

British Bankers Association, 31, 273
brokers
  advice on, 179–180
  advisory services, 159
  charges for, 163–164
  choosing, 157–160
  commission, 163
  discretionary services, 158
  execution-only services, 159–160
  fixed fees, 163
  mortgage, 170
  overview, 157
  regulation of, 157–158
  types of services, 158–160
budgets
  creating, 17–19
  overview, 95
  surplus, 18
*Buying a Home on a Budget For
  Dummies* (Bien), 167–168
buying shares, 160

• *C* •

CA08 *Voluntary National Insurance
  Contributions* leaflet, 193
CAB (Citizens Advice Bureau), 87, 94,
  98, 273
Cahoot, Internet banking, 35
calculating
  additional mortgage fees, 169–172
  annuities, 240–241
  debts, 11–12
  interest, 66–67
  loan cost, 82
  mortgage affordability, 168–169
  overdraft interest, 56–57
  required income, 189–190
  retirement age, 190–191
Callcredit, credit reference agency,
  75, 275
CAM (current account mortgage),
  177–178
capital bonds, 130
capital gains tax (CGT), 152, 164
capital growth from shares, 162
capped mortgage rates, 176
car insurance, 51–52

card payment protection (store
  card), 91
cash
  access to retirement, 196–197
  advances on credit cards, 72
  as investment choice, 226
cash individual savings account. *See*
  individual savings accounts
  (ISAs)
cashback
  credit cards, 70
  mortgage, 178–179
CCJs (county court judgments), 74
CeMap (Certificate in Mortgage
  Advice and Practice), 25
certification
  Advanced Financial Planning
    Certificate (AFPC), 25
  Certificate in Financial Planning
    (Cert.FP) exam, 24
  Certificate in Mortgage Advice, 25
  Certificate in Mortgage Advice and
    Practice (CeMap), 25
  CFP (Certified Financial Planner)
    licence, 25
CGT (capital gains tax), 152, 164
Chancellor of the Exchequer, 113
Charcol mortgage brokers, 181
charges. *See also* costs; fees
  annual credit card, 72
  for bouncing payments, 58
  brokers, 163–164
  early settlement, 82–83
  investment, 125
  pooled investments, 150
  share transactions, 163–164
  stakeholder pensions, 221
  unit trusts, 142–143
cheques/cheque cards, 35
child trust fund, 263
Christmas bonus, 195
CIC (critical illness cover), 45, 48–49
Citizens Advice Bureau (CAB), 87, 94,
  98, 273
Citizens Advice Northern Ireland, 273
Citizens Advice Scotland, 273
Citywire website, 166
clearing debt, 12–13

closed-ended, 145
CML (Council of Mortgage Lenders), 274
cold weather payments, 195
collective funds
   corporate bond funds, 147–148
   costs of, 139
   exchange traded funds (ETF), 148–149
   pooled investments, 137–139, 149–152
   with-profits investment bonds, 146–147
commission
   broker, 163
   plus fees broker charges, 163
   trail, 26
company pensions. *See also* pensions; personal pensions
   additional voluntary contributions (AVCs), 215
   allowance limits, 213–216
   beneficiaries of, 205–206
   benefits of, 204–205
   changing jobs, 217–218
   company schemes, 207–208
   contribution ceiling, 213–214
   death in service benefit, 205–206
   final salary pension schemes, 208–210
   freestanding AVCs (FSAVCs), 215–216
   group personal pension (GPP), 211–212
   increasing contributions, 215–216
   limits, 213–216
   money purchase pension schemes, 210–211
   occupational pension schemes, 207–208
   overview, 203–204, 207–208
   personal pensions compared with, 224
   stakeholder pension schemes, 212
   State Second Pension (S2P) scheme, 216–217
   for surviving partners, 206
   tax relief, 214

   transfer value, 217–218
   types of, 207–212
compulsory insurance, 183
Computershare Investor Service, 132
connected accounts, 38
consolidation loan, 92–93
Consumer Credit Act (1974), 73, 79, 80
Consumer Credit Counselling Service, 87, 99, 273
contacting creditors, 97
contents insurance, 51
contracting in/out of State Second Pension (S2P) scheme, 216–217
contributions
   ceiling, 213–214
   increasing pension, 215–216
   personal pensions, 227–229
   stopping personal pension, 229
conventional gilts, 133
convertible bonds, 134
convertible term (term assurance), 46
conveyancing, 171
corporate bonds, 126, 134–135, 147–148
costs. *See also* charges; fees
   collective funds, 139
   financial adviser, 21
   loan, 82
   mortgage, 181–183
   pooled investments, 138
Council of Mortgage Lenders (CML), 274
council tax and housing benefit, 195
county court judgements (CCJs), 74
creating budgets, 17–19
credit
   available, 67
   limit, 67–68
   reference agencies, 75, 84, 275–276
   score, 74, 76, 84
credit cards. *See also* store cards
   activities to avoid, 72–73
   added benefits, 71
   affinity, 71
   Air Miles, 71
   annual charges, 72

ATMs, 67
available credit, 67
balance clearing perks, 70–71
balance transfers, 69
calculating interest, 66–67
cash advances, 72
cashback, 70
credit card protection, 72–73
credit limits, 67–68
credit rating, 73–76
credit references agencies, 75, 84,
    275–276
destroying, 255
footprint, 75
interest-free, 256
introductory rates, 11, 69
low lifetime balance, 70
loyalty points, 71
minimum payment, 68
overview, 66
protecting purchases, 73
replacing, 96–97
transferring balances, 12, 66,
    96–97, 256
credit file
ordering copies of, 75–76
overview, 84
credit rating
correcting mistakes, 74–76
credit scoring, 74
failing, 76
interest, 57
overview, 73–74
creditors, contacting, 97
critical illness cover (CIC), 45, 48–49
current accounts
access to, 34–36
accruing interest, 36
application form, 37–38
balances, 32–33, 36
changeover period, 39
charges, 31–32
direct debit list, 38
emergency savings and, 104–105
fee-free overdraft buffers, 60–61
finding, 33–37
interest, 30
interest-free overdraft buffers, 60–61

introductory offers for overdrafts,
    61–62
mortgage (CAM), 177–178
overdrafts, 36–37, 60–62
overview, 29–30
packaged accounts, 32
safety and security, 31
switching, 37–39
switching with overdrafts, 62
taxes, 30

• *D* •

daily charges (overdrafts), 58
Data Protection Act (1988), 75
death benefits, 231–232
death in service benefit, 205–206
debenture stocks, 134
debit card, 30
debt
advice, 98–99
budgeting, 95
calculating, 11–12
clearing, 12–13
contacting creditors, 97
going bankrupt, 97–98
mortgages, 96
overview, 94–95
prioritising, 19, 95
replacing store/credit cards, 96–97
savings, 95–96
seeking free advice, 98–99
tips for clearing, 255–259
debt consolidation firms
consolidating debts, 92–93
high rates and fees, 93–94
overview, 92
Debt Management Office, 132
decreasing term (term assurance), 46
default arrangement, 226
deferred period, 48
defined benefit pension schemes
final salary plan, 209
money purchase schemes, 210–211
overview, 208–210
defined contribution pension
    schemes, 210–211
deflation, 242

demutualised, 11
Department of Work and
    Pensions, 225
dependants, providing for, 271
deposit, mortgages with no, 169
derivatives, 157
Digital Look website, 166
direct debit
    defined, 30
    list, 38
    for store cards, 91
discount mortgage rates, 176
discretionary service, 158
discretionary trust, 202
diversify, 156
dividends
    basic-rate taxpayers, 164
    defined, 154
    distributions, 151
    final, 163
    generating, 162–163
    higher-rate taxpayers, 164
    income tax on, 164
    interim, 163
    non-taxpayers, 164
    unclaimed, 162
    vouchers, 163
    yields from stocks, 155
domestic warranty cover, 71
double-dated conventional gilts, 133
downsizing property, 248–249
duty, stamp, 164, 172

• E •

E111 form, 52
early redemption penalties,
    82–83, 182
early retirement, 237, 266
early settlement charges, 82–83
easy access account, 108
Egg, Internet banking, 35
80+ annual payment, 195
EIRIS (Ethical Investment Research
    Service), 146, 274
emergency savings, 13, 103–104, 107
employee share-ownership plans, 165
Equifax credit reference agency,
    75, 276

equities. *See also* shares
    ISAs (individual savings accounts),
        114–119
    releasing, 249–251
    types of returns from, 162
escalating annuity, 242
establishing financial goals, 13–14,
    19–20
ETF (exchange traded fund), 148–149
Ethical Investment Research Service
    (EIRIS), 146, 274
European Economic Area, Internet
    banking safety, 36
excess (insurance), 43
exchange traded fund (ETF), 148–149
execution-only service, 159–160
execution only unit trusts, 141
executors, 200
Experian credit reference agency,
    76, 276
expression of wish form, 231
extended redemption penalty, 182

• F •

family income benefit (term
    assurance), 46
fee-free overdraft buffers, 60–61
fees. *See also* charges; costs
    ATMs, 34–35
    current account, 31–32
    debt consolidation firms, 93–94
    fixed broker, 163
    legal, 171
    lender's, 170
    loading, 73
    mortgage broker, 180
    overdraft, 58–59
    procuration, 170
fees-only advice, 25
Fidelity FundsNetwork, 119
final dividends, 163
final pensionable salary, 208
final salary pension schemes
    accrual rate, 208
    demise of, 209
    overview, 207

financial advice
  benefits of, 20–21
  combining fees and commission, 26
  commission, 26
  fees-only, 25–26
  going it alone, 26–27
financial adviser. *See also*
      independent financial adviser
      (IFA)
  benefits of using, 20–21
  costs, 21
  experience, 25
  independent, 21–23
  keyfacts documents, 21
  multi-tied, 24
  overview, 15
  qualifications of, 24–25
  tied, 23–24
  types of, 21
financial goals
  establishing, 13–14, 19–20
  prioritising, 20
financial management
  benefits of, 9–10
  golden rules for, 267–272
Financial Ombudsman Service (FOS)
  dispute settlement, 31
  insurance policies, 43–44
  overview, 274
  website, 22, 274
Financial Services Authority (FSA)
  brokers, 157
  Central Register, 22
  current accounts, 31
  Firm and Person Check Service, 150
  holding shares, 161
  independent financial advisers
      (IFAs), 22
  money laundering, 161
  overview, 274
  pension comparisons, 222
  unit trust ISAs (individual savings
      accounts), 118, 141
  website, 274
Financial Services Compensation
    Scheme (FSCS)
  brokers, 157–158
  current accounts, 31
  overview, 274

savings security, 112, 141
  website, 274
Financial Times (newspaper), 165
fixed fees (broker), 163
fixed interest funds, 226
fixed-interest securities, 134–135
fixed-rate interest, 81, 109
fixed-rate mortgage, 175
flat annuity, 242
flexible mortgages, 177
footprint, 75
forms
  current account application, 37–38
  E111, 52
  cxpression of wish, 231
  pooled investments, 138
  store card application, 90
FOS (Financial Ombudsman Service)
  dispute settlement, 31
  insurance policies, 43–44
  overview, 274
  website, 22, 274
free purchase protection
      insurance, 71
free travel accident insurance, 52, 71
freestanding additional voluntary
      contributions (FSAVCs), 215–216
FSA (Financial Services Authority)
  brokers, 157
  Central Register, 22
  current accounts, 31
  Firm and Person Check Service, 150
  holding shares, 161
  independent financial advisers
      (IFAs), 22
  money laundering, 161
  overview, 274
  pension comparisons, 222
  unit trust ISAs (individual savings
      accounts), 118, 141
  website, 274
FSCS (Financial Services
      Compensation Scheme)
  brokers, 157–158
  current accounts, 31
  overview, 274
  savings security, 112, 141
  website, 274

full structural survey, 171
fully comprehensive insurance, 51
fund manager
  investment style, 142
  paying for, 139
FundChoice, 119
funds. *See also* collective funds
  child trust, 263
  fixed interest, 226
  hedge, 128
  managed, 226
  passive, 143
  property, 226
  stock market, 225
  tracker, 143–144, 225

• *G* •

G60, financial adviser qualification, 25
G70, financial adviser qualification, 25
generating
  additional retirement income,
    248–251
  dividends, 162–163
gilts. *See also* government bonds
  Bank of England commission
    rates, 132
  conventional, 133
  double-dated conventional, 133
  index-linked, 133
  strips, 134
  undated, 133
  ways to deal in, 132
GL23 *Social security benefit rates*
    leaflet, 192
goals
  establishing financial, 13–14, 19–20
  prioritising, 20
government agencies, 274–275
government bonds, 131–134. *See
    also* gilts
GPP (group personal pension), 204,
    211–212
Griswold, Robert, *Renting Out Your
    Property For Dummies,* 199
group personal pension (GPP), 204,
    211–212
growth stocks, 155

guaranteed rate, 48
'Guide to Ethical and Socially
    Responsible Investment Funds,
    A' (Investment Management
    Association), 146

• *H* •

Halifax, Internet banking, 25
health insurance, 44
hedge funds, 128
Hemscott website, 166
high risk investments, 127–128,
    156–157
high-yield bonds, 134
higher lending charge (HLC), 169,
    181–182
higher-rate taxpayers
  dividends, 164
  pensions, 214
  private pensions, 196
HIP (home information pack), 171
HLC (higher lending charge), 169,
    181–182
HM Revenue & Customs
  becoming self-employed, 258, 265
  CA08 *Voluntary National Insurance
    Contributions* leaflet, 193
  downloading tax forms, 108
  GL23 *Social security benefit rates*
    leaflet, 192
  ISAs (individual savings
    accounts), 114
  overview, 275
  PC1L *Pension Credit, Do I qualify and
    how much could I get?* leaflet, 195
  pension contribution limits, 213
  pension schemes, 228
  retirement lump sums, 209, 231
  self-assessment tax return, 271
  tax codes, 262
  tax relief listings, 214
  tax treatment of investments, 152
  website, 14, 275
holding shares, 160–161
home information pack (HIP), 171
home insurance, 50–51
home reversion scheme, 249, 250

homebuyer's report, 171
HSBC, current accounts, 33

● *I* ●

ideal balance, maintaining, 32–33
identity, proving, 161
IFA (independent financial adviser)
  benefits of using, 10–11, 22
  disadvantages of, 22
  finding, 22–23
  importance of using, 270–271
  overview, 21
  personal pensions, 224–225
IFA Promotion (IFAP), 23, 117, 150,
    155, 217, 225, 245, 274
IHT (inheritance tax), 201–202
IMA (Investment Management
    Association), 144, 151, 274
IMC (Investment Management
    Certificate), 25
impaired life annuity, 243
income
  calculating required, 189–190
  drawdown, 231, 246–247
  drawing from personal pensions,
    231
  generating more retirement,
    248–251
  multiples for mortgages, 168–169
  protection, 47–48
  retirement, 240
  from shares, 162
  stocks, 155
  tax on dividends, 164
  withdrawal, 246–247
increasing term (term assurance), 46
independent financial adviser (IFA)
  benefits of using, 10–11, 22
  disadvantages of, 22
  finding, 22–23
  importance of using, 270–271
  overview, 21
  personal pensions, 224–225
index-linked annuity, 242
index-linked gilts, 133
index tracker fund, 143, 225

individual savings accounts (ISAs)
  as alternatives to pensions, 199
  contributing to, 114
  equity, 114–119
  investment components, 115–118
  investment tax returns, 151
  mortgages, 173–174
  overview, 15, 113–114
  selecting, 118
  self-select, 118
  transferring, 119
  types of, 114
inflation
  final salary pension schemes, 208
  risk of, 31
inheritance tax (IHT), 201–202
insolvency practitioner, 97
instant access account, 108
insurance
  accident, sickness, and
    unemployment (ASU), 49
  acute conditions, 49
  arranging cover, 41–44
  claims, 43–44
  compulsory, 183
  contents, 51
  cost-saving tips, 44
  critical illness cover (CIC), 45, 48–49
  deferred period, 48
  excess, 43
  fully comprehensive, 51
  health and protection, 44–50
  home, 50–52
  income protection, 47–48
  information disclosure, 42
  life, 45–47
  medical history, 50
  moratorium option, 50
  motor, 51–52
  overview, 41
  policy, 43
  premiums, 48
  private medical (PMI), 49–50
  purchase protection, 71
  risk, 272
  shopping for, 42–43
  term assurance, 45–47
  terms, 45
  travel, 52, 71

Insurance *(continued)*
  types, 42
  websites, 43
  whole of life, 47
Intelligent Finance, Internet
    banking, 25
Interactive Investor website, 166
interest
  accruing in current accounts, 36
  calculating, 66–67
  credit rating, 57
  current account, 30
  fixed-rate, 81, 109
  loan, 81–82
  overdraft, 56–57
  savings, 108
interest-free credit cards, 256
interest-free overdraft buffers, 60–61
interest-only mortgage, 173–174
interest rates
  debt consolidation firms, 93–94
  fixed-rate, 109
  store cards, 90
  tiered, 109
interim dividend, 163
Internet
  banking, 35–36
  mortgage research, 180–181
  savings accounts research, 111
intestate, 199
introductory rates (credit card), 69
investing
  default arrangement, 226
  lifestyle option, 226
investment bonds, with-profits,
    146–147
investment-grade bonds, 134
investment-linked annuity, 244
Investment Management Association
    (IMA), 144, 151, 274
Investment Management Certificate
    (IMC), 25
investment portfolios
  balancing, 128–130
  basics, 128
  bonds, 130–135
  building, 14

charges, 125
cutting your losses, 129–130
evaluating risk level, 125–128
management services, 158
reviewing holdings, 129
share, 135–136, 145–146
strategy planning, 124–125
investment trusts, 140
investments
  amount used for, 124
  balanced risk, 126–127
  charges, 125
  herd mentality, 143
  high risk, 127–128, 156–157
  length of, 124
  medium-risk, 126–127
  no-risk, 126
  pooled, 127, 137–139, 149–152
  purpose of, 124
  reviewing, 10–12
  socially responsible, 146
  strategies, 124–125
  tax breaks, 14–15
  tax-free, 113
  trusts, 145–146
Investors Chronicle (newspaper), 165
investors, types of, 124
ISAs (individual savings accounts)
  as alternatives to pensions, 199
  contributing to, 114
  equity, 114–119
  investment components, 115–118
  investment tax returns, 151
  mortgages, 173–174
  overview, 15, 113–114
  selecting, 118
  self-select, 118
  transferring, 119
  types of, 114
item charges (overdrafts), 58

• *J* •

Jobcentre Plus, 47
John Lewis store cards, 91
joint life annuity, 243
junk bonds, 128, 134

• K •

key features document, 223
keyfacts documents, 21

• L •

late retirement, 237–238
legal fees, 171
legislation
  Consumer Credit Act (1974),
    73, 79, 80
  Data Protection Act (1988), 75
lender's fee, 170
lender's valuation, 170–171
level annuity, 242
level term (term assurance), 46
life assurance, 45–47
life events
  children, 263, 264
  coping with, 261–266
  divorce, 264
  early retirement, 266
  first job, 262
  leaving home, 261
  marriage, 262–263
  redundancy, 265
  self-employment, 265
  university costs, 261–262
life insurance, 45–47
lifestyle option, 226
lifetime allowance limits, 213, 238
lifetime mortgage, 249–250
Liffe (London International Financial
    Futures Exchange), 157
Lloyds TSB, current accounts, 33
loading fee, 73
loans
  annual percentage rate (APR),
    81–82, 85
  applying for, 81–82, 84–85
  calculating cost of, 82
  consolidation, 92–93
  early redemption penalties, 82–83
  flexibility of, 83
  interest, 81–82
  loan sharks, 94
  overview, 79

payment protection insurance,
    86–87
poor/no credit history, 85
regulated, 79–80
repayment mortgage, 172–174
repayment problems, 87–88
second charge, 80–81
shopping for, 83–84
student, 262
terms, 81
tuition fee, 262
unsecured compared with secured,
    79–81, 85, 92
when not to use, 78–79
when to use, 77–78
London & Country mortgage
    brokers, 181
London International Financial
    Futures Exchange (Liffe), 157
London Stock Exchange (LSE), 156,
    157, 274
long term, 13
low risk investments, 126
lower earnings limit, 194
loyalty points, 71
LSE (London Stock Exchange), 156,
    157, 274

• M •

managed funds, 226
managing pooled investments, 138
market research, 165
market value reduction (MVR), 147
medical history, 50
medium-risk investments, 126–127
minimum payments, 68
Money Box (radio programme), 165
Money Extra website, 43
Money Facts website, 43
money laundering, 161
Money Observer (newspaper), 165
money purchase pension schemes
  overview, 207, 210–211
  surviving partners, 206
  switching, 209
  transfer value, 218

Moneywise (newspaper), 165
monitoring pooled investments, 151
monthly savings account, 106–107
monthly usage fees (overdrafts), 59
moratorium option, 50
mortgage payment protection
    insurance, 49
mortgages. *See also* property
    investments
  adjustments, 96
  advice, 179–180
  affordability, 168–169
  applying online, 181
  base rate tracker, 175
  brokers, 170
  calculating additional fees, 169–172
  calculating affordability, 168–169
  capped rates, 176
  cashback, 178–179
  Charcol mortgage brokers, 181
  compulsory insurance, 183
  costs, 181–183
  current account (CAM), 177–178
  discount rates, 176
  downsizing property, 248–249
  early redemption penalties, 182
  fixed-rate, 175
  flexible, 177
  higher lending charge (HLC),
    181–182
  income multiples, 168–169
  interest-only, 173–174
  ISAs (individual savings accounts),
    173–174
  legal fees, 171
  lenders fee, 170
  lender's valuation and survey,
    170–171
  lifetime, 249–250
  no deposit, 169
  offset accounts, 110
  offsetting, 177–178
  online research, 180–181
  overview, 12, 167
  paying brokers, 170, 180
  rates, 174–179
  repayment loans, 173–174

  shopping for, 179–181
  stamp duty, 172
  standard variable rate (SVR),
    174–175
  types of, 172–174
Motley Fool website, 166
motor insurance, 51–52
multi-tied agents, 24
MVR (market value reduction), 147

• N •

National Debtline, 87, 99, 274
National Insurance Contribution
    (NIC), 192–193, 216, 237, 266
National Savings Certificates, 120
National Savings and Investments
    (NS&I), 15, 112, 120
Nationwide Flex account, 73
NatWest, current accounts, 33
NIC (National Insurance
    Contribution), 192–193, 216, 237,
    266
nil-rate band, 201
no notice account, 108
no risk investments, 126
nominee account, 161
non-taxpayers, dividends, 164
notice periods, 108–109
NS&I (National Savings and
    Investments), 15, 112, 120

• O •

occupational pension schemes,
    204–205, 207–212
Oeics (open-ended investment
    companies)
  focus of, 140
  overview, 144–145
  taxes on, 151–152
OFEX (Off Exchange) shares, 156
offer, 142
Office of Fair Trading (OFT), 90
Office of the Pensions Advisory
    Service (Opas), 231
Official Receiver, 97

offset account, 110
offset mortgage, 177–178
OFT (Office of Fair Trading), 90
Opas (Office of the Pensions Advisory Service), 231
open-ended, 141
open-ended investment companies (Oeics)
  focus of, 140
  overview, 144–145
  taxes on, 151–152
open market option, 211, 231, 245
overdrafts
  authorised, 56–57
  calculating interest, 56–57
  choosing current accounts for, 60–62
  defined, 56
  fees, 58–59
  introductory offers, 34
  overview, 55
  pros and cons, 59–60
  reducing, 62–63
  requesting permission, 56
  switching current accounts with, 62
  typical rate for, 57
  unauthorised, 56–57
  viewing, 36–37
overhang, 182
own occupation, income protection, 48

• *P* •

packaged account, 32
passive fund, 143
pay raises, pensions, 270
payment protection insurance, 86–87
payments
  charges for bouncing, 58
  cold weather, 195
  80+ annual, 195
  minimum credit card, 68
  sample annuity, 241
  smoothing, 147
  winter fuel, 195

PC1L *Pension Credit, Do I qualify and how much could I get?* leaflet, 195
penalties
  early redemption, 82–83, 182
  extended redemption, 182
Pension Credit, Do I qualify and how much could I get? leaflet (PC1L), 195
pension planning. *See* retirement planning
Pension Service, 195, 217, 225
pensions. *See also* company pensions; personal pensions
  alternatives to, 197–199
  amounts at different ages, 236
  annual allowance limits, 214
  credit, 195
  dividends, 214
  key features document, 223
  overview, 14
  pay raises, 270
  property compared with, 198–199
  stakeholder, 197, 221–222
  state, 192–193
  state second (S2P), 194
  supplementing state with personal, 196–197
Peps (personal equity plans), 114
permanent health insurance. *See* income protection
personal equity plans (Peps), 114
Personal Finance Society, 23
personal loans
  annual percentage rate (APR), 81–82, 85
  applying for, 81–82, 84–85
  calculating cost of, 82
  consolidation, 92–93
  early redemption penalties, 82–83
  flexibility of, 83
  interest, 81–82
  loan sharks, 94
  overview, 79
  payment protection insurance, 86–87
  poor/no credit history, 85
  regulated, 79–80

personal loans *(continued)*
  repayment mortgage, 172–174
  repayment problems, 87–88
  second charge, 80–81
  shopping for, 83–84
  student, 262
  terms, 81
  tuition fee, 262
  unsecured compared with secured,
    79–81, 85, 92
  when not to use, 78–79
  when to use, 77–78
personal pensions. *See also* company
    pensions; pensions
  advice on, 224–225
  annuities, 230–231
  best scheme, choosing, 222–226
  company pensions compared
    with, 224
  contribution limits, 227–228
  death benefits, 231–232
  dividends, 196
  drawing income from, 231
  expression of wish form, 231
  independent financial adviser (IFA),
    224–225
  investment choices, 225–226
  making contributions to, 227–229
  overview, 219–221
  paid up, 229
  phased retirement, 231
  process, 220–221
  receiving, 230–232
  searching for, 223–224
  self-invested (Sipp), 232–233
  stakeholder pensions, 221–222
  stopping contributions, 229
  topping up contributions, 228
  transferring funds, 229
phased retirement, 231, 245–246
phone banking, 36
PMI (private medical insurance),
    49–50
pooled investments
  advantages of, 138
  charges, 138, 150
  checking authorisation, 150

defined, 127
disadvantages, 139
drip-feeding money, 151
goals, 150
monitoring, 151
overview, 137–138
past performance, 149
taxes, 151–152
portfolios
  balancing, 128–130
  basics, 128
  bonds, 130–135
  building, 14
  charges, 125
  cutting your losses, 129–130
  evaluating risk level, 125–128
  management services, 158
  reviewing holdings, 129
  share, 135–136, 145–146
  strategy planning, 124–125
posting, for information on savings
    accounts, 111
preference shares, 163
premium, 41
price promise cover, 71
prioritising
  debts, 19, 95
  financial goals, 20
private medical insurance (PMI),
    49–50
private pensions. *See also* company
    pensions; pensions
  advice on, 224–225
  annuities, 230–231
  best scheme, choosing, 222–226
  company pensions compared with,
    224
  contribution limits, 227–228
  death benefits, 231–232
  dividends, 196
  drawing income from, 231
  expression of wish form, 231
  independent financial adviser (IFA),
    224–225
  investment choices, 225–226
  making contributions to, 227–229
  overview, 219–221
  paid up, 229

phased retirement, 231
process, 220–221
receiving, 230–232
searching for, 223–224
self-invested (Sipp), 232–233
stakeholder pensions, 221–222
stopping contributions, 229
topping up contributions, 228
transferring funds, 229
private reversion company, 250
procuration fee, 170
professional organisations, 273–274
profit-sharing schemes, 165
proof of identity, 37
property
  downsizing, 248–249
  funds, 226
  investing in, 269
  pensions compared with, 198–199
property investments. *See also*
    mortgages
  as alternatives to pensions, 197–199
  calculating cost of, 169–172
  legal fees, 171
  lender's fee, 170
  lender's valuation and survey,
    170–171
  paying mortgage brokers, 170
  stamp duty, 172
protected discount policy, 52
Prudential, Internet banking, 35
purchase protection (credit card), 73
purchase protection insurance, 71
purchased life annuity, 239

• *Q* •

qualifications (financial adviser),
  24–25
quarterly usage fees, overdrafts, 59

• *R* •

rates
  capped mortgage, 176
  comparisons, 268
  guaranteed, 48

mortgage, 174–179
  reviewable, 48
rebate, State Second Pension (S2P)
    scheme, 216–217
regulated loans, 79–80
regulations, broker, 157–158
releasing equity, 249–251
remortgaging, 96
renewable term (term assurance), 46
*Renting Out Your Property For
    Dummies* (Bien and
    Griswold), 199
repayment loans, 172–174
replacing credit cards, 96–97
reports
  annual, 166
  homebuyer's, 171
research
  annuities, 245
  market, 165
  mortgages online, 180–181
  savings accounts, 110–112
Retail Price Index-linked (RPI-linked)
    annuity, 242
Retail Price Index (RPI), 133
retirement. *See also* retirement
    planning
  age, 188, 235–238
  annuities, 239–245
  calculating current status, 190–191
  early, 237, 266
  everyday outgoings, 189–190
  final salary pension schemes,
    208–209
  generating bigger retirement
    income, 248–251
  gradual, 245–246
  income, 240
  late, 237–238
  money purchase pension
    scheme, 211
  phased, 231
  planning, 14
  tax-free lump sum, 238–239
  trivial commutation, 247–248
  wish list, 190
  withdrawing income, 246–247

The Retirement Pension Forecasting
    Team, 193, 266
retirement planning. *See also*
    retirement
  access to cash, 196–197
  alternatives to pensions, 197–199
  calculating current position,
    190–191
  calculating required income,
    189–190
  guaranteeing income, 197
  inheritance tax (IHT), 201–202
  other benefits, 195
  overview of factors determining, 188
  pension credit, 195
  retirement age, 188
  reviewing, 191–192
  starting to save, 191
  state pension, 192–193
  state second pension (S2P), 194
  supplementing state pensions,
    196–197
  tax breaks, 196
  wills, 199–201
returns
  from equities, 162
  maximising, 136
Reuters website, 166
reversionary bonus, 146
reviewable rate, 48
reviewing assets, 10–12
rising annuity, 242
risk
  assessing, 14
  attitude to, 124
  balanced, 126–127
  bonds, 131
  corporate bonds, 147–148
  high, 156–157
  inflation, 31
  insurance, 272
  minimising, 135
  pooled investments, 138
  savings, 105
  shares, 154–156
  VCT, 121
risk evaluation
  balanced approach, 126–127
  high risk, 127–128

low/no risk, 126
  overview, 125
RPI (Retail Price Index), 133

• *S* •

safeguarding savings, 112
salary-related pension schemes,
    208–210
Save As You Earn (SAYE) scheme, 165
Savills Private Finance mortgage
    brokers, 181
savings
  accessibility of, 105
  advantages, 104–105
  calculator website, 110
  determining amount for, 106
  emergency, 13, 103–104, 107
  interest, 108
  minimising risk, 105
  overview, 95–96
  safeguarding, 112
  starting, 12–13, 268
  starting retirement, 191
  tax breaks, 14–15
savings accounts
  bonuses, 109
  cash individual, 107
  fixed-rate and term, 109
  interest, 108
  monthly account, 106–107
  notice periods, 108–109
  offsetting savings, 110
  overview, 106
  researching, 110–112
  shopping for, 110–112
  tiered rates, 109
SAYE (Save As You Earn) scheme, 165
second charge loan, 80–81
secured loans, 79–81, 85, 92
securities, fixed-interest, 134–135
security
  current account, 31
  Internet banking, 36
  proving identity, 161
self-invested personal pension (Sipp),
    232–233
self-select ISA (individual savings
    account), 118

Selftrade online trading service, 157
selling shares, 160
Separately Traded and Registered
    Interest and Principal Securities
    (strips), 134
SERPS (State Earnings-Related
    Pension Scheme), 194
services, financial adviser, 21
shares
  buying, 160
  capital gains tax (CGT), 152, 164
  capital growth from, 162
  certificates, 160–161
  charges, 163–164
  choosing brokers, 157–160
  dividends, 162–163
  employee share-ownership
    plans, 165
  growth compared with income, 155
  holding, 160–161
  income from, 162
  investing basics in, 154–155
  OFEX (Off Exchange), 156
  paying duty, 164
  portfolio, 135–136
  preference, 163
  prices of, 154
  proving identity, 161
  risks, 154–156
  selecting, 155–160
  selling, 160
  tracking, 164–166
  transaction charges, 163–164
  windfall, 11
Sharesave scheme, 165
short term, 13
single-life annuity, 230
Sipp (self-invested personal pension),
    232–233
smoothing payments, 147
Social security benefit rates leaflet
    (GL23), 192
socially responsible investment
    (SRI), 146
specialist unit trusts, 127
SRI (socially responsible investment),
    146

stakeholder pensions. *See also*
    personal pensions
  advantages of, 212
  charges, 221
  group personal pension (GPP)
    compared with, 204
  overview, 197, 221–222
  transferring, 229
stamp duty, 164, 172
standard annuity, 242
standard variable rate (SVR)
    mortgage, 174–175
standing order, 30
State Earnings-Related Pension
    Scheme (SERPS), 194
state pension, 192–193
state Second Pension (S2P) scheme,
    194, 216–217
statutory sick pay, 47
stock market funds, 225
stocks. *See also* shares
  debenture, 134
  growth compared with income, 155
  unsecured loan, 134
store cards. *See also* credit cards
  advantages of, 90–91
  annual percentage rate (APR), 90
  applying for, 90
  avoiding, 269
  card protection, 91
  clearing debt, 91–92
  defined, 89
  destroying, 255
  direct debit for, 91
  interest rates, 90
  overview, 12
  payment protection, 91
  pressure from, 93
  replacing, 96–97
  transferring balances, 92, 96–97
strips (Separately Traded and
    Registered Interest and Principal
    Securities), 134
student loan for maintenance, 262
surplus, budget, 18
SVR (standard variable rate)
    mortgage, 174–175

• T •

tax
  capital gains (CGT), 152, 164
  credit, 164
  current account, 30
  on dividends, 164
  inheritance, 201–202
  on part-time earnings, 258
  on pooled investments, 151–152
  relief on pensions, 214
  return filing, 271
tax breaks
  for private pensions, 196
  on property investments, 198
  savings and investments, 14–15
  VCT, 121
tax-exempt special savings accounts
      (Tessas), 114, 117
tax-free lump sum, 238–239
tax-free savings/investments
  individual savings account (ISA),
      113–119
  National Savings Certificates, 120
  overview, 113
  venture capital trusts (VCT),
      120–122
taxpayers. *See* basic-rate taxpayers;
      higher-rate taxpayers
telephoning for savings account
      information, 111
term assurance
  disadvantages of, 46
  overview, 45–46
  re-evaluating periodically, 46–47
  types, 46
terms, loan, 81
Tessa-only ISA (Toisa), 117
Tessas (tax-exempt special savings
      accounts), 114, 117
third-party cover, 51
third-party fire and theft, 51
tied agent, 23–24
tiered interest rates, 109
tips for clearing debt, 255–259
Toisa (Tessa-only ISA), 117
tracker funds, 143–144, 225
tracker mortgages, 175

tracking shares, 164–166
trade organisations, 273–274
Trades Union Congress (TUC), 191,
      230, 266
trail commission, 26
transfer value, 217
transferring
  credit card balances, 66, 69
  ISAs (individual savings
      accounts), 119
travel cover, 52, 71
trivial commutation (pensions),
      247–248
trustee, 141
trusts
  discretionary, 202
  investment, 140
  unit, 140–143, 151–152
TUC (Trades Union Congress), 191,
      230, 266
tuition fee loan, 262

• U •

UK Retail Price Index (RPI), 133
unauthorised overdraft, 32, 56–57
Unclaimed Assets Register, 162
unclaimed dividends, 162
undated gilts, 133
unit-linked annuity, 244
unit trusts
  best fund, choosing, 141–142
  charges, 142–143
  focus of, 140
  index tracker fund, 143
  overview, 140–141
  passive tracker fund, 143
  specialist, 127
  taxes on, 151–152
unsecured loans, 79–80, 85, 92, 134
upper accrual point, 194
upper earnings limit, 194

• V •

variable rate interest, 82
VCT (venture capital trust), 120–121

Voluntary National Insurance Contributions leaflet (CA08), 193
vouchers, 163

• *W* •

Websites
  Association of British Insurers (ABI), 147, 273
  Association of Investment Trust Companies (AIC), 273
  Association of Private Client Investment Managers and Stockbrokers (APCIMS), 157, 273
  Bank of England Brokerage Service, 132
  bank overdraft comparisons, 60
  best buy calculator, 34
  Bloomberg, 166
  British Bankers Association, 31, 273
  Callcredit, 75, 275
  Charcol, 181
  Citizens Advice Bureau, 98, 273
  Citizens Advice Northern Ireland, 273
  Citizens Advice Scotland, 273
  Citywire, 166
  comparison, 115
  Computershare Investor Services, 132
  Consumer Credit Counselling Service, 87, 99, 273
  Council of Mortgage Lenders (CML), 274
  credit card research, 256
  Debt Management Office, 132
  Department of Work and Pensions, 225
  Digital Look, 166
  EIRIS (Ethical Investment Research Service), 146, 274
  employee share ownership schemes, 165
  Equifax, 75, 276
  Experian, 76, 276
  Fidelity FundsNetwork, 119
  Financial Ombudsman Service, 22, 43–44, 274
  Financial Services Authority (FSA), 31, 118, 161, 222, 274
  Financial Services Compensation Scheme (FSCS), 274
  FSA Central Register, 22
  FSA Firm and Person Check Service, 150
  FundChoice, 119
  Hemscott, 166
  HM Revenue & Customs, 14, 108, 152, 193, 214, 258, 262, 275
  IFA Promotion (IFAP), 23, 117, 150, 155, 217, 225, 245, 274
  insurance, 43
  Insuresupermarket, 275
  Interactive Investor, 166
  Investment Management Association (IMA), 144, 146, 151, 274
  Jobcentre Plus, 47
  loan shopping, 83
  London & Country, 181
  London International Financial Futures Exchange (Liffe), 157
  London Stock Exchange, 157, 274
  Moneysupermarket, 275
  Motley Fool, 166
  National Debtline, 87, 99, 274
  National Savings and Investments (NS&I), 120
  news services, 166
  Pension Service, 195, 217, 225
  Personal Finance Society, 23
  private investor resources, 166
  rate comparisons, 268
  redundancy help, 265
  redundancy pay calculator, 265
  The Retirement Pension Forecasting Team, 193, 266
  Reuters, 166
  Savills Private Finance, 181
  savings account comparisons, 111
  savings calculator, 110
  Selftrade, 157
  Trades Union Congress, 191, 230, 266
  Unclaimed Assets Register, 162
  Up My Street, 275

whole of life insurance, 47
wills
  delaying, 200
  inheritance tax (IHT), 201–202
  overview, 199
  process of writing, 200–201
windfall shares, 11
winter fuel payments, 195
with-profits
  annuity, 244
  investment bonds, 146–147

Work and Pensions, Department
  of, 225
workplace pensions. *See* company
  pensions

 • *y* •

yields, dividends from stocks, 155
Young Person's Railcard, 33

FOR DUMMIES®

Do Anything. Just Add Dummies

UK editions

BUSINESS

Starting a Business DUMMIES

978-0-470-51806-9

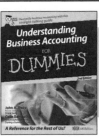

Understanding Business Accounting DUMMIES

978-0-470-99245-6

Business Plans DUMMIES

978-0-7645-7026-1

FINANCE

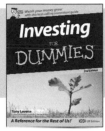

Investing DUMMIES

978-0-470-99280-7

Tax DUMMIES

978-0-470-99811-3

Bookkeeping DUMMIES

978-0-470-05815-2

PROPERTY

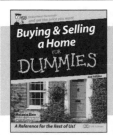

Buying & Selling a Home DUMMIES

978-0-470-99448-1

Property Investing ALL-IN-ONE DUMMIES

978-0-470-51502-0

DIY & Home Maintenance ALL-IN-ONE DUMMIES

978-0-7645-7054-4

Body Language For Dummies
978-0-470-51291-3

Building Self-Confidence for Dummies
978-0-470-01669-5

Children's Health For Dummies
978-0-470-02735-6

Cognitive Behavioural Coaching For Dummies
978-0-470-71379-2

Counselling Skills For Dummies
978-0-470-51190-9

Digital Marketing For Dummies
978-0-470-05793-3

Divorce for Dummies
978-0-7645-7030-8

eBay.co.uk For Dummies, 2nd Edition
978-0-470-51807-6

Emotional Freedom Technique For Dummies
978-0-470-75876-2

English Grammar For Dummies
978-0-470-05752-0

Fertility & Infertility For Dummies
978-0-470-05750-6

Genealogy Online For Dummies
978-0-7645-7061-2

Golf For Dummies
978-0-470-01811-8

Green Living For Dummies
978-0-470-06038-4

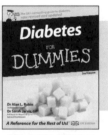
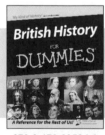
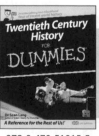
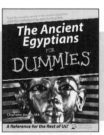

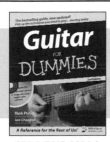

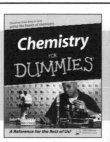

FOR DUMMIES®

Helping you expand your horizons and achieve your potential

COMPUTER BASICS

Computers For Seniors For Dummies
978-0-470-24055-7

PCs For Dummies
978-0-470-13728-4

Windows Vista For Dummies
978-0-471-75421-3

DIGITAL LIFESTYLE

Digital Photography For Dummies
978-0-7645-9802-9

iPod & iTunes For Dummies
978-0-470-17474-6

iPhone For Dummies
978-0-470-17469-2

WEB & DESIGN

Creating Web Pages For Dummies
978-0-470-08030-6

Photoshop CS3 For Dummies
978-0-470-11193-2

Dreamweaver CS3 For Dummies
978-0-470-11490-2

Access 2007 For Dummies
978-0-470-04612-8

Adobe Creative Suite 3 Design Premium All-in-One Desk Reference For Dummies
978-0-470-11724-8

AutoCAD 2008 For Dummies
978-0-470-11650-0

C++ For Dummies, 5th Edition
978-0-7645-6852-7

Excel 2007 All-in-One Desk Reference For Dummies
978-0-470-03738-6

Flash CS3 For Dummies
978-0-470-12100-9

Laptops For Dummies, 2nd Edition
978-0-470-05432-1

Mac OS X Leopard For Dummies
978-0-470-05433-8

Macs For Dummies, 9th Edition
978-0-470-04849-8

Networking All-in-One Desk Reference For Dummies, 3rd Edition
978-0-470-17915-4

Office 2007 All-in-One Desk Reference For Dummies
978-0-471-78279-7

Search Engine Optimization For Dummies, 2nd Edition
978-0-471-97998-2

Second Life For Dummies
978-0-470-18025-9

The Internet For Dummies, 11th Edition
978-0-470-12174-0

Visual Studio 2008 All-in-One Desk Reference For Dummies
978-0-470-19108-8

Web Analytics For Dummies
978-0-470-09824-0

Windows XP For Dummies, 2nd Edition
978-0-7645-7326-2

Available wherever books are sold. For more information or to order direct go to www.wiley.com or call +44 (0) 1243 843291